Dear Reader,

My introduction to Chinese food came in the 1960s—a time when chop suey and egg rolls were considered exotic. But there was something about Chinese food that transcended the overly sweet sauces found at the town's only Chinese restaurant.

My love affair with Chinese cooking really took off when I had the good fortune to work with a group of women who recently emigrated from Hong Kong. On weekends we toured Asian markets together, and they introduced me to the delights of a dim sum brunch. During this time I became intrigued both with Chinese food and its symbolic importance in Chinese culture.

Today, Chinese cooking has never been more popular. A search for ingredients often takes you no farther than the local supermarket, where chili paste and hoisin sauce are readily available, and vegetables with exotic names such as amaranth share space with the cabbage in the produce section. With a little practice, it's easy to prepare home-cooked Chinese dishes that are tasty and healthful. I enjoyed putting my wok to use preparing the recipes for this book. I hope they provide you with a helpful introduction to the fascinating world of Chinese cuisine.

Rhonda Lauret Parkinson

The EVERYTHING® Series

Editorial

Publishing Director	Gary M. Krebs
Managing Editor	Kate McBride
Copy Chief	Laura MacLaughlin
Acquisitions Editor	Bethany Brown
Development Editor	Julie Gutin
Production Editor	Khrysti Nazzaro

Production

Production Director	Susan Beale
Production Manager	Michelle Roy Kelly
Series Designers	Daria Perreault
	Colleen Cunningham
Cover Design	Paul Beatrice
	Frank Rivera
Layout and Graphics	Colleen Cunningham
	Rachael Eiben
	Michelle Roy Kelly
	Daria Perreault
	Erin Ring
Series Cover Artist	Barry Littmann

Visit the entire Everything® Series at everything.com

THE
EVERYTHING®
CHINESE
COOKBOOK

From Wonton Soup to Sweet and
Sour Chicken—300 succulent recipes
from the Far East

Rhonda Lauret Parkinson

A

Adams Media Corporation
Avon, Massachusetts

An Everything® Series Book.
Everything® and everything.com® are registered trademarks of F+W Publications, Inc.

Published by Adams Media, an F+W Publications Company
57 Littlefield Street, Avon, MA 02322 U.S.A.
www.adamsmedia.com

ISBN: 1-58062-954-7
Printed in the United States of America.

J I H G F E D C B

Library of Congress Cataloging-in-Publication Data
Lauret Parkinson, Rhonda.
The everything Chinese cookbook / Rhonda Lauret Parkinson.
p.   cm.
(An everything series book)
ISBN 1-58062-954-7
1. Cookery, Chinese. I. Title. II. Series: Everything series

TX724.5.C5L3767 2003
641.5951–dc21

2003004469

This publication is designed to provide accurate and authoritative information with regard to the subject matter covered. It is sold with the understanding that the publisher is not engaged in rendering legal, accounting, or other professional advice. If legal advice or other expert assistance is required, the services of a competent professional person should be sought.

—From a *Declaration of Principles* jointly adopted by a Committee of the American Bar Association and a Committee of Publishers and Associations

Many of the designations used by manufacturers and sellers to distinguish their products are claimed as trademarks. Where those designations appear in this book and Adams Media was aware of a trademark claim, the designations have been printed with initial capital letters.

This book is available at quantity discounts for bulk purchases.
For information, call 1-800-872-5627.

Contents

Dedication

To my parents: a great cook and a great writer.

Introduction

▶ WHAT MAKES CHINESE CUISINE SO APPEALING? Restaurant classics such as Mu Shu Pork and Kung Pao Chicken captivate our senses. Even an order of the ubiquitous Chicken Balls with Sweet-and-Sour Sauce from the local Chinese takeout has its own special appeal.

What is it that makes Chinese food so special? It's not the exotic vegetables and seasonings—a skilled chef can prepare a meal that epitomizes the best of Chinese cooking using only native ingredients. It's not the equipment, either. Many tasty stir-fries have been born in a frying pan instead of a wok.

The true secret to Chinese cuisine lies in a harmonious blending of flavors, textures, and colors. Take Basic Sweet-and-Sour Pork (page 139), for example. The sweet and sour flavors balance each other nicely, and the reddish sauce provides a nice contrast to the pineapple and green bell peppers.

This characteristic isn't limited to entrées, either. The same satisfying balance can be found in many Chinese dishes, such as Wonton Soup (page 54), where pork-filled wonton wrappers are swimming in a rich broth.

So, why aren't more people stir-frying noodles and boiling dumplings? A common misconception is that it takes a skilled chef working with state-of-the-art equipment to prepare good Chinese food. Fortunately, that's not true. Stir-frying, steaming, and deep-frying—the three primary Chinese cooking techniques—are all easily mastered with practice.

Another common complaint is that the recipes are too complex, taking too long to make. The sight of a lengthy ingredient list can be a little daunting. But on closer inspection you'll find that many of the ingredients go into preparing a marinade or sauce. Subtract those, and the basic recipe is frequently quite simple.

As for time involved, most of the work lies in preparation. Time spent actually cooking can be mere minutes, especially if you're stir-frying. And once you've cooked a few dishes you'll find yourself falling into a routine—cutting vegetables while the meat is marinating, preparing a sauce while waiting for the oil to reach the required temperature for deep-frying. Other handy time-savers include washing vegetables in the morning—giving them all day to dry—and marinating meat ahead of time and refrigerating it until you're ready to cook.

What are the pluses of cooking Chinese food at home? Besides the obvious advantage to your wallet, it's often healthier than restaurant fare, since you control the fat and calorie count. You can let your own creativity come into play, adjusting a recipe to add favorite foods or seasonal local ingredients. Cooking Chinese food at home also allows you to modify a recipe to suit your family's tastes; substituting parsley for cilantro, for example.

An added bonus is that there is something about cooking Chinese food that brings families together. Many pleasurable evenings can be spent filling dumplings or making pancakes. Appetizers such as egg rolls can often be baked as well as deep-fried, making it easier to involve young children.

This book is designed to help you incorporate home-cooked Chinese meals into your daily life. Tips on purchasing equipment, cooking techniques, and stocking the pantry are all here. Recipes include popular favorites such as Mu Shu Pork, and less well-known dishes such as MaPo Dofu, a tofu dish. Information on cooking with more exotic ingredients such as Szechwan peppercorns and fermented black beans is provided, along with suggestions for substitutes where possible.

Chapter 1

Let's Get Started

Chinese cuisine can seem very exotic after a dim sum brunch or dinner at a Chinatown restaurant, but it's easy to prepare many Chinese recipes at home. All it takes is a good wok, mastery of a few simple cooking skills, and stocking the pantry with basic ingredients, many of which are available on local supermarket shelves.

At the Asian Market

To supplement your regular shopping, you may want to visit the local Asian grocery store. When you enter, you'll be hit with the pungent aromas of exotic ingredients. Then, you'll note the profusion of unusual sights and sounds. Live lobster and crab swim in tanks, competing for your attention with strange fruits and vegetables. You wander past, taking note of the brightly decorated red lanterns hanging from the ceiling and the pleasant sounds of Oriental music in the background.

To the uninitiated, a visit to the Asian market can seem like a trip to a foreign land, minus a map or guidebook. But structure and organization do exist. Unlike the typical large supermarket, Asian groceries share much in common with the shops of days gone by, when several businesses shared the same general space. Most groceries have a butcher shop, where slabs of glazed barbequed pork hang from hooks. A fishmonger sells the freshest fish possible, preferably caught earlier that day. Most stores have a bakery that offers fresh-baked bread and buns. All of these businesses normally operate independently from the main grocery store.

QUESTION?

What about monosodium glutamate (MSG)?
You don't need to add MSG to home-cooked dishes; fresh ingredients will provide plenty of flavor. However, since many restaurants use MSG, you may find it difficult to reproduce the taste of your favorite restaurant dish without it.

As for the main grocery area, the most important thing to remember is that the space allocation for various products is different from that in Western supermarkets. One aisle may be set aside for the myriad sauces and seasonings used in Chinese cooking, while another contains a varied assortment of noodles, flour, and starch. And where else would you find an entire aisle devoted to tea, China's national drink?

Two areas that may prove challenging are spices and fresh vegetables. It is very common for grocers to provide only the Cantonese names for produce. Similarly, bags of spices may have Chinese writing on the label, leaving you unsure of their English equivalent. At this point you may notice another difference in Asian markets; there tends to be fewer staff on the floor to ask for help. Don't worry. The checkout cashier will gladly assist you, even if it means temporarily leaving the till.

An added plus to shopping at the Asian market is that you can stock up on ingredients and purchase the tools you need to begin cooking Chinese food at the same time. While most supermarkets carry a few cooking tools, in Chinese markets it is very common for several aisles to be set aside for everything from woks to harder-to-find accessories such as cooking chopsticks.

FACT

In Chinese cooking, the fresher the better! It is quite possible that the fish you see on a slab of ice was killed mere hours before being delivered to the market. Freshness is particularly important in Cantonese cuisine. It is a point of pride with Cantonese cooks to create dishes that retain as much of the natural flavor and texture of the food as possible.

Staple Ingredients

Certain flavors such as ginger and garlic feature prominently in Chinese cooking. While on occasion you may find yourself scouring Chinatown for a seldom-used ingredient such as shark's fin, keeping the pantry stocked with the items below will allow you to whip up a stir-fry any night of the week, using whatever combination of meat and vegetables you have on hand.

In southern China the day begins and ends with a bowl of steaming rice. While noodles are the grain of choice in China's colder northern regions, rice is consumed there as well. Long grain rice is favored for main dishes, but medium grain rice is an acceptable substitute. Short grain rice is used primarily in desserts.

Chinese noodles are not much different from Italian pasta. Most types of noodles are very user-friendly, often requiring only a quick soaking to soften before use. A chart of Chinese noodles and cooking times is included on the following page.

Cooking Chinese Noodles		
Noodle Type	Cooking Method	Cooking Time
Cellophane/Bean Thread Noodles	Soak in Hot Water	15 minutes
Egg Noodles, Fresh	Boil	3–5 minutes
Egg Noodles, Dried	Boil	4–5½ minutes
Rice Noodles	Soak in Hot Water	15–20 minutes
Rice Paper	Soak in Hot Water	1 minute
Wheat Flour, Fresh	Boil	3–5 minutes
Wheat Flour, Dried	Boil	4–5 minutes

Fresh Is Best

Always use the freshest ingredients possible; nothing can replace the bite of freshly ground white pepper, or ginger that has gone straight from garden to kitchen, bypassing the market.

- *Ginger:* Used for everything from seasoning oil to masking fishy odors in seafood dishes. Be sure to use fresh instead of powdered.
- *Garlic:* The mainstay of northern Chinese dishes, where cooks rely on hardy vegetables that can tolerate cold winters and a short growing season. Like ginger, it is also used to flavor hot oil before stir-frying.
- *Green onions:* Also called spring onions and scallions, these are used in cooked dishes and as a garnish.
- *Celery:* Celery's crisp texture makes a nice contrast with other vegetables in stir-fries.
- *White pepper:* Freshly ground white pepper lends a sharp bite to soups and stir-fries. Use sparingly at first or according to taste.

The Chinese also use hundreds of dried ingredients, from tangerine peel to lily buds. The most commonly used are dried black mushrooms—you'll frequently find these stacked in bins at the entrance to Asian markets. Don't worry about purchasing the most expensive brands, but do look for mushrooms with a nice curl to them.

Sauces and Oils

A good sauce is a key component in Chinese cooking. Savory sauces like oyster and hoisin sauce add their own intriguing blend of flavors to a sauce or marinade, while soy sauce is used both to flavor and color the food. Here are some of the sauces most commonly used in Chinese cooking:

- *Dark soy sauce:* This sauce is used primarily to lend a darker color to marinades, sauces, and heavier dishes. The recipe will state if dark soy sauce is required.
- *Light soy sauce:* Saltier and aged for a shorter period of time, light soy sauce makes a frequent appearance in soups, stir-fries, and deep-fries. When a recipe calls for soy or soya sauce, use light soy sauce.
- *Oyster sauce:* This rich sauce adds a savory flavor to dishes such as Broccoli with Oyster Sauce (page 242).
- *Hoisin sauce:* Made from seasoned soybean paste, the sweet and savory flavor of hoisin sauce is an indispensable tool of northern Chinese cooks.
- *Chili paste and chili sauce:* Fiery Szechuan cuisine wouldn't be the same without hot chilies. Just remember that a little goes a long way!

Versatile cornstarch has many uses, from binding liquid ingredients in meat marinades to coating food during deep-frying. Mixed with water, it's frequently used to thicken sauces during the final stages of cooking.

Both stir-frying and deep-frying require oils with a high smoking point. While Chinese cooks favor peanut oil, it can go rancid if there is too long a period between stir-fries. Vegetable oils such as canola and corn oil are an acceptable substitute. Sesame oil is used to add a unique nutty flavor to soups and fried dishes—just drizzle a few drops into the dish in the final stages of cooking.

You will also need to get Chinese rice wine, which is valued for its sweet flavor and ability to mask strong odors in marinades and stir-fries.

(Generally, pale dry sherry is an acceptable substitute.) In marinades and special sauces where the flavor of each ingredient counts more, stick with Chinese rice wine or make sure to use a higher quality pale dry sherry.

Cooking Equipment

You don't need to splurge on a bunch of fancy gadgets to cook Chinese food. All it takes is a wok and a few basic utensils. The versatile wok is a steamer, frying pan, deep-fryer, and roasting pan all rolled into one. A good chef's knife can be used instead of a Chinese cleaver, and you don't need a rice cooker to boil rice, but a wok is the one piece of equipment that you should definitely consider purchasing before you begin cooking Chinese food.

It would be stretching the truth to say that you absolutely must have a wok to cook Chinese food. Many satisfactory meals of chop suey and chow mein have been born in a frying pan. The main thing is to use a heavy skillet that can take the high heats required for stir-frying. Cast iron and Calphalon hard anodized pans are both good choices. Still, if it's possible, a wok is preferable. Here are a few tips on choosing a good wok.

Material Matters

Originally, woks were large round vessels made of cast iron, with handles on either side for easy lifting in and out of the conventional Chinese oven. Over the centuries, woks have evolved to meet changing needs. Today, most Asian cooks favor woks made of carbon steel. Inexpensive and easy to handle, carbon steel woks can take the high heat needed for stir-frying and deep-frying. Properly seasoned and cleaned, they will last for years.

Still, modern technology has provided other options. It's now possible to purchase woks made with a nonstick coating. There are several advantages to cooking with a nonstick wok. For one thing, it's healthier since you don't need to use as much oil. For another, there is less cleanup. It can be frustrating to interrupt cooking dinner to wash the remains of a meat marinade from the wok before starting to stir-fry the vegetables. A nonstick coating means less fuss and muss.

The one potential drawback with nonstick woks is that the coating may warp under higher temperatures. Be prepared to pay extra for hard-anodized aluminum or carbon steel woks with a nonstick coating that can take the high heats needed for stir-frying.

Wok Design

As a general rule, the type of stove you have will influence your choice of wok design. Traditional round-bottomed woks don't sit properly on an electric stove element. Originally, wok manufacturers tried to solve the problem by devising a round "collar" to sit on the burner and hold the wok in place. However, a better solution for an electric stove is a wok with a flat bottom. In addition to being safer, flat-bottomed woks ensure that the food cooks quickly and evenly. Both round and flat-bottomed woks work on gas stoves.

FACT

Purchase a wok that is too small, and you'll be spending extra time in the kitchen, stir-frying and deep-frying in batches. While fascinating to look at, the mammoth woks favored by Chinese restaurant chefs are designed to feed a crowd, and aren't necessary for home cooking. For most families, a 14-inch wok is a good choice.

Pay Attention to the Cover

Be sure that the wok you purchase comes with a lid. Unlike the conventional frying pan cover, wok lids are bowl-shaped, with a handle on top. Use them to cover foods during braising and steaming, and as a large bowl for tossing food prior to cooking.

Other Kitchen Accessories

Just because you're learning an ancient cuisine doesn't mean you can't take advantage of modern technology. Here are a number of handy tools and gadgets that will make your cooking go more smoothly.

- *Cleaver or chef's knife:* It doesn't need to be a Chinese cleaver, but it must be sharp and able to cut everything from meat to mushrooms.
- *Mandoline:* Great for cutting potatoes and other root vegetables julienne style. There are also miniature mandolines that do a nifty job of shredding garlic and ginger.
- *Food processor:* Invaluable for mixing sauces and crushing ingredients.
- *Wire mesh skimmer:* A large wire mesh spoon that makes transferring deep-fried food from wok to plate much easier.
- *Cooking chopsticks:* Longer than regular chopsticks, these are great for lightly beating eggs, mixing marinade ingredients, and maneuvering individual pieces of food in the wok.
- *Cutting board:* Chinese chefs favor thick, round wooden cutting boards, but acrylic is also acceptable. Avoid plastic, as it can damage your knife.
- *Chinese spatula:* With a wide handle shaped like a child's toy shovel, this utensil is the perfect size and shape for moving large quantities of food through the wok while stir-frying, ensuring that the food lands back in the pan and not on the stove or floor.

Peeling garlic is easy with a Chinese cleaver. Use the edge of the cleaver to separate one clove from the rest, then smash the clove using the side of the cleaver. Peel the garlic and chop or mince according to the directions in the recipe.

Cooking Techniques

While anyone can learn to prepare Chinese food, it helps to master a few basic techniques. Whether you're stir-frying chicken for four or making egg rolls for twenty, here are a few general tips to keep in mind when cooking Chinese food:

- *Start small.* Try preparing a stir-fry entrée accompanied by steamed rice, or a vegetable side dish to serve with your main meal. Later, you can work up to an entire Chinese meal complete with appetizer, soup, and dessert.

- *Try to create meals that provide an interesting variety of textures, colors, and flavors.* The goal of Chinese cooking is to strike a pleasing balance, with no one ingredient overpowering the others.
- *Use fresh ingredients wherever possible.* If a recipe calls for a certain ingredient that is out of season, substitute whatever is available locally.
- *Think about texture as well as color when making substitutions.* Zucchini stands in nicely for a Chinese gourd, while crisp broccoli makes a good substitute for bok choy.
- *Be creative with leftovers.* Leftover vegetables can liven up a dish of fried rice, while chicken bones can be used to make chicken stock.
- *Leaving the meat partially frozen will make it easier to cut.*
- *Always marinate fresh meat before cooking.* Use the time while the meat is marinating to cut vegetables and mix sauces.
- *Keep a supply of paper towels on hand to drain stir-fried and deep-fried food.*
- *Don't use dark soy sauce unless the recipe specifically calls for it.* Light soy sauce has a higher salt content than dark; substituting one for the other will affect the flavor of the dish.
- *Never use more cornstarch than the recipe calls for; a little goes a long way.*
- *Trust your judgment.* Something as minor as varying salt levels between different brands of soy sauce can affect the flavor of a dish. Always do a taste test at the end of cooking and adjust the seasonings if you think it is necessary.

Stir-frying

It may look daunting when we watch a television chef skillfully maneuvering food in a wok, but anyone can learn to stir-fry. The key to successful stir-frying is high heat combined with vigorous stirring.

Make sure all your ingredients are prepared ahead of time. The average stir-fry takes less than seven minutes, leaving little time for last minute slicing and dicing. Always leave stir-frying until the end of cooking. Stir-fries are meant to go straight from wok to table.

Cut all the ingredients to a uniform size, to ensure that they cook at the same rate. If you're improvising instead of following a recipe, a good rule of thumb is to cut everything into bite-sized pieces.

If you are using a carbon steel wok, preheat the wok for 1 minute before adding oil. If you are using a wok made out of a different type of material, or a wok or frying pan with a nonstick coating, check the manufacturer's instructions first to ensure that preheating will not cause any damage.

FACT

Stir-frying may be China's most famous cooking technique, but it was not the first. Stir-frying came into vogue during the Han dynasty, when fuel shortages forced people to adopt a speedy cooking method that used oil sparingly.

When adding oil, pour it so that it swirls around the sides of the wok before reaching the bottom. Test to see if the oil is hot by standing a cooking chopstick straight up in the wok's center. If the oil sizzles all the way around the chopstick, you can start cooking. If you don't have a chopstick, a small piece of bread works also.

Before adding other ingredients, try flavoring the oil with a few slices of ginger and/or garlic. Stir-fry until they are aromatic. Then, add other ingredients. To stir-fry, simply move the spatula through the wok and stir the ingredients every few seconds.

When you cook meat, sear it briefly before stir-frying. To make sure all of it comes into contact with the pan, it's important not to overcrowd the wok. Cook meat in batches, if necessary.

ESSENTIAL

When it comes to cooking temperatures for stir-frying, be prepared to do a bit of experimenting. Every stove is different, and it may take a few attempts before you find the optimum temperature for stir-frying on your make and model.

Never pour a cornstarch-and-water mixture directly over the food in the wok. Instead, push the food up to the sides of the wok and add the cornstarch and water in the middle. Turn up the heat and stir vigorously to thicken. Once it has thickened you can mix it with the other ingredients.

Most importantly, don't panic. If you feel things are moving too fast, just take the wok or frying pan off the heat and give yourself a moment to relax and refocus. Stir-frying is a very forgiving art.

Deep-frying

Deep-frying has gotten a bad rap in recent years, thanks to visions of oil-splattered stoves and concern over high cholesterol levels. But there is nothing like deep-frying for sealing in meat's juices and adding a crispy coating to dishes such as Ginger Beef (page 127).

The trick to deep-frying is keeping the temperature constant during cooking. Too low temperatures will lead to greasy food loaded with extra fat and calories. The following tips will help you prepare deep-fried dishes that are crisp and full of flavor.

First of all, make sure the wok is securely attached to the stand. Next, pour in enough oil to completely cover the food being cooked, while leaving a couple of inches of room at the top of the wok. Unless the recipe states otherwise, the temperature of the oil should rise to about 350–375°F.

Slide the food in carefully, so that it doesn't splatter when it meets the hot oil. Leave plenty of room in the wok for the food to move around. Deep-fry in batches, if necessary. As soon as the food is added, check the temperature of the oil. Turn and separate the individual pieces of food while they are cooking.

ALERT!

Continue to monitor the oil temperature while deep-frying. The easiest way to do this is with a deep-fry thermometer with a clamp that can attach to the side of the wok. That way, your hands remain free for cooking while you're checking the temperature.

Use a slotted spoon or a mesh skimmer to carefully remove the deep-fried food from the wok. Drain the deep-fried food on paper towels. If the recipe calls for food to be deep-fried twice, retest the temperature and make sure the oil is hot enough before you begin deep-frying the second time.

To reuse cooked oil, let it cool and then strain and store in a sealed container in the refrigerator. Cooked oil can be reused up to five times. Throw it out if the color darkens or it begins to smell rancid.

Even with these tips, you may find that using a wok to deep-fry is not for you. Wok deep-frying demands your undivided attention. If you have small children at home, or frequent interruptions are the norm, consider using a deep-fat fryer instead.

Steaming

Steaming, or cooking food by placing it over boiling or simmering water, is the third and the simplest Chinese cooking technique. The key to successful steaming lies in ensuring that the hot water never touches the food.

When it comes to equipment, a set of bamboo steamers is ideal. Bamboo steamers allow you to prepare multiple layers of food at the same time. In contrast to aluminum steamers, the natural texture of bamboo acts to prevent condensation from getting into the food. The cooked food can move straight from wok to table, with the steaming baskets doing double duty as cooking utensil and serving dish.

FACT

Steaming is the least intrusive cooking technique; the flavor, color, and texture of the steamed food remain closer to what nature intended. Nutritionally speaking, steamed food retains more nutrients and vitamins, and is generally lower in fat and calories, than food cooked by other methods.

Steaming with bamboo is easy if you keep the following tips in mind:

- Before placing the food in the bamboo steamer, line the steamer with cabbage leaves, bamboo or banana leaves, or cheesecloth. This prevents the food from sticking.
- Be sure to leave approximately an inch between the water and food to be steamed.

- For smaller items such as dumplings, place the bamboo base or trivet in the water, with the steaming basket on top. Place the food in the basket, cover, and cook. For larger items such as meat and seafood dishes, either move to a larger set of bamboo steamers or substitute a heatproof dish. Also placed on the bamboo base, the heatproof dish can be anything from a dinner plate to an aluminum pie plate. The wok lid makes an ideal cover.
- When choosing a bamboo steamer, inspect it carefully to make sure none of the parts are connected with staples. If you find staples, choose another brand.
- Prior to its first use, give the steamer a thorough washing with soap and hot water. Dry completely before using.
- For best results, always use the freshest ingredients possible.

Tea Time

Dine at a Chinese restaurant, and chances are that before you've placed your order, the waitress will appear at your table with a steaming pot of tea. In China, tea is more than merely a hot drink. Over centuries, tea drinking has gone from being a refined pastime stretching several hours to an essential part of every meal.

A Brief History of Tea in China

According to a charming legend, tea was discovered when an Emperor fell asleep underneath a tea bush and awoke to find that a brown leaf had drifted into his cup of boiled water. This legend places the discovery of tea to 2737 B.C. Whether or not the story is true, there is no doubt that the Chinese were cultivating tea by A.D. 350.

However, it took the publication of a scholarly work to transform tea from merely a hot brew into China's national drink. Late in the eighth century, Lu Yu published *The Classic Art of Tea Drinking*. A poet and performer who had been educated by Buddhist monks, Lu Yu attempted to provide a complete overview of the history, cultivation, processing, and drinking of tea. The result was a definitive tome that is still consulted by tea experts today.

ALERT!

Brewing the perfect cup of green tea is a tricky process. With improper handling, those same polyphenols that protect the body against cancer and other diseases can ruin the tea's flavor. Allow boiled water to cool to a temperature of no more than 175°F before pouring over the tea. Steep for 2 to 3 minutes before drinking. Plan on using 1–2 teaspoons of green tea per cup.

Tea's popularity skyrocketed following the publication of Lu Yu's work. Buddhist monks introduced tea to the Japanese, although its use in Japan didn't become widespread until the 1200s. Today, teahouses are scattered throughout cities in China. Each has its own atmosphere; you can play chess at one, listen to music played on ancient Chinese instruments at another. The one thing that remains constant is the quality of the tea.

Tea Tapping

When dining at a Chinese restaurant, you may have noticed diners tapping the table each time their teacup is refilled. "Tea tapping" is a charming custom that originated during the Qing dynasty. According to legend, one of the emperors during this period was fond of traveling throughout the country incognito with his servants. During one trip they stopped at a teahouse. In order to preserve his disguise, the emperor took a turn at pouring the tea.

His traveling companions wanted to thank the emperor by bowing. However, this would have revealed the emperor's true identity. Instead, the emperor asked his companions to show their appreciation by tapping their fingers on the table each time he poured the tea. He suggested they tap the table three times, with one tap representing their bowed head and the two remaining taps their outstretched arms.

The custom has survived to this day. It's an easy way to thank someone for refilling your teacup without disrupting the conversation at the table.

Types of Tea Available

When you consider the different types of teas available, it's easy to believe that they come from different plants. In fact, all tea comes from the *Camellia sinensis* plant. In general, tea is categorized both by the way it is processed and its country of origin.

When it comes to tea, not all water is created equal. Tea just won't taste the same if it is made with water that contains impurities or has been treated with chlorine. A good water filter helps here, and bottled water is always preferable. According to the sage of Chinese tea, Lu Yu, pure water from natural springs is best for making tea, followed by river water and well water, in that order.

There are literally hundreds of varieties of Chinese teas, many named after the region where they were first cultivated. However, the majority fall into one of these five categories:

- *Green tea:* Probably the most famous Chinese tea due to its reputed health benefits, green tea is made from unfermented tea leaves. The leaves are dried immediately after picking. This prevents oxidation, leaving the chemical properties of the tea intact.
- *Oolong tea:* Made from larger tea leaves, this is a tea that has been partially fermented, so that full oxidization of the leaves does not take place. After drying in the sun, the leaves are heated to stop the oxidation process. This gives them a greenish-black color. Because fermentation can be stopped at any point, the flavor of different types of oolong tea vary.
- *Black tea:* Black tea consists of tea leaves that have been rolled and then fully dried and fermented, giving them a darker color. Black tea is more popular in the west than in Asia. It is often used in cooking dishes, such as Tea Smoked Chicken (page 175).
- *Scented teas:* These are made by adding flowers to the tea leaves during the fermentation process. The most popular scented teas are jasmine and chrysanthemum.

- *White tea:* Like green tea, white teas are unfermented. However, instead of steam drying, the tea leaves are dried naturally in the sun. White tea is believed to have even more health benefits than green tea.

Health Benefits of Tea

In recent years, scientists have been paying a great deal of attention to the health benefits of drinking green tea. What sets green tea apart from other teas? Green teas contain a polyphenol called epigallocatechin gallate (EGCG), which is known to be a powerful antioxidant.

Since antioxidants inhibit the growth of free radicals found in cancer cells, it's not surprising that most of the research on green tea has focused on its ability to prevent cancer. However, EGCG has other health benefits as well. Green tea has been shown to lower blood pressure and reduce high cholesterol levels. It is also believed to lower the risk of stroke.

QUESTION?

Which is better, tea bags or loose-leaf tea?
Loose-leaf teas are preferable to bagged tea. Made with a lower grade of tea leaves known as "fannings," bagged teas tend to have less flavor. Many higher quality teas aren't available in bags. Still, bagged tea does have its advantages if you're in a hurry or want a quick cup of tea at the office.

While most of the research has focused on green tea, scientists are discovering that there are also health benefits to be derived from drinking black tea. Black teas contain another type of polyphenol called theaflavin-3'-monogallate (TF-2). Like EGCG, TF-2 is believed to inhibit the growth of cancer cells. Research is also being conducted on the use of black tea to treat arthritis.

CHAPTER 2
Common Dipping Sauces

Hot Mustard Dip

Yields ⅓ cup

Hot mustard's bite makes a great combination with Egg Rolls (page 32) and less highly spiced appetizers such as Gow Gees (page 45).

3 tablespoons hot mustard
3 tablespoons water
1 teaspoon rice vinegar
½ teaspoon sugar

Combine all the ingredients. Use immediately.

What Makes Hot Mustard Hot?

A better question would be, why aren't all mustards hot? The secret behind hot mustard's fiery flavor lies in the chemical reaction that occurs when mustard seeds come in contact with a liquid such as water or salad oil. Commercially prepared mustards tone down the reaction by adding ingredients such as flour. The strength and flavor of mustard also depends on the type of mustard seeds used.

Hot Mustard Sauce

Yields about ¼ cup

This is a little runnier than a paste. Use in a salad like Chinese Potato Salad (page 69).

2 tablespoons mustard powder
2 tablespoons rice vinegar
1 teaspoon brown sugar
1 tablespoon vegetable oil
3 drops sesame oil

Mix all the ingredients and use immediately.

Plum Sauce

1 12-ounce can prune plums,
  drained
2 tablespoons brown sugar
4 tablespoons rice vinegar
1 slice ginger

1 clove garlic
½ cup canned juice from the
  drained plums
½ cup water

1. Remove the plum pits. In a medium saucepan, bring all ingredients to a boil. Simmer, covered, for about 2 hours, or until the plums are soft.
2. Remove the ginger and garlic. Process the sauce in a blender or food processor until smooth. Cool and chill in the refrigerator. Use within a few days.

Brown Sauce

1 tablespoon plus 1 teaspoon
  oyster sauce
3 teaspoons hoisin sauce
1 teaspoon sherry
1 teaspoon soy sauce
½ teaspoon sugar

½ cup beef broth or juices
  from cooked meat
2 tablespoons water
1 tablespoon cornstarch

1. Combine all the ingredients, adding the cornstarch last. Bring to a boil.
2. Cook on medium to medium-low heat, stirring constantly to thicken mixture. The sauce should be neither too thin nor too runny, but thick enough to use as a dip, if desired.

Peanut Sauce

Yields 1 cup

Use this spicy sauce with Gado Gado Salad (page 70) or to liven up a plain garden salad.

½ cup chicken broth
½ cup peanut butter
2 garlic cloves, minced
2 tablespoons red onion, minced
2 teaspoons brown sugar
4 tablespoons soy sauce
½ teaspoon chili sauce
2 tablespoons plus 2 teaspoons rice vinegar
2 tablespoons water
1 teaspoon chopped cilantro (optional)

1. Combine all the ingredients except for the cilantro and purée in a food processor.
2. Bring to a boil in a small saucepan. Stir in the cilantro. Use immediately.

Szechwan Salt and Pepper Mix

Yields about ⅓ cup

For variety, try using this flavorful mix in place of plain salt and pepper, even when you're not eating Chinese food.

2 tablespoons Szechwan peppercorns
1 teaspoon black peppercorns
½ teaspoon white peppercorns
¼ cup salt

1. Brown the peppercorns and salt in a heavy skillet on medium to medium-low heat, shaking the pan occasionally, until the Szechwan peppercorns are fragrant and the salt turns a light brown color.
2. Grind the cooled mixture in a blender. Store in a sealed jar and use as a dip or condiment.

Don't Let the Name Fool You
Szechwan peppers aren't peppers at all! They are distinctive reddish brown berries that come from the prickly ash native to Szechwan province.

Sweet-and-Sour Worcestershire Sauce

¼ cup white rice vinegar
2 tablespoons black rice vinegar
½ cup brown sugar
1 tablespoon Worcestershire sauce
¼ cup ketchup

½ cup pineapple juice
¼ cup water
2 teaspoons cornstarch mixed
*   with 4 teaspoons water*

1. In a medium saucepan, bring the white rice vinegar, black rice vinegar, brown sugar, Worcestershire sauce, ketchup, pineapple juice, and water to a boil.
2. Add the cornstarch-and-water mixture, stirring vigorously to thicken.

Yields about 1¼ cups

Use this flavorful sauce wherever you might normally use a sweet-and-sour sauce.

Hoisin Satay Sauce

3 tablespoons hoisin sauce
2 teaspoons dark soy sauce
1 teaspoon rice vinegar
1 teaspoon orange marmalade

Up to ¼ teaspoon cayenne
*   pepper flakes*
1 clove garlic, chopped
¼ cup peanuts, crushed

Combine all the ingredients. Serve with Beef Satay (page 116).

Yields ⅓ cup

Orange marmalade lends flavor to a traditional hoisin-based sauce in this fusion recipe. For a different taste, substitute 1 tablespoon of honey.

Quick and Easy Sweet-and-Sour Sauce

½ cup vinegar

1 tablespoon and 1 teaspoon sugar

1 large clove garlic, minced

1 teaspoon cornstarch

4 teaspoons water

In a medium saucepan, bring all the ingredients to a boil, stirring to thicken.

Sweet-and-Sour Sauce with Ketchup

⅓ cup rice vinegar

¼ cup brown sugar

2 tablespoons ketchup

1 tablespoon soy sauce

¼ cup water

4 teaspoons cornstarch mixed with 4 teaspoons water

1. In a small saucepan, combine the rice vinegar, brown sugar, ketchup, soy sauce, and water and bring to a boil.
2. Stir in the cornstarch-and-water mixture, stirring vigorously to thicken.

Hot Chili Oil

6 red chili peppers   1 cup vegetable oil
1 tablespoon sesame oil

1. Cut the chili peppers in half and remove the seeds. Chop coarsely.
2. Mix the oils and heat in a wok or heavy skillet.
3. Add the chopped chili peppers and cook over low heat for about 5 minutes, or until the oil turns red.
4. Cool the oil and strain into a sealed jar. Store in the refrigerator.

✿ Handling Hot Chilies
When handling chili peppers, it's important to make sure that none of the chemical gets in your eyes. For extra safety, wear rubber gloves.

> **Yields ⅞ cup**
>
> Chili Oil makes an excellent dipping sauce for Potstickers with Rice Wine (page 41). Use it whenever you want to add heat to your meal.
>
> ⌣ · ✿ · ⌣

Spicy Szechwan Peanut Sauce

3 tablespoons peanut butter   1 clove garlic, chopped
3 tablespoons soy sauce   1–2 tablespoons Hot Chili Oil
4 teaspoons sugar   (page 23)
3 tablespoons black rice vinegar
1 tablespoon sesame oil

Process all the ingredients in a food processor.

> **Yields ½ cup**
>
> Use as a dipping sauce or in Szechwan dishes such as Bang Bang Chicken (page 163). For best results, use within a few days.
>
> ⌣ · ✿ · ⌣

Mild Szechwan Peanut Sauce

Yields ⅓ cup

Want to enjoy
Szechwan cooking
without experiencing
the extreme heat? Use
this sauce instead of
Spicy Szechwan
Peanut Sauce
(page 23).

3 tablespoons peanut butter
3 tablespoons soy sauce
4 teaspoons sugar
3 teaspoons black rice vinegar

1 teaspoon sesame oil
1 clove garlic, chopped
2 teaspoons chili sauce

Process all the ingredients in a food processor.

Hot Food Antidote
Tempted to reach for a glass of water after tasting fiery Szechwan food? Try a forkful of rice instead. Oil and water don't mix, and a glass of water will roll right over the chili oils that add heat to Szechwan cooking. Rice, milk, or even beer all provide more immediate relief than a glass of water.

Soy Hoisin Dressing

Yields about ⅓ cup

This savory dressing
makes a great dip
and adds flavor to
vegetable and
noodle salads.

2 teaspoons Chinese rice wine
  or dry sherry
1 teaspoon minced ginger

2 teaspoons hoisin sauce
2 tablespoons soy sauce
2 tablespoons dark soy sauce

Combine all the ingredients.

Storing Homemade Dips
Unlike their store-bought counterparts, homemade dipping sauces have a relatively short life span. Store them in a sealed container in the refrigerator, and use within a few days. Waiting a few hours or even overnight (refrigerated) before using a sauce gives the flavors a chance to blend.

Soy Ginger Dressing

2 tablespoons soy sauce
2 teaspoons rice vinegar
1 teaspoon grated ginger

A few drops sesame oil
    (about ⅛ teaspoon)

Combine all the ingredients.

🌿 Worcestershire Sauce

It may have been invented by two British chemists in the 1800s, but Worcestershire sauce wouldn't be the same without an Asian influence. The secret ingredient in Worcestershire sauce is tamarind, an acid-tasting fruit that gives many Thai sauces their sharp bite. Today, Worcestershire sauce makes a frequent appearance in Chinese dipping sauces.

Yields about ⅓ cup

The clean flavor of ginger gives this dressing a sharp bite. Use as a dip with Chinese dumplings such as Gow Gees (page 45).

Soy Vinegar Dressing

3 tablespoons soy sauce
2 teaspoons rice vinegar
¼ teaspoon minced ginger

Combine all the ingredients in a small bowl.

Yields about ¼ cup

This dressing takes mere minutes to make. Drizzle over vegetables and rice, or use as a dipping sauce for Mini Spring Onion Pancakes (page 48).

Asian Vinaigrette

Yields about ½ cup

This dressing nicely complements a simple tossed green salad. Stored in a sealed container and refrigerated, it will keep for a few days.

4 tablespoons salad oil
2 tablespoons black rice vinegar
2 teaspoons soy sauce

½ teaspoon sugar
A few drops sesame oil

Combine all the ingredients in a jar and shake to mix thoroughly. Drizzle over the salad.

Stocking Up on Asian Ingredients

If the local grocery store doesn't carry a certain ingredient, and there is no Asian market nearby, try the Internet. Several online grocery stores carry a broad range of Asian ingredients and cooking equipment. Just be sure to check out availability and shipping rates for your area before ordering.

Speedy Sweet Chili Sauce

Yields ½ cup

A quick and easy recipe for those days when you don't have any chili peppers on hand.

¼ cup rice vinegar
4 tablespoons sugar
1½ teaspoons chili sauce, or to taste

1 teaspoon cornstarch mixed with 4 teaspoons water

1. In a small saucepan, bring the rice vinegar, sugar, and chili sauce to a boil.
2. Add the cornstarch-and-water mixture, stirring vigorously to thicken.

Sweet Green and Red Chili Sauce

3 jalapeno peppers
1/4 red bell pepper
1/4 cup rice vinegar

4 tablespoons sugar
1 teaspoon cornstarch
4 teaspoons water

1. Cut the jalapeno peppers in half lengthwise. Remove the seeds and chop. Wash the red bell pepper and cut into squares.
2. Process the rice vinegar, sugar, jalapeno peppers, and red pepper in a blender or food processor.
3. In a small saucepan, bring the liquid to a boil. As it simmers for a few minutes, mix the cornstarch and water.
4. Stir in the cornstarch mixture, until the sauce thickens.

> **Yields 2/3 cup**
>
> This dip will give a burning sensation in the back of your mouth, but without the sweating and watery eyes associated with hotter peppers.

Northern Noodle Sauce

1 small clove garlic, chopped
1/2 green onion, mainly white
    part, thinly sliced
1/4 cup dark soy sauce
2 teaspoons black rice vinegar
1 teaspoon Hot Chili Oil
    (page 23)

1/2 teaspoon sugar
1/4 teaspoon sesame oil
1 teaspoon cornstarch mixed
    with 4 teaspoons water

1. Combine garlic clove and green onion with the dark soy sauce, black rice vinegar, Hot Chili Oil, sugar, and sesame oil. Process in a blender or food processor until smooth.
2. In a small saucepan, bring the sauce to a boil. Give the cornstarch-and-water mixture a quick stir. Add to the sauce, stirring vigorously to thicken. Cool and serve as a dip or serve hot with noodles.

> **Yields 1/3 cup**
>
> This spicy sauce adds bite to noodle and tofu dishes. For a milder sauce, leave out the chili oil.

Potsticker Dipping Sauce

Yields ⅓ cup

Feel free to serve this spicy sauce with other Chinese dumplings besides Potstickers (page 41).

2 tablespoons dark soy sauce
2 tablespoons light soy sauce
¼ teaspoon sesame oil
1 teaspoon oyster sauce
2 teaspoons black rice vinegar

1 teaspoon sugar
1 teaspoon Hot Chili Oil (page 23)
1 teaspoon cilantro leaves, finely chopped

Combine all the ingredients.

Intriguing XO Sauce
For an exotic twist, try adding a teaspoon of XO sauce to your favorite dipping sauce recipe. First served at Hong Kong Chinese restaurants, this flavorful sauce is an intriguing mix of seafood and spicy seasonings such as hot chilies and garlic.

Jazzed Up Black Bean Sauce

Yields about ¾ cup

This is a savory sauce that can be used with pancakes, noodles, and steamed buns.

1½ tablespoons black bean sauce
2 teaspoons sugar
1 tablespoon oyster sauce
1 teaspoon Chinese rice wine or dry sherry

¼ teaspoon chili sauce with garlic
½ cup water

Combine all the ingredients.

Jazzed Up Hoisin Sauce

½ cup hoisin sauce
1 clove garlic, finely chopped
1 teaspoon finely chopped
    ginger
1 teaspoon black rice vinegar,
    or to taste
½ teaspoon sesame oil

Combine all the ingredients.

What about Duck Sauce?

Not sure whether to serve duck sauce or plum sauce with your mandarin pancakes? Actually, both terms refer to the same sweet and spicy sauce. Plum sauce was nicknamed "duck sauce" after Western Chinese restaurants began serving it with Peking Duck, under the mistaken impression that this was an authentic practice. In reality, Peking Duck is traditionally served with hoisin sauce. But whatever name it goes by, the thick reddish sauce makes an excellent dipping sauce for Egg Rolls (page 32) and goes well with sparerib and chicken dishes.

Yields about ½ cup

Serve as a dipping
sauce with dumplings,
or snacks such as
Mandarin Pancakes
(page 268) or Mini
Spring Onion
Pancakes (page 48).

Asian Appetizers and Dim Sum

Egg Rolls

¼ cup canned bamboo shoots, sliced
1 tablespoon oyster sauce
1 tablespoon chicken broth or stock
½ teaspoon sugar
2 tablespoons oil for stir-frying
6 large fresh mushrooms, thinly sliced
1 stalk celery, thinly sliced on the diagonal

¼ cup water chestnuts, thinly sliced
1 cup fresh mung bean sprouts, drained
2 green onions, thinly sliced on the diagonal
½ pound barbecued pork
15 egg roll wrappers
3 tablespoons cornstarch mixed with 2 tablespoons water
4–6 cups oil for frying

1. Thinly slice the bamboo shoots. Combine the oyster sauce, chicken broth, and sugar. Set aside.
2. Add 2 tablespoons oil to a preheated wok or skillet. When oil is hot, add the mushrooms and stir-fry for about 1 minute. Add the celery, then the water chestnuts, then bamboo shoots, stir-frying each for about 1 minute in the middle of the wok before adding the next vegetable. (If the wok is too crowded, stir-fry each vegetable separately.) Add more oil as necessary, pushing the vegetables up to the side of the wok until the oil is hot. Add the bean sprouts and the green onions.
3. Add the sauce to the middle of the wok and bring to a boil. Add the barbequed pork. Heat everything through. Cool.
4. Heat 4–6 cups oil to 375°F. While the oil is heating, prepare the wrappers. To wrap, spread a heaping tablespoon of filling in the middle of the wrapper, evenly spread out but not too close to the edges. Coat the top edge and the sides with the cornstarch/water mixture. Fold the bottom half over the filling. Fold the top half over, making sure the 2 sides overlap. Press down to seal all the edges. Continue with the remainder of the egg rolls. (Prepare more cornstarch and water if necessary.)
5. Deep-fry the egg rolls until they turn golden brown (2–3 minutes). Drain on paper towels.

Deep-fried Wontons

3 medium dried mushrooms
1½ cups ground pork
½ cup canned bamboo shoots, shredded
1½ green onions, thinly sliced
1 slice ginger

2 teaspoons black rice vinegar
2 teaspoons soy sauce
1 teaspoon sugar
1 teaspoon sesame oil
1 package wonton wrappers
4–6 cups oil for deep-frying

Yields 30–35 wontons

Have more filled wontons than you need? Freeze and use the next time you're making Wonton Soup (page 54). Thaw before adding to the soup.

1. Soak the dried mushrooms in hot water for at least 20 minutes to soften. Drain, remove the stems, and slice finely. Shred the bamboo shoots.
2. Combine the ground pork, bamboo shoots, green onions, dried mushrooms, ginger, black rice vinegar, soy sauce, sugar, and sesame oil.
3. Add oil to a preheated wok and heat to 375°F. While waiting for the oil to heat, wrap the wontons. Lay the wrapper in a square shape in front of you. Place 1 teaspoon of filling in the middle of the wrapper. Fold the wonton wrapper in half lengthwise, making sure the ends meet. Roll the wonton wrapper over again, being sure to keep the filling centered. Wet the ends. Bring the corners together so that one overlaps the other, and seal. Continue with the remainder of the wontons. Cover the completed wontons with a damp towel to prevent drying.
4. Carefully slide a few wontons at a time into the wok. Deep-fry until they turn golden (about 2 minutes). Remove with a slotted spoon and drain on paper towels.

Maintaining Oil Temperature During Deep-frying

To prevent greasy food, it's important to keep the oil temperature from dropping substantially during deep-frying. This can be tricky, since it is normal for the temperature to drop when food is first added to the wok. One solution is to heat the oil to a higher temperature than called for in the recipe. For example, if the instructions state the food should be deep-fried at 350°F, wait until the oil temperature reaches 355–360°F before starting to deep-fry.

Wonton Wrappers

Yields 24–28 wrappers

Stuffed wonton wrappers feature prominently in soups and dim sum dishes. They can even replace egg roll wrappers in the recipe for Bowties (page 272-273).

½ teaspoon salt
2¼ cups flour
⅔ cup water

1 medium egg
1 teaspoon vegetable oil

1. Sift the salt into the flour. Add the remaining ingredients, adding the water slowly and not using more than necessary. Form the batter into a dough and knead until smooth. Cover the dough and let it rest for 30 minutes.
2. Cut the dough in half. Form each half into a cylinder. Lightly score the dough into ½-inch pieces and cut (you should have 12–14 pieces). Repeat with the other half of the dough.
3. On a lightly floured surface, roll each piece out into a 3½-inch square. Store wrapped in plastic in the refrigerator or freeze until ready to use.

Water Chestnut Appetizer

Yields 20 appetizers

This simple but tasty appetizer works best with fresh chestnuts. For quicker cooking, broil the water chestnuts for 5–6 minutes instead of baking.

20 fresh water chestnuts
½ cup soy sauce
10 slices raw bacon

½ cup brown sugar
20 toothpicks

1. Peel the water chestnuts. Rinse and drain well. Place the soy sauce in a plastic bag. Add the water chestnuts and seal. Marinate for 3 hours, turning occasionally to cover completely.
2. Preheat the oven to 350°F. Cut each slice of bacon in half. Spread the brown sugar out on a piece of waxed paper.
3. Remove the water chestnuts from the bag, reserving the marinade. Roll each water chestnut in the brown sugar. Wrap a slice of bacon around each water chestnut and secure with a toothpick.
4. Bake the water chestnuts at 350°F for 45 minutes. After 20 minutes, turn the water chestnuts over and pour the reserved marinade over. Continue baking.

Spring Rolls

½ pound pork tenderloin, shredded
2 tablespoons oyster sauce, divided
½ teaspoon baking soda
6 dried mushrooms
1 carrot
1 tablespoon chicken broth or stock
½ teaspoon sugar
1 cup mung bean sprouts, rinsed
    and drained

2 green onions, thinly sliced on
    the diagonal
¼ teaspoon sesame oil
12 spring roll wrappers
2 tablespoons cornstarch mixed
    with 1 tablespoon water
4–6 cups oil for frying

Yields 12 Spring Rolls

Both barbecued pork
and chicken mari-
nated in oyster sauce
also work well in
this recipe.

1. Marinate the pork in 1 tablespoon oyster sauce and baking soda for
   30 minutes.
2. Soak the dried mushrooms in hot water to soften; drain and thinly
   slice. Wash and grate the carrot until you have ¼ cup.
3. Combine the remaining 1 tablespoon oyster sauce, chicken broth, and
   sugar. Set aside.
4. Add 2 tablespoons oil to a preheated wok or skillet. When oil is hot,
   add the pork. Stir-fry briefly until it changes color and is nearly
   cooked through. Remove from the wok.
5. Add 1½ tablespoons oil. When oil is hot, add the dried mushrooms.
   Stir-fry for 1 minute, then add the bean sprouts, grated carrot, and the
   green onion. Add the sauce in the middle of the wok and bring to a
   boil. Add the pork and mix through. Drizzle with the sesame oil. Cool.
6. Heat 4–6 cups oil to 375°F. While oil is heating, prepare the spring
   rolls. To wrap, lay the wrapper in a diamond shape. Place a tablespoon
   of filling in the middle. Coat all the edges with the cornstarch-and-water
   mixture. Roll up the wrapper and tuck in the edges. Seal the tucked-in
   edges with cornstarch and water. Continue with the remainder of the
   Spring Rolls. (Prepare more cornstarch and water as necessary.)
7. Deep-fry the spring rolls, 2 at a time, until they turn golden. Drain on
   paper towels.

Crab Rangoon

48 wonton wrappers
1 cup fresh or canned crabmeat
1 cup cream cheese
½ teaspoon Worcestershire sauce
½ teaspoon soy sauce
⅛ teaspoon freshly ground white pepper, or to taste
2 teaspoons minced onion
1½ green onions, thinly sliced
1 large clove garlic, minced
Water for wetting wontons
4 cups oil for deep-frying

1. Cover the wonton wrappers with a damp towel to prevent drying. Set aside.
2. If using canned crabmeat, drain thoroughly. Flake the crabmeat with a fork. Add the cream cheese, then mix in the Worcestershire sauce, soy sauce, white pepper, onion, green onion, and garlic.
3. To prepare the Crab Rangoon: lay a wrapper in a diamond shape or circle, depending on the shape of wonton wrappers you are using. Add a heaping teaspoon of filling in the middle, spread out evenly but not too near the edges. Spread the water along all 4 sides. Fold the bottom over the top to form a triangle (round wrappers will form a half moon). Seal the edges, adding more water if needed. Cover filled wontons with a damp towel to prevent drying.
4. Heat 4 cups oil in a preheated wok to 375°F. Slide in the wonton wrappers a few at a time, and deep-fry for 2–3 minutes, until they turn golden brown. Remove with a slotted spoon and drain on paper towels. Cool and serve.

Make-Ahead Crab Rangoon

Want to get a head start on making cocktail appetizers? Crab Rangoon can be prepared ahead of time up to the deep-frying stage and frozen. Thaw the filled wontons before deep-frying.

Lettuce Wraps

1 pound boneless, skinless chicken breasts

1 head iceberg lettuce

1 red bell pepper

½ 8-ounce can water chestnuts, rinsed and drained

½ 8-ounce can bamboo shoots, rinsed and drained

1 tablespoon soy sauce

2 tablespoons oyster sauce

1 tablespoon Chinese rice wine

1 teaspoon sugar

4 tablespoons oil for stir-frying

1 teaspoon minced garlic clove

1 teaspoon minced ginger

1 stalk celery, thinly sliced on the diagonal

1 tablespoon cornstarch mixed with 2 tablespoons water

2 green onions, thinly sliced on the diagonal

1 teaspoon sesame oil

Yields 12 wraps

Serve lettuce wraps as an appetizer, or as a main course with stir-fried rice vermicelli.

1. Wash the chicken and pat dry. Pound lightly to tenderize. Cut the chicken into thin slices approximately 2½ inches long.

2. Wash the lettuce, and dry and separate the leaves. Remove the seeds from the red pepper and chop into bite-sized pieces. Slice the water chestnuts and bamboo shoots into 1-inch pieces.

3. Mix together the soy sauce, oyster sauce, Chinese rice wine, and sugar. Set aside.

4. Add 2 tablespoons oil in a preheated wok or heavy skillet. When oil is hot, add the garlic and ginger. Stir-fry briefly, then add the chicken. Stir-fry until it is browned and nearly cooked through. Remove from the wok and drain on paper towels.

5. Add 2 tablespoons oil. When oil is hot, add the water chestnuts and celery. Stir-fry for about 1 minute, then add the red pepper. Add the bamboo shoots. Stir-fry until the vegetables are brightly colored and tender. Add the sauce. Give the cornstarch/water mixture a quick stir and add in the middle, stirring quickly to thicken. Stir in the green onions. Drizzle with sesame oil.

6. To prepare lettuce wrap, lay a lettuce leaf flat. Place one-twelfth of the chicken combined with the vegetable/sauce mixture into the middle and roll up the lettuce leaf.

Paper Wrapped Chicken

24 chicken packages

This popular appetizer also makes a satisfying meal when served with green salad. Cooking parchment or cellophane paper can be used instead of aluminum foil.

2 large boneless, skinless chicken breasts, 6–8 ounces each
4 large Chinese dried mushrooms
1½ green onions
2 tablespoons oyster sauce
2 tablespoons soy sauce
1 slice ginger, shredded
1 teaspoon sesame oil

1 tablespoon Chinese rice wine or dry sherry
2 teaspoons sugar
Salt and pepper to taste
24 6-inch squares of aluminum foil

1. Wash the chicken and pat dry. Cut the chicken into thin slices approximately 2½ inches long. You want to have 48 strips, or 2 strips for each packet. (With a larger breast you may have more chicken than you need, so you can make more packets.)
2. Soak the dried mushrooms in hot water for 20 minutes, or until they are softened. Squeeze gently to remove excess water, and cut into 24 thin slices, or 6 slices per mushroom. Thinly slice the green onions on the diagonal, so that you have 48 pieces, or 2 slices per packet.
3. In a small bowl, combine the oyster sauce, soy sauce, shredded ginger, sesame oil, Chinese rice wine, sugar, salt and pepper, and green onions. Add to the chicken and marinate for 45 minutes. Add the mushrooms and marinate for another 15 minutes.
4. Preheat oven to 350°F.
5. To wrap the chicken, lay out a square of foil so that the lower corner is pointing toward you. Place 2 chicken slices, 1 mushroom slice, and 2 green onion slices in the middle. Bring the bottom corner up over the chicken. Roll this corner once. Fold the right corner over toward the middle, and then the left corner, so that one is overlapping the other. Tuck the triangle at the top into the flap.
6. Place the wrapped parcels on a baking sheet and bake at 350°F for 15 minutes. Allow to cool before serving.
7. To serve, do not unwrap the chicken packets, but serve heaped on a large platter for guests to open.

Gift Wrapped Beef

½ pound flank steak
1 teaspoon oyster sauce
¼ teaspoon baking soda
6 large dried mushrooms
1 bok choy
2 tablespoons hoisin sauce
2 tablespoons water

½ teaspoon sugar
1 bunch cilantro
2 tablespoons sesame oil
12 6-inch squares of aluminum
  foil

24 beef packages

Serve the beef packets piled on a serving dish with a cilantro garnish. Like Paper Wrapped Chicken, Gift Wrapped Beef can be deep-fried instead of baked.

1. Preheat oven to 350°F.
2. Cut the beef into thin slices 2–3 inches long. You want to have about 3 slices for each packet. Add the oyster sauce and baking soda. Marinate the beef for 30 minutes.
3. Soak the dried mushrooms in hot water for 20 minutes, or until they are softened. Squeeze gently to remove any water, and cut into 48 thin slices, or 8 slices per mushroom. Wash the bok choy, drain thoroughly, and shred. You want to have 3–4 pieces for each packet.
4. Mix the hoisin sauce, water, and sugar and set aside.
5. To wrap the beef, lay out a square of foil so that it forms a diamond shape. Add 3 of the beef slices, 2–3 slices of mushroom, a few shreds of bok choy, and a few sprigs of cilantro in the middle, being sure to keep the filling in the center and not near the edges. Mix in ¼ teaspoon of sesame oil and ½ teaspoon of the hoisin and water mixture.
6. Bring the bottom corner up over the beef. Roll this corner once. Fold the right corner over toward the middle, and then the left corner, so that one is overlapping the other. Tuck the triangle at the top into the flap.
7. Place the wrapped parcels on a baking sheet and bake at 350°F for 15 minutes. Allow to cool before serving. Serve wrapped on a platter, unopened.

Shrimp Stuffed Mushrooms

Yields 20 mushrooms

Large portobello mushrooms work well in this recipe. Garnish with cilantro or parsley sprigs before serving.

20 large fresh mushrooms
1 teaspoon baking powder
¾ cup flour
½ teaspoon sugar
¼ teaspoon salt
2 tablespoons vegetable oil

¾ cup water
½ batch Shrimp Paste
(page 216)
¼ cup cornstarch
4–6 cups oil for deep-frying

1. Wash the mushrooms, dry thoroughly, and remove the stems.
2. Sift the baking powder into the flour. Stir in the sugar, salt, and vegetable oil. Add the water slowly, adding more or less as necessary to make a smooth batter.
3. Add oil to a preheated wok and heat to 350°F. While oil is heating, spread up to ½ teaspoon of the Shrimp Paste on the inside of the mushroom. Lightly dust the outside of the cap with cornstarch. Use your fingers to coat the outside with the batter.
4. When oil is hot, deep-fry the mushrooms, adding a few at a time. Deep-fry until the batter turns a golden brown. Drain on paper towels.

How to Use Chopsticks

It may look tricky, but chopsticks are really quite easy to use. Hold the chopsticks slightly above the middle, making sure that the ends don't cross. Position them so that the top chopstick is between your thumb and index finger, and the lower chopstick between your middle and fourth fingers. To pick up food, use your thumb and index finger to raise and lower the upper chopstick. Think of it as a type of lever, and you've got the idea. One final tip: Stick to wood or bamboo chopsticks if possible, as food can slide off chopsticks made of plastic.

Potstickers with Rice Wine

1½ cups ground pork
3 teaspoons Chinese rice wine
  or dry sherry
3 teaspoons soy sauce
1½ teaspoons sesame oil
1½ tablespoons chopped onion

1 package round wonton
  (gyoza) wrappers
½ cup water for boiling
  potstickers
Oil for frying as needed

**Yields 30–35
potstickers**

For a different flavor,
try steaming the pot-
sticker dumplings in
chicken broth instead
of water.

1. Combine the ground pork, rice wine, soy sauce, sesame oil, and chopped onion.
2. To make the potstickers: Place 1 teaspoon of filling in the middle of the wrapper. Wet the edges of the wrapper, fold over the filling, and seal, crimping the edges. Continue with the remainder of the potstickers. Cover the completed potstickers with a damp towel to prevent drying.
3. Add 2 tablespoons of oil to a preheated wok or skillet (1 tablespoon if using a nonstick pan). When oil is hot, add a few of the potstickers, smooth side down. Do not stir-fry, but let cook for about 1 minute.
4. Add ½ cup of water. Do not turn the potstickers over. Cook, covered, until most of the liquid is absorbed. Uncover, and cook until the liquid has evaporated.
5. Loosen the potstickers with a spatula and serve with the burnt side facing up. Serve with Potsticker Dipping Sauce (page 28).

Potsticker Origins
Potstickers are dumplings that are pan-fried on the bottom and steamed on top. According to legend, they were invented by a imperial court chef who panicked after realizing he'd accidentally burnt a batch of dumplings. With no time to make more, he served them anyway, and the rest is history. When cooking potstickers, it's important to add enough steaming water. While a crispy brown bottom is desirable, potstickers aren't supposed to stick too firmly to the bottom of the pot!

Sticky Rice in Cabbage Leaves

Serves 4

Don't like cabbage? You can also wrap the sticky rice in aluminum foil or waxed paper before steaming.

1 cup short grain (sticky) rice
4 large cabbage leaves
4 dried mushrooms
4 Chinese sausages
2 tablespoons oyster sauce
2 tablespoons Chinese rice wine or dry sherry

2 tablespoons chicken broth or stock
2 tablespoons oil for stir-frying
1 garlic clove, finely chopped
2 slices ginger, finely chopped
2 green onions, finely chopped

1. Cover the sticky rice in warm water and let soak for at least 2 hours, preferably overnight. Drain well. In a medium-sized saucepan, bring the sticky rice and 2 cups of water to a boil. Simmer, covered, for 20 minutes or until rice is cooked. Remove from the element and let cool for 15 minutes. Fluff up the rice before removing from the pot. Split the rice into 4 equal portions and set aside.

2. Blanch the cabbage leaves in boiling water. Drain thoroughly. Soak the dried mushrooms in hot water for at least 20 minutes to soften. Drain, giving them a gentle squeeze to remove any excess water. Cut into thin slices.

3. Chop the Chinese sausages into small pieces. Combine the oyster sauce, rice wine, and chicken broth.

4. Add the oil to a preheated wok or skillet. When oil is hot, add the garlic and ginger. Stir-fry briefly until aromatic. Add the sausage. Stir-fry for about 2 minutes, then add the mushrooms. Stir in the green onion. Make a well in the middle of the wok and add the sauce, bringing to a boil. Mix everything together, then remove from the heat and allow to cool.

5. Split the filling into 4 equal portions. Take a cabbage leaf and add a quarter of the rice and the filling, layering it so that there is rice at the top and bottom, with the meat and vegetable filling in the middle. Roll up the cabbage leaf as in cabbage rolls. Repeat with the remaining 3 cabbage leaves.

6. Steam the cabbage wraps, covered, on a heatproof plate in a bamboo steamer for 15 minutes, or until they are done.

Sticky Rice in Lotus Leaves

1 cup short grain (sticky) rice
4 lotus leaves
4 dried mushrooms
2 Chinese sausages
½ cup chicken meat
2 tablespoons oyster sauce
2 tablespoons rice wine

2 tablespoons chicken broth
  or stock
2 tablespoons oil for stir-frying
1 garlic clove, finely chopped
2 slices ginger, finely chopped
2 green onions, finely chopped

Serves 4

Steaming imparts the delicate flavor of lotus leaves to the sticky rice in this popular dim sum dish.

1. Cover the sticky rice in warm water and let soak for at least 2 hours, preferably overnight. Drain well. In a medium-sized saucepan, bring the sticky rice and 2 cups of water to a boil. Simmer, covered, for 20 minutes or until rice is cooked. Let cool for 15 minutes. Fluff up the rice before removing from the pot. Split the rice into 4 equal portions.

2. Blanch the lotus leaves in boiling water and drain. Soak the dried mushrooms in hot water for at least 20 minutes to soften. Drain, giving them a gentle squeeze to remove any excess water. Cut into thin slices.

3. Chop the sausages into small pieces. Thinly slice the chicken. Combine the oyster sauce, rice wine, and chicken broth and set aside.

4. Add the oil to a preheated wok or skillet. When oil is hot, add the garlic and ginger. Stir-fry briefly until aromatic. Add the chicken, and then the sausage. Stir-fry for about 2 minutes, then add the mushrooms. Stir in the green onion. Make a well in the middle of the wok and add the sauce, bringing to a boil. Mix everything together, then remove from the heat and allow to cool.

5. Take a lotus leaf and add a quarter of the rice and the filling, layering it so that there is rice at the top and bottom, with the meat and vegetable filling in the middle. Form a square parcel with the lotus leaf and tie it up with twine. Repeat with the remaining lotus leaves.

6. Steam the lotus leaf wraps, covered, on a heatproof plate in a bamboo steamer for 15 minutes, or until they are done.

Spicy Potstickers

**Yields 30–35
potstickers**

Out of round wonton wrappers? Cut square wonton wrappers into a circular shape.

¼ pound (4 ounces) fresh
  shrimp
½ cup canned bamboo shoots,
  shredded
3 medium dried mushrooms
1 cup ground pork
1½ green onions, thinly sliced
2 teaspoons Worcestershire
  sauce

2 teaspoons soy sauce
1 teaspoon sugar
1 teaspoon sesame oil
1 package round wonton
  (gyoza) wrappers
½ cup water for boiling
  potstickers
Oil for frying as needed

1. Wash and devein the shrimp, and chop finely. Shred the bamboo shoots. Soak the dried mushrooms in hot water for at least 20 minutes to soften. Drain, remove the stems, and slice finely.
2. Combine the ground pork, shrimp, bamboo shoots, green onions, dried mushrooms, Worcestershire sauce, soy sauce, sugar, and sesame oil.
3. To make the potstickers: Place 1 teaspoon of filling in the middle of the wrapper. Wet the edges, fold the wrapper over the filling and seal, crimping the edges. Continue with the remainder of the wontons. Cover the completed wontons with a damp towel to prevent drying.
4. Add 2 tablespoons oil to a preheated wok or skillet (1 tablespoon if using a nonstick pan). When oil is hot, add a few of the potstickers, smooth side down. Do not stir-fry, but let cook for about 1 minute. Add ½ cup of water. Do not turn the dumplings over.
5. Cook, covered, until most of the liquid is absorbed. Uncover, and cook until the liquid has evaporated. Loosen the potstickers with a spatula and serve with the burnt side facing up. Serve with Potsticker Dipping Sauce (page 28).

Traditional Gow Gees

¼ pound (4 ounces) shrimp
3 medium dried mushrooms
1 cup ground pork
1 napa cabbage leaf, shredded
1½ green onions, thinly sliced
¼ teaspoon minced ginger
2 teaspoons Chinese rice wine
   or dry sherry

2 teaspoons soy sauce
1 teaspoon sugar
1 teaspoon sesame oil
1 package round wonton
   (gyoza) wrappers
4–6 cups oil for deep-frying

> **Yields 30–35 gow gees**
>
> Serve with soy sauce or a dipping sauce such as Sweet-and-Sour Worcestershire Sauce (page 21).
>
>

1. Wash, devein, and finely chop the shrimp. Soak the dried mushrooms in hot water for at least 20 minutes to soften. Drain, remove the stems, and slice finely.

2. Combine the ground pork, shrimp, cabbage, green onions, dried mushrooms, ginger, rice wine, soy sauce, sugar, and sesame oil.

3. Add oil to a preheated wok and heat to 375°F. Wrap the gow gees while waiting for the oil to heat. Place 1 teaspoon of filling in the middle of the wrapper. Wet the edges of the wrapper, fold over the filling and seal, crimping the edges. Continue with the remainder of the wontons. Cover the completed wontons with a damp towel to prevent drying.

4. Carefully slide gow gees into the wok, a few at a time. Deep-fry until they turn golden (about 2 minutes). Remove with a slotted spoon and drain on paper towels.

Avoid Drying Out the Wrappers

It's important to cover filled wontons with a damp towel while preparing the rest, as they have a tendency to dry out quickly. For extra protection, also cover wrappers that haven't been used yet.

Crisp Chinese "Seaweed"

¼ pound bok choy
¼ cup unblanched almonds
¼ teaspoon salt
1 teaspoon brown sugar
2 cups oil for deep-frying

1. Wash the bok choy and drain well. While the bok choy is drying, crush the unblanched almonds in a food processor and set aside.
2. Separate the bok choy leaves from the stalks. Roll the leaves up like a cigar or sausage, and cut into thin shreds. Discard the stalks or save for another dish.
3. Heat wok and add oil. When the oil is heated to between 300°F and 320°F, add the bok choy shreds. Fry them very briefly, until they turn crispy but do not brown. (This will take only a few seconds.) Remove from the wok with a slotted spoon and drain on paper towels.
4. Toss the salt and brown sugar over the "seaweed" and add the crushed almonds.

Chinese "Seaweed"
People are often surprised to discover that this elegant dish is made from everyday Chinese greens! Crisp Chinese "Seaweed" takes its name from the crisp texture and bright green color of the bok choy, which resembles dried seaweed after deep-frying. Serve as an appetizer, or as a colorful side dish with fish.

Deep-fried Mushrooms

20 fresh mushrooms
1 teaspoon baking powder
¾ cup flour
½ teaspoon sugar
¼ teaspoon salt

2 tablespoons vegetable oil
¾ cup water
¼ cup cornstarch
4 cups oil for deep-frying

1. Wipe the mushrooms with a damp cloth and cut off the stems.
2. To make the batter: In a medium bowl, sift the baking powder into the flour. Add the sugar, salt, and vegetable oil, stirring. Add the water, and stir into a smooth batter. Add a bit more water if the batter is too dry, or flour if it is too wet. Use a wooden spoon to test the batter—it should drop slowly, and be able to coat the back of the spoon.
3. Lightly dust the mushrooms with cornstarch and coat with the batter, using your fingers.
4. Add the oil to a preheated wok and heat to 350°F. When the oil is ready, add about 5 mushrooms at a time, and deep-fry until golden brown. Drain on paper towels. Cool and serve.

Flavorful Mushrooms

If you normally enjoy mushrooms raw in a salad, try adding a little heat. A little known fact is that many varieties of mushrooms contain over 90 percent water. Deep-frying causes the water to evaporate and seals in the mushroom's natural juices.

Mini Spring Onion Pancakes

1 cup flour
2½ teaspoons salt, divided
½ cup boiling water
2 teaspoons sesame oil

4 green onions, thinly sliced
4–6 tablespoons oil for frying

1. Place the flour in a medium bowl. Sift ½ teaspoon salt into the flour. Stir in a small amount of the boiling water. Add more water and begin forming into a dough. Add the rest of the water and mix in. Cover the dough with a damp towel and let it rest for 30 minutes.
2. Knead the dough until it is smooth. Cut the dough in half.
3. Roll one-half of the dough out until it is no more ¼ inch thick. Spread 1 teaspoon of sesame oil over the dough. Sprinkle with half the green onion slices.
4. Roll the dough up like a jelly roll and cut into 6 pieces. Take a piece of cut dough, use your fingers to lengthen it a bit, and then form it into an *L* shape. Push down on the top of the *L* with the palm of your hand to form a circle. The pancake should be about 2–3 inches in diameter. Continue with the remainder of the dough.
5. Add 2 tablespoons oil to a preheated wok or skillet. Add half the pancakes and fry until brown on both sides. Sprinkle with the remainder of the salt while cooking. Add more oil as needed.

Gow Gees with Ground Turkey

1½ cups ground turkey
1½ tablespoons oyster sauce
¾ teaspoon sugar
2 teaspoons soy sauce
1 teaspoon sesame oil
1½ green onions, minced
1 tablespoon minced ginger

1 package round wonton
  (gyoza) wrappers
4–6 cups oil for deep-frying

Yields 30–35 gow gees

These dumplings taste delicious served with Hot Mustard Dip (page 18), Soy Ginger Dressing (page 25), or chili paste.

1. Combine the ground turkey, oyster sauce, sugar, soy sauce, sesame oil, green onions, and ginger.
2. Add oil to a preheated wok and heat to 375°F. Wrap the gow gees while waiting for the oil to heat. Place 1 teaspoon of filling in the middle of the wrapper. Wet the edges of the wrapper, fold over the filling, and seal, crimping the edges. Continue with the remainder of the wontons. Cover the completed wontons with a damp towel to prevent drying.
3. Carefully slide gow gees into the wok, a few at a time. Deep-fry until they turn golden (about 2 minutes). Remove with a slotted spoon and drain on paper towels.

Dim Sum Isn't Always Dim Sum
Australians refer to dumplings cooked in the Chinese style as "dim sim." Meanwhile, at Chinese-American restaurants you can order a pu pu platter filled with juicy spareribs, fried wontons, and other Chinese finger foods. In Hawaii, pu pu platters also feature local ingredients such as taro and pineapple.

Siu Mai (Cook and Sell) Dumplings

Yields 15–18 dumplings

Adding oil before steaming helps prevent the Siu Mai from sticking to the heatproof plate.

¼ pound (4 ounces) fresh shrimp
3 medium dried mushrooms
1 cup ground pork
1½ green onions, thinly sliced
½ cup canned bamboo shoots, shredded
2 teaspoons oyster sauce
2 teaspoons soy sauce
1 teaspoon sugar
1 teaspoon sesame oil
1 package Siu Mai or wonton wrappers
Oil for coating heatproof plate

1. Wash and devein the shrimp, and chop finely. Soak the dried mushrooms in hot water for at least 20 minutes to soften. Drain, remove the stems, and slice finely.
2. Combine the ground pork, shrimp, green onions, dried mushrooms, bamboo shoots, oyster sauce, soy sauce, sugar, and sesame oil.
3. To wrap the Siu Mai: Place 2 teaspoons of filling in the middle of the wrapper. **Do not** fold the wrapper over the filling. Gather up the edges of the wrapper and gently pleat the sides so that it forms a basket shape, with the top open.
4. Lightly coat a heatproof plate with oil. Place the dumplings on the plate. Place the plate on a bamboo steamer in a wok set up for steaming. Steam the dumplings for 5–10 minutes or until they are cooked.

Mix and Match

Feel free to experiment by trying the different fillings with any of the dumplings. For example, potsticker fans could use this recipe to make potstickers instead of siu mai. The sticky rice recipes also work well in dumplings or with other wrappers such as banana leaves.

Turkey Fried Wontons

1½ cups ground turkey
2 teaspoons dark soy sauce
1½ tablespoons oyster sauce
1 large garlic clove, minced

½ cup chopped spinach leaves
1 package wonton wrappers
4 cups oil for deep-frying

1. Combine the ground turkey, dark soy sauce, oyster sauce, garlic, and spinach leaves.
2. Add oil to a preheated wok and heat to 375°F. While waiting for the oil to heat, wrap the wontons (see the Deep-fried Wontons recipe on page 33 for instructions).
3. Carefully slide a few wontons at a time into the wok. Deep-fry until they turn golden (about 2 minutes). Remove with a slotted spoon and drain on paper towels.

Yields 30–35 wontons

For this recipe, there is no need to blanch the spinach leaves prior to cooking. You can substitute chopped bok choy leaves for the spinach.

Translucent Dumpling Dough

1 cup wheat starch
¼ teaspoon salt

1 cup boiling water
1 tablespoon lard

1. Place the wheat starch in a medium-sized bowl. Sift in the salt.
2. Slowly pour in the boiling water. Pour in only as much as you need. Stir with a wooden spoon or chopsticks until you have a sticky dough. Let the dough rest and cool for 30 minutes.
3. Add 1 tablespoon lard to the dough, a portion at a time, gradually working it in. Knead the dough until it is smooth and satiny. Make sure the lard is fully mixed in. Use as called for in the recipe.

Yields 22–24 dumplings

This dough is used for Har Gow Dumplings (page 52). Vegetable oil can be substituted for the lard.

Har Gow Dumplings

Yields 22–24 dumplings

These taste delicious with Hot Chili Oil (page 23). For variety, replace half the bamboo shoots with 2 tablespoons minced water chestnuts.

Translucent Dumpling Dough (page 51)
6 ounces raw shrimp
4 tablespoons shredded canned bamboo shoots
1 teaspoon oyster sauce
1 teaspoon sugar
¾ teaspoon Chinese rice wine or dry sherry
¼ teaspoon sesame oil

1. Peel and devein the shrimp. Mince finely. Rinse the bamboo shoots in warm water. Drain well. Combine the shrimp and bamboo shoots with the oyster sauce, sugar, rice wine, and sesame oil. Chill.
2. Work the rested dough if necessary. Cut into quarters. Roll each quarter into a cylinder. Cut into 6 equal pieces (each piece should be approximately 1 inch thick and 1 inch wide). You should now have 24 pieces.
3. On wax paper, roll each piece of dough into a circle 2½–3 inches in size. Cover with a towel while rolling out the remainder to prevent drying.
4. Prepare the wok for steaming. Place up to 1 teaspoon of the filling in each dumpling. Carefully fold the dough over the filling and pleat the edges.
5. Place the dumplings 1 inch apart for steaming. Steam, covered, on medium heat for 15–20 minutes, or until the dumplings are done.

Wonton Soup

Serves 4

This recipe calls for ready-made wontons you can buy at your local Asian grocery store, but you can also try making your own.

Water for boiling wontons
24 filled wonton dumplings
6 cups chicken broth or stock

½ cup shredded napa cabbage
Salt and pepper, to taste
1 green onion, thinly sliced

1. Bring a large pot of water to a boil. Add the wonton dumplings, making sure there is enough room for them to move about freely. Boil for at least 5 minutes, until the wontons rise to the top and the filling is cooked through. Remove from the pot with a slotted spoon.
2. Bring the chicken stock to a boil. Add the cabbage and cook until tender. Season the broth with salt and pepper. Add the cooked wontons and bring the soup back to a boil. Remove the pot from the heat and add the green onion. When serving, allow 6 wontons per person.

Watercress Soup

Serves 4

If you don't have time to prepare the chicken stock, you may substitute 2 cups of canned chicken broth mixed with 2 cups of water.

1 bunch watercress
4 cups chicken stock
1 pinch salt

¼ teaspoon sugar
⅜ teaspoon white pepper

1. Wash the watercress and drain thoroughly. In a large saucepan, add the chicken stock and bring to a boil.
2. Add the salt, sugar, and white pepper. Add the watercress, and cook for another 2–3 minutes. Serve hot.

Canned Broth or Homemade Stock?

Many recipes in the book call for chicken broth. Nothing beats a good homemade stock, but canned chicken broth is an acceptable alternative. If possible, choose brands labeled "reduced sodium."

Hot and Sour Soup

6 dried mushrooms
¼ cup dried lily buds
1 cake firm tofu
6 cups chicken stock, or
    5 cups stock and 1 cup
    mushroom soaking liquid
¼ cup ground pork
1 teaspoon salt
2 tablespoons soy sauce

2 tablespoons mildly sweetened
    rice vinegar
½ teaspoon white pepper,
    or to taste
1 tablespoon tapioca starch
¼ cup water
1 egg white, lightly beaten
1 green onion, minced
A few drops of sesame oil

> **Serves 4–6**
>
> This popular soup is reputed to be good for colds. Serve with Kung Pao Stir-fry (page 166) or Restaurant-Style Mu Shu Pork (page 144).

1. Soak the dried mushrooms in hot water for 20 minutes to soften. Give the mushrooms a little squeeze to remove excess water and cut into thin slices. Reserve the soaking liquid if desired. Soak the dried lily buds in hot water for 20 minutes. Drain.
2. Cut the tofu into cubes.
3. In a large saucepan, bring the chicken stock or stock and mushroom liquid mixture to a boil. When it is boiling, add the mushrooms, lily buds, tofu, and the ground pork.
4. Bring back to a boil and add the salt, soy sauce, rice vinegar, and white pepper.
5. Mix the tapioca starch and water and slowly pour it into the soup, stirring. When the soup thickens, turn off the heat.
6. Pour in the egg white and stir quickly to form thin shreds. Stir in the green onion. Drizzle with sesame oil. Give a final stir.

Freezing Instructions

This dish can be prepared ahead of time and frozen. Prepare the soup, leaving out the tofu and egg. When ready to serve, thaw the soup, add the tofu, and bring to a boil. When the soup is boiling, add the beaten egg white.

Quick and Easy Hot and Sour Soup

Serves 4–6

This modified version of the famous Szechwan soup contains ingredients that are all available at the local supermarket.

1 cup chicken broth
6 cups water
1 teaspoon salt
1 teaspoon sugar
2 tablespoons soy sauce
½ cup canned bamboo shoots, rinsed and drained
2 shiitake mushrooms, sliced
½ cup cooked pork or chicken, cut as desired

3 tablespoons rice vinegar
White pepper to taste
1 tablespoon cornstarch
¼ cup water
1 egg, lightly beaten
1 green onion, minced
A few drops sesame oil

1. In a large saucepan, bring the chicken broth and water to a boil. When it is boiling, add the salt, sugar, soy sauce, bamboo shoots, mushrooms, and cooked meat.
2. Bring back to a boil and add the rice vinegar and white pepper. Test the broth and adjust the taste if required. Mix the cornstarch and water and slowly pour it into the soup, stirring. When the soup thickens, turn off the heat.
3. Pour in the beaten egg and stir quickly to form thin shreds. Stir in the green onion. Drizzle with the sesame oil. Give a final stir and serve hot.

How Do You Drop?

The most challenging part of preparing Egg Drop Soup is streaming the egg into the soup. First, turn off the heat: this prevents the eggs from developing a rubbery texture. Next, hold a fork twelve inches above the pot and slowly pour the beaten egg through the tines. Stir rapidly in a clockwise direction to form thin shreds; gently to form long streams.

Egg Drop Soup

4 cups chicken broth or stock
⅛ teaspoon white pepper
¼ teaspoon salt
¼ teaspoon sugar
1 teaspoon Chinese rice wine
    or dry sherry

2 eggs, lightly beaten
2 green onions, minced
A few drops of sesame oil

1. Bring the chicken stock or broth to a boil.
2. When the broth is boiling, add the white pepper, salt, sugar, and rice wine. Cook for another minute.
3. Turn off the heat and pour the eggs into the soup in a steady stream, stirring rapidly in a clockwise direction until they form thin strands.
4. Add the green onions and sesame oil. Give the soup a final stir. Serve hot.

Serves 4

For contrast, serve Egg Drop Soup with a more strongly spiced main dish and a colorful stir-fried vegetable.

Walnut Soup

6 whole walnuts
4 cups water
2 slices ginger

2 tablespoons plus 1 teaspoon
    sugar

1. In a medium saucepan, bring to a boil the walnuts and 4 cups water. Turn down the heat and simmer for 30 minutes.
2. Add the ginger slices. Simmer for at least another 30 minutes. Stir in the sugar. Remove the walnuts. Leave in the ginger or remove as desired.

Serves 4

This soup does double duty as a nourishing hot broth, or chilled and served as a dessert soup.

Cream Corn Soup

Serves 4

This soup tastes delicious served with Beef with Broccoli (page 113) and cooked rice.

4 cups chicken stock or broth
¼ teaspoon salt
¼ teaspoon sugar
¼ teaspoon white pepper, or to taste
1 teaspoon Chinese rice wine or dry sherry
1 can creamed corn

2 slices cooked ham, diced
1 tablespoon cornstarch
4 tablespoons water
2 egg whites, lightly beaten
2 green onions, minced
A few drops of sesame oil

1. Bring the broth or stock to a boil.
2. Add the salt, sugar, white pepper, rice wine, corn, and cooked ham. Bring the broth back to a boil.
3. Mix the cornstarch and water and pour into the soup, stirring to thicken. When the soup has thickened, turn off the heat.
4. Pour the egg whites into the soup in a steady stream, and quickly stir in a clockwise direction until they form thin shreds.
5. Add the green onions and sesame oil. Give the soup a final stir.

Make Your Own Stock
It's easy! Bring 2½–3 pounds of chicken bones, a sliced green onion, and a few slices of ginger to a boil in a large pot of water (about 8 cups). Skim off the foam that rises to the top. Reduce the heat and simmer the stock, uncovered, for at least 2 hours. Cool before using.

Chicken Velvet Soup

4 ounces skinless, boneless
   chicken breast
1 tablespoon water
2 teaspoons Chinese rice wine
   or dry sherry, divided
4 cups chicken stock or broth
¼ teaspoon salt

⅛ teaspoon white pepper
1 can creamed corn
1 tablespoon cornstarch mixed
   with 4 tablespoons water
2 eggs whites, lightly beaten
2 green onions, sliced

1. Cut the chicken into chunks and place in a food processor. Add the water and 1 teaspoon rice wine, and mince the chicken into a fine paste.
2. Bring the broth or stock to a boil. Add the salt, white pepper, 1 teaspoon rice wine, and creamed corn. Add the chicken paste, stirring so that the chicken breaks up into small pieces. Cook until the chicken turns white.
3. Mix the cornstarch and water, and pour the mixture into the soup, stirring to thicken. Turn off the heat.
4. Pour the eggs into the soup in a steady stream, and quickly stir in a clockwise direction until they form thin shreds.
5. Add the green onions and give the soup a final stir.

Serves 4

In a pinch, you can make chicken stock from chicken bones that have been boiled for as little as thirty minutes, but the flavor won't be as strong.

Tomato Egg Flower Soup

Serves 4

Beef and tomato are a natural combination. For a heartier soup, add ½ cup of ground beef or lean beef.

4 cups beef broth
2 medium tomatoes
⅛ teaspoon white pepper
¼ teaspoon salt
½ teaspoon sugar
1 teaspoon Chinese rice wine
   or dry sherry

1 tablespoon cornstarch
4 tablespoons water
1 egg white, lightly beaten
2 green onions, minced
A few drops of sesame oil

1. Bring the 4 cups of beef broth to a boil.
2. Bring a large pot of water to a boil. Blanch the tomatoes briefly in the boiling water. (This will make it easier to remove the peel.) Peel the tomatoes and cut each into 6 equal pieces.
3. When the beef broth comes to a boil, add the white pepper, salt, sugar, rice wine, and tomatoes. Bring the broth back to boiling.
4. Mix the cornstarch and water, and pour it into the soup, stirring to thicken. Turn off the heat.
5. Pour the egg white into the soup and quickly stir in a clockwise direction to form thin shreds.
6. Add the green onions and a few drops of sesame oil. Give the soup a final stir.

Cholesterol Concerns
Using egg whites instead of eggs in the Egg Drop Soup-type recipes helps reduce the amount of cholesterol. Another option is to forego the egg altogether—heartier soups such as Chicken Velvet Soup taste fine without it.

Winter Melon Soup

2 Chinese dried mushrooms
1 pound winter melon
3½ cups water
2½ cups chicken stock or
  1 cup chicken broth mixed
  with 1½ cups water
½ cup barbequed pork, diced

2 slices ginger
1 teaspoon Chinese rice wine
  or dry sherry
1 pinch salt

1. Cut the stems off the dried mushrooms and soak in hot water for
   20 minutes. Give the mushrooms a little squeeze to remove excess
   water and cut into thin slices.
2. Wash the winter melon and remove the green rind, seeds, and the
   pulp. Cut into slices approximately 2 inches long and ½ inch thick.
   In a large saucepan, add the winter melon to 3½ cups water and
   bring to a boil. Simmer for 20 minutes or until the melon is tender.
3. Add the chicken stock or chicken broth and water mixture, barbequed
   pork, dried mushrooms, and ginger.
4. Add the rice wine and salt. Simmer for another 15 minutes. Serve hot.
   Leave the ginger slices in or remove as desired.

Drink Your Soup!
*The Chinese believe that cold drinks and hot food don't mix, so
soup normally takes the place of a beverage at meals. It's customary
in Chinese restaurants for the waitress to bring a steaming pot of tea
as soon as you're seated, but traditionally tea was looked upon as
a digestive aid, to be consumed at the conclusion of a meal.*

Cucumber and Carrot Soup

1 cucumber
4 shiitake mushrooms
1 carrot, diced
½ cup cooked ham, diced
1 teaspoon Chinese rice wine
  or dry sherry

⅛ teaspoon salt
4 cups chicken broth
1 green onion, minced
A few drops sesame oil

1. Peel the cucumber, remove the seeds, and dice. Wash the shiitake mushrooms and cut into thin slices.
2. In a large saucepan, add the cucumber, mushrooms, diced carrot, diced ham, rice wine, and salt to the chicken broth.
3. Bring the soup to a boil and cook over low heat for about 20 minutes.
4. Turn off the heat and add the green onion. Drizzle with the sesame oil.

Pork and Spinach Soup

1 tablespoon soy sauce
1 teaspoon Chinese rice wine
  or dry sherry
1 tablespoon cornstarch
½ cup ground pork
¾ cup spinach leaves

5 cups chicken stock or 4 cups
  canned broth mixed with
  1 cup water
½ teaspoon sugar
¼ teaspoon salt

1. Add the soy sauce, rice wine, and cornstarch to the ground pork. Marinate the pork for 15 minutes.
2. Blanch the spinach in boiling water briefly, just until the leaves begin to wilt. Drain well.
3. Bring the chicken stock or broth to a boil. Add the marinated pork and simmer for about 10 minutes. Add the sugar, salt, and spinach. Heat through and serve hot.

Emerald Soup

15 leaves of spinach
1 boneless, skinless chicken
   breast
1 slice ginger
1 tablespoon oil for stir-frying
¼ teaspoon salt
¼ teaspoon sugar

4½ cups chicken stock or broth
1 teaspoon soy sauce
1 teaspoon Chinese rice wine
   or dry sherry

Serves 4

Made with spinach, ginger, and chicken broth, this soup is great for fighting colds. Blanching the spinach before stir-frying preserves its brilliant green color.

1. Wash the spinach leaves and cut off the ends. Blanch the leaves briefly in boiling water, just until the leaves begin to wilt. Remove and sprinkle with cold water.
2. Cut the chicken into thin slices. Blanch briefly in boiling water with the ginger until it turns white. Remove from the water and set aside.
3. Heat a wok or frying pan and add oil for stir-frying. When the oil is ready, stir-fry the spinach very briefly (under 1 minute), adding the salt and sugar.
4. Add the chicken broth to the spinach. Add the soy sauce and rice wine and bring to a boil.
5. Add the chicken and bring back to a boil. Serve hot.

Cilantro
Also called Chinese parsley, cilantro is the common name for the leaves of the coriander plant. Indispensable in Chinese cooking, cilantro leaves lend a pleasantly musky odor to soups, salads, and stir-fries. Just remember that, like garlic, a little goes a long way. Substitute parsley leaves if you find the flavor too overpowering.

Sizzling Rice Soup

Serves 4

Success lies in keeping the soup hot while deep-frying the rice, so that the rice crackles and pops when it meets the heated broth.

10 squares Rice Crisps
   (page 82)
6 large dried black mushrooms
⅓ pound cooked shrimp
1 large chicken breast
6 cups chicken stock or 5 cups
   broth with 1 cup water
½ 8-ounce can water chestnuts,
   drained and sliced

½ cup frozen peas
1 teaspoon salt
1 tablespoon Chinese rice wine
   or dry sherry
White pepper to taste (optional)
1 teaspoon sesame oil
4–6 cups oil for deep-frying

1. Two hours ahead of time, begin preparing the Rice Crisps.
2. Soak the mushrooms in hot water for 20 minutes to soften. Give a gentle squeeze to remove any excess liquid. Cut into thin slices. Rinse the shrimp in warm water and pat dry.
3. Bring a large pan of water to a boil and poach the chicken very briefly in the boiling water. Drain. Cut the chicken into thin slices.
4. Bring the chicken stock or broth and water mixture to a boil. Add the chicken, water chestnuts, mushrooms, shrimp, and peas. Bring the soup back to a boil.
5. While waiting for the soup to boil, begin heating oil for deep-frying the Rice Crisps.
6. Add the salt, rice wine, and white pepper to the soup, if desired. Drizzle with sesame oil. Pour the soup into a large tureen or serving bowl. Keep warm.
7. When the oil is hot, add the Rice Crisps. Deep-fry until the pieces puff up and turn brown. Remove from the wok and drain on paper towels.
8. At the table, slide the sizzling rice into the soup. The rice will make crackling sounds.

West Lake Beef Soup

1 tablespoon soy sauce
1 teaspoon Chinese rice wine
* or dry sherry*
½ teaspoon salt, divided
1 tablespoon cornstarch
½ cup lean ground beef
5 cups chicken or beef broth
1 teaspoon sugar

1½ tablespoons cornstarch
* mixed with ⅓ cup water*
2 egg whites, lightly beaten
¼ teaspoon sesame oil

Serves 4

Pair this dish with Beef
and Bean Sprouts in
Black Bean Sauce
(page 115) and
steamed rice for a
quick and easy dinner.

---

1. Add the soy sauce, rice wine, ¼ teaspoon salt, and cornstarch to the ground beef, adding the cornstarch last. Marinate for 15 minutes.
2. Bring the chicken or beef broth to a boil. Stir in the marinated ground beef. Bring back to a boil and add the sugar and ¼ teaspoon salt.
3. Boil for 5 more minutes and add the cornstarch mixed with water, stirring to thicken. When the soup has thickened, turn off the heat.
4. Pour the egg whites into the soup in a steady stream, and quickly stir in a clockwise direction until they form thin shreds.
5. Drizzle with the sesame oil. Give the soup a final stir. Serve hot.

Thick or Thin?

In Chinese cooking, thin soups are soups in which the meat and vegetables are added to the heated broth during the final stages of cooking. With thick soups, the ingredients are all added together and the soup is slowly simmered, giving the flavors time to blend.

Bean Curd Soup

2 cakes firm tofu
1 green onion
4 fresh water chestnuts
1 tablespoon oil
1 teaspoon shredded ginger

5½ cups chicken stock or broth
¼ teaspoon salt
1 teaspoon Chinese rice wine or dry sherry

1. Drain the tofu, and cut into 1-inch cubes. Slice the green onion on the diagonal into thirds. Cut the top off the water chestnuts, peel the skin, and chop.
2. In a large saucepan heat the oil on medium-low heat. Add the ginger and cook briefly until aromatic.
3. Add the chicken stock or broth and bring to a boil. Add the salt, rice wine, tofu, and water chestnuts. Bring back up to a boil and simmer for about 10 minutes. Stir in the sliced green onion.

Creamy Fruit Salad

½ cup plain yogurt
¼ teaspoon cinnamon
2½ teaspoons honey

1 half section of cantaloupe or other melon

Process the yogurt, cinnamon, and honey until smooth. Spoon into the middle of the cantaloupe.

Bird's Nest Soup

4 ounces bird's nest
Basic Chicken Velvet (page
    160), use the amounts
    specified in the recipe
6 cups stock or broth
1 ½ teaspoons Chinese rice
    wine or dry sherry
½ teaspoon salt

½ teaspoon sugar
⅛ teaspoon white pepper,
    or to taste
2 green onions, minced
¼ cup ham, chopped

Serves 6

Be sure to take extra care when preparing this expensive delicacy. Combine bird's nest with rock sugar and water for a sweet dessert soup.

1. To prepare the bird's nest, soak overnight in water. Drain thoroughly. Spread out the bird's nest and use tweezers to carefully remove any foreign materials or dirt. Bring a large pot of water to a boil and simmer the bird's nest for 5 minutes. Drain thoroughly and check again for any foreign material.
2. Prepare the Basic Chicken Velvet.
3. Bring stock or broth to a boil. Add the bird's nest and simmer for 30 minutes. Add the rice wine, salt, and sugar.
4. Fold in the Basic Chicken Velvet and bring the soup back up to a boil. Add the white pepper. Stir in the green onions and ham or add after serving as a garnish.

Exotic Bird's Nest
Not keen to try a soup filled with twigs and branches? Actually, bird's nest isn't made from traditional nesting materials. Instead, the swiftlet—a type of swallow—makes a nest using its own saliva, which hardens upon exposure to air. The swiftlet inhabits remote caves in China and Southeast Asia. Retrieving the nests can be hazardous; the men who perform this task often come from families that have been earning their living in this manner for generations.

Sweet Red Bean Paste Soup

Serves 3

This simplified version of a famous Chinese wedding soup can be served as a snack or as a sweet dessert soup.

4 cups water
1 piece dried tangerine peel,
    2-3 inches wide

½ cup Sweet Red Bean Paste
    (page 269)
⅓ cup sugar

1. In a medium saucepan, add the 4 cups water and the dried tangerine peel. Bring to a boil and simmer for about 30 minutes.
2. Add the Sweet Red Bean Paste. Continue simmering for another 30 minutes. Add the sugar, stirring to dissolve. Chill before serving.

Chinese Wedding Soup

Traditionally, sweet red bean paste soup is made with raw adzuki beans and contains lotus seeds, a symbol of fertility in Chinese culture.

Sweet Almond Soup

Serves 4

Traditionally this dessert would be made with Chinese almonds, which are actually apricot pits.

½ cup unblanched almonds
3 tablespoons long grain rice
2 tablespoons Chinese dates

2 tablespoons vegetable oil
2½ cups milk
2 tablespoons sugar

1. Process the almonds in a blender or food processor into a fine powder. Combine 3 tablespoons of the processed almonds with the white rice and process again. Add water, a few drops at a time, to form a paste.
2. Process the Chinese dates into small pieces and set aside.
3. Add oil to a preheated wok or heavy skillet. When oil is hot, add the milk and heat until it is almost, but not quite, boiling. Add the almond and rice paste and cook for 10 minutes at a near boil, stirring frequently.
4. Bring the milk to a boil. Add the sugar, stirring. Add the Chinese date pieces. Serve chilled.

Chinese Potato Salad

4 potatoes
2 eggs
3 tablespoons mayonnaise
1½ tablespoons soy sauce
1½ teaspoons chopped cilantro
    leaves
¾ teaspoon Hot Mustard Sauce
    (page 18)
¾ teaspoon sugar

¼ teaspoon plus a few drops
    of sesame oil
1 cup shredded napa cabbage
⅓ cup chopped red onion

Serves 6–8

For extra bite, add
up to ½ teaspoon
of curry paste to
the potato salad
before serving.

---

1. Boil the potatoes and hard-boil the eggs. Drain and peel the potatoes, and cut them into bite-sized squares. Slice the hard-boiled eggs.
2. Mix together the mayonnaise, soy sauce, cilantro leaves, Hot Mustard Sauce, and sugar. Stir in the sesame oil.
3. Mix the potatoes, eggs, shredded cabbage, and chopped red onion together in a large bowl. Mix in the mayonnaise sauce. Keep in a sealed container in the refrigerator until ready to serve.

Main Dish Salad

The common tossed green salad is unknown in Chinese cuisine. A salad can be hot or cold, an appetizer or part of the main meal. It may even take the place of a sorbet when served between courses.

Chinese-Style Gado Gado Salad

Serves 4

This Chinese take on the popular Indonesian salad features peanut sauce without the lime juice. Serve with scented rice for a light supper.

Peanut Sauce (page 20)
2 red potatoes
2 hard-boiled eggs
½ English cucumber
½ cup snow peas

½ cup cauliflower
½ cup spinach leaves
½ cup carrots, chopped
½ cup mung bean sprouts

1. Boil the potatoes with their skins on and slice. Boil the eggs and cut into thin slices. Peel the cucumber and cut into thin slices. String the snow peas. Chop the cauliflower.
2. Blanch the snow peas, spinach leaves, carrots, and bean sprouts.
3. Arrange the vegetables on a platter, working from the outside in. You can arrange the vegetables in any order, but the boiled egg slices should be placed on top.
4. Pour the Peanut Sauce over the salad. Serve immediately.

Steamed Beef Salad

Serves 6

This is an excellent dish to serve on summer days when you want something more substantial than chicken wings or potato salad.

Spicy Steamed Beef (page 124)
1 bunch Romaine lettuce leaves
1 carrot, shredded
1 cup raw cherry tomatoes,
  halved

2 tablespoons red rice vinegar
2 teaspoons soy sauce
1 teaspoon sugar
A few drops sesame oil

1. Prepare the steamed beef. Place the cooked beef in a sealed container in the refrigerator and leave overnight.
2. Place the vegetables in a medium-sized bowl and toss with the red rice vinegar, soy sauce, sugar, and sesame oil.
3. Serve the steamed beef on a plate with the salad arranged around it.

Watermelon and Watercress Salad

¼ cup rice vinegar
½ teaspoon lemon juice
¼ teaspoon chili sauce
¼ teaspoon sesame oil
1 tablespoon sesame paste
    or peanut butter
2 tablespoons water
2 cups watercress
1 small tomato

1 leaf Romaine lettuce,
    shredded
10 1-inch cubes of watermelon,
    green peel and seeds
    removed

Serves 2

For extra flavor, add a few Spicy Roasted Peanuts (page 274) to the dressing before processing. The dressing yields ⅓ cup.

1. For the dressing, place the rice vinegar, lemon juice, chili sauce, sesame oil, sesame paste, and water in a blender and process until smooth. Place in a bowl and set aside.
2. Wash the watercress. Drain thoroughly, and remove the stems. Cut the tomato into thin slices.
3. Toss the watercress with the Romaine lettuce and tomato. Place in a serving bowl and add the watermelon cubes. Drizzle the dressing over. Refrigerate leftover dressing in a sealed jar. It will keep for 3–4 days.

Peanut Butter Is a Substitute

The more authentic version of this dish uses sesame paste. Made from toasted sesame seeds, sesame paste has a sweet flavor similar to peanut butter, which makes a convenient substitute. Although it is also made from ground sesame seeds, the Middle Eastern tahini is not a good substitute for sesame paste: It is made with untoasted sesame seeds, giving it a very different flavor.

Hot Spiced Cucumbers

Serves 2

Rice vinegar and rice
wine vinegar both
mean the same thing.
Rice vinegar is simply
rice wine that has
been allowed to
ferment.

½ English cucumber
½ teaspoon salt
1 teaspoon grated ginger
1 garlic clove, finely minced

1 tablespoon plus 1 teaspoon
* red rice vinegar*
1 tablespoon sugar
¼ teaspoon chili paste

1. Peel the cucumber and cut into thin slices. Place in a bowl and toss with the salt and leave for 15 minutes.
2. Combine the remaining ingredients in a bowl. Place the cucumber in a clean bowl and pour the sauce mixture over. Serve immediately or chill.

Creamy Cucumber Salad

Serves 2

This is a wonderful
picnic dish. For a less
spicy version, leave
out the chili paste.

1 English cucumber
¼ teaspoon salt
1 clove garlic, minced
½ cup plain yogurt
½ teaspoon cilantro leaves

1 teaspoon honey
1 teaspoon freshly squeezed
* lemon juice*
¼ teaspoon chili paste
1 Asian pear

1. Peel the cucumber and slice. Place in a bowl and toss with salt, allowing to stand for 15 minutes.
2. Place the garlic, yogurt, cilantro leaves, honey, lemon juice, and chili paste in the blender and process until smooth. Makes ⅓ cup.
3. Serve the cucumber slices on a plate with the dressing on the side. Garnish with Asian pear slices.

Bean Sprout and Carrot Salad

2 cups mung bean sprouts,
    rinsed and drained
½ carrot, shredded
1 tablespoon red rice vinegar
1 teaspoon sugar
1 tablespoon soy sauce

1 teaspoon chili with garlic
    sauce
¼ teaspoon sesame oil

1. Trim the ends of the bean sprouts if desired. Combine with the shredded carrot.
2. Mix together the red rice vinegar, sugar, soy sauce, chili with garlic sauce, and sesame oil. Drizzle over the mixture of bean sprouts and carrot, and refrigerate for at least 2 hours before serving.

Green Onion Brushes
This attractive garnish is easy to make. Simply slice a green onion into 1½-inch pieces, then, starting in the middle and going left, cut several slits with a pin. Repeat in the other direction. (Leave a small section in the middle untouched so that the green onion doesn't fall apart.)

> **Serves 3–4**
>
> For an attractive presentation, trim the ends of the bean sprouts and serve on a plate of Romaine lettuce leaves decorated with green onion brushes.
>
>

Cold Asparagus Salad with Garlic

Serves 4

This dish tastes excellent refrigerated and served the next day with a beef stir-fry and rice.

1 pound fresh asparagus
1 clove garlic, chopped
2 tablespoons black rice vinegar
2 teaspoons white sugar

1 tablespoon soy sauce
⅛ teaspoon sesame oil

1. Wash the asparagus and drain well. Cut off the ends and cut diagonally into 1½-inch pieces.
2. Bring a large pot of water to a boil. Parboil the asparagus, and plunge into cold water. Drain well.
3. Mix together the garlic clove, black rice vinegar, sugar, soy sauce, and sesame oil. Toss with the asparagus.

Black Rice Vinegar

With its intriguing combination of tart and sweet, black rice vinegar is the crème de la crème of the rice vinegars. The most famous comes from southern China's Chinkiang region. If you enjoy black rice vinegar's distinctive smoky flavor, try substituting it in any recipe where rice vinegar is called for.

Hot Chicken Salad

*4 boneless, skinless chicken
  breasts
½ cup soy sauce, divided
1 head Romaine lettuce
1 red bell pepper
4 tablespoons red rice vinegar
3 teaspoons sesame oil*

*2 green onions, minced
2 teaspoons sugar
½ teaspoon chili paste
2 tablespoons toasted sesame
  seeds*

Serves 4

For an interesting contrast in taste and texture, serve this dish with hard Chinese noodles such as Chow Mein or Deep-fried Vermicelli (page 99).

1. Marinate the chicken in ¼ cup soy sauce for 1 hour. Steam the chicken in a bamboo steamer in a wok until it is cooked through. Cool. Shred the cooked chicken meat.
2. Wash the Romaine lettuce leaves and drain well. Wash the red bell pepper and cut into thin slices.
3. Mix together ¼ cup soy sauce, the red rice vinegar, sesame oil, green onions, sugar, and chili paste.
4. Arrange the lettuce and red bell pepper on a plate. Add the shredded cooked chicken. Drizzle with the red rice vinegar dressing and top with toasted sesame seeds.

How to Shred Meat
Hold the cleaver parallel to the cutting board and slice the meat horizontally into thin sections. Lay the cut pieces on top of each other, position the cleaver perpendicular to the board, and cut the meat lengthwise into thin slices, from ¼- to ⅛-inch thick. For easier shredding, partially freeze the meat ahead of time.

Basic Cooked Rice

Serves 4–6

Most Chinese recipes call for long grain rice, although medium grain rice is also acceptable. Short grain rice is reserved for desserts.

2 cups long grain rice
3¼ cups water

1. If necessary, rinse the rice to remove any excess starch.
2. In a large saucepan, bring the rice and water to a boil on medium heat.
3. Once the rice is boiling, turn down the heat to medium low. Put the lid at an angle on the pot, so that the pot is partially covered but some steam can escape.
4. When the water has evaporated to the point where you can see holes in the rice, put the lid fully on.
5. Simmer the rice on low heat for 15 more minutes.

The Knuckle Method of Measuring Water
This really works! Stick your finger on the top of the rice and begin adding water. You know you've added enough when the water reaches your first knuckle.

Basic Fried Rice

3 medium or large eggs
2½ tablespoons oyster sauce,
  divided
⅛ teaspoon salt, divided
⅛ teaspoon pepper, divided

3–4 tablespoons oil for frying,
  divided
4 cups cold cooked rice

Serves 4

This recipe is very adaptable—enjoy as is, or add your favorite meat and vegetable combinations.

1. Lightly beat the eggs and add 1 tablespoon oyster sauce and a small amount of salt and pepper to taste.
2. Add 2 tablespoons oil to a preheated wok or heavy skillet and turn the heat on high. When oil is hot, add the egg mixture. Scramble gently until the eggs are almost cooked but still moist. Remove from the heat and let sit for 1 minute before removing from the pan.
3. Wipe the wok clean and add 2 tablespoons oil. When oil is hot, add the rice, stirring to separate the grains. Stir-fry for 2–3 minutes, then blend in the scrambled egg. Add 1½ tablespoons oyster sauce, and salt and pepper to taste. Mix through and serve hot.

Eggs and Rice
There are many ways to cook the beaten egg in fried rice. You can scramble it, or fry it whole and cut into strips to serve on top of the fried rice. For added variety, try scrambling half the beaten egg and frying the other half.

Basic Scented Rice

Serves 4–6

The trick to making scented rice is to reduce the amount of water used, so that the rice is steamed rather than boiled.

2 cups jasmine or balsamic
    scented rice
3 cups water

1. Rinse the rice thoroughly to remove any excess starch. The water should be clear and not milky.
2. In a large saucepan, bring the rice and water to a boil.
3. When the rice has boiled, turn down the heat to very low. Cover and simmer for about 20 minutes, or until the rice is cooked.
4. Remove the pot from heat. Let the rice cool for 15 minutes before removing from the pot. Fluff and serve.

Fried Glutinous Rice

Serves 4

Serve this fragrant dish where you would normally serve Thai scented rice. The sauce is similar to the sauce for Beef with Broccoli (page 113).

2 cups glutinous rice
2 tablespoons oil for stir-frying
½ cup beef broth

2 tablespoons oyster sauce
1 teaspoon brown sugar
2 tablespoons water

1. Rinse the rice several times, and soak for several hours or overnight, if possible. Drain well.
2. Add oil to a preheated heavy skillet or wok. When the oil is hot, add the rice and stir-fry for 2–3 minutes. Add the remaining ingredients and mix through.

Pork-filled Rice Balls

½ cup glutinous rice
1 green onion
2 dried mushrooms
1 green leaf from Stir-fried Bok
    Choy (page 235), optional
¼ teaspoon salt
1 tablespoon soy sauce

1 tablespoon soaking liquid
    from the mushrooms
1 tablespoon Chinese rice wine
    or dry sherry
¼ teaspoon sugar
1 tablespoon cornstarch
1 cup ground pork

Yields 12 rice balls

Serve this delicate appetizer to guests with Crisp Chinese "Seaweed" (page 46) for an interesting contrast of colors, textures, and flavors.

1. Rinse the rice several times, and soak for several hours or overnight, if possible. Drain well.
2. Chop the green onion very thinly into small rounds. Reconstitute the dried mushrooms by soaking in hot water for at least 20 minutes. Reserve the soaking liquid. Cut the mushrooms into thin slices. Thinly slice the bok choy leaf, if desired.
3. Combine the salt, soy sauce, mushroom liquid, rice wine, sugar, and cornstarch in a small bowl. Set aside.
4. In a medium bowl, mix the ground pork with the mushrooms, green onion, and bok choy leaf. Add the cornstarch mixture, 1 tablespoon at a time, and work it into the pork with your hands.
5. Place a piece of waxed paper on the counter and spread out the dried glutinous rice. Use your hands to shape the pork mixture into a ball roughly the size of a golf ball. Roll the ball over the rice, making sure it is covered with rice. Repeat with the remainder of the pork.
6. Steam the pork balls for about 30 minutes, or until they are firm and cooked through. Serve warm or cold.

Fungus Fun
The Chinese believe dried mushrooms can lower blood pressure and they are also thought to be an aphrodisiac! Meanwhile, cloud ear, strange-looking fungus that does vaguely resemble a human ear, is thought to improve blood circulation. Any kind of mushroom will add texture to a variety of dishes, from soups to stir-fries.

Rice Crisps

Yields 8–10 squares

Crispy rice is used to make Wor Wonton Soup, a popular restaurant dish with seafood and vegetables swimming in a rich broth.

1 cup short grain rice
1 cup water

1. Bring rice and water to boil, uncovered, in a medium saucepan.
2. Cover and simmer on low heat for 30 minutes. Remove from the burner and allow to cool.
3. Spread the rice out on a baking sheet, making sure it is no more than ¼ inch thick.
4. Bake at 300°F for 50 minutes or until dry. When cooled, cut into 2-inch squares and store in a canister to use as needed.

Rinsing Rice

In the past, cooks always rinsed the rice to remove impurities and to soften it, making the grains easier to separate. Today, raw rice is cleaner, and rinsing does remove some of the nutrients. If you're uncertain about whether or not to rinse, check the directions on the bag or box. (Thai scented rice and glutinous rice should always be rinsed.) To rinse, place the rice in a large bowl and cover with cold water. Use your fingers to swirl the rice around, then drain. Repeat this process 2 or 3 times, until the water comes out clear and is not cloudy.

Beef Fried Rice

2 large eggs
2½ tablespoons oyster sauce
⅛ teaspoon salt
⅛ teaspoon pepper
½ red bell pepper
1 green onion
6–7 tablespoons oil for
  stir-frying
2 garlic cloves, minced

½ onion, chopped
4 mushrooms, sliced
4 cups cold cooked rice
1 pound cooked beef, cut as
  desired
1 tablespoon mushroom soy
  sauce
½ teaspoon sugar

Serves 4–6

Concerned about cholesterol? Serve the fried rice without the strips of cooked egg on top.

1. Lightly beat the eggs. Stir in the oyster sauce and salt and pepper to taste.
2. Remove the seeds from the red pepper and cut into bite-sized cubes. Cut the green onion into 1-inch slices on the diagonal.
3. Add 2 tablespoons oil to a preheated wok or skillet. When oil is hot, pour the egg mixture into the pan. Cook on medium to medium-high heat, using 2 spatulas to turn it over once. Don't scramble. Remove and cut into thin strips. Set aside.
4. Clean out wok, if necessary. Add 2–3 tablespoons oil. When oil is hot, add the garlic cloves and stir-fry until aromatic. Add the onion. Stir-fry for 1 minute, then add the mushrooms, and then the red pepper. Stir-fry the vegetables until they are tender. Remove.
5. Add 2 tablespoons oil to the wok. When oil is hot, add the rice, stirring to separate the grains. Stir-fry on medium heat for 2–3 minutes, then blend in the vegetables and beef. Stir in the mushroom soy sauce and sugar. Stir in the green onion. Serve hot, topped with the egg strips.

Chicken Fried Rice

Serves 4

Thick soy sauce is thickened with molasses. Restaurants frequently rely on it to add flavor to fried rice and noodle dishes.

2 large eggs
2½ tablespoons oyster sauce, divided
⅛ teaspoon salt
⅛ teaspoon pepper
5–6 tablespoons oil for stir-frying
2 stalks celery, diced

½ cup chopped onion
4 cups cold cooked rice
1½ cups cooked chicken, chopped
2 teaspoons thick soy sauce
2 green onions, minced

1. Lightly beat the eggs. Stir in 1 tablespoon oyster sauce and salt and pepper to taste.
2. Add 2 tablespoons oil to a preheated wok or skillet. When oil is hot, pour the egg mixture into the pan. Cook on medium to medium-high heat, using 2 spatulas to turn it over once. Don't scramble. Remove and cut into thin strips. Set aside.
3. Clean out wok, if necessary. Add 1–2 tablespoons oil. When oil is hot, add the celery. Stir-fry for 1 minute, then add the onion. Stir-fry the vegetables until they are tender. Remove.
4. Add 2 tablespoons oil. When oil is hot, add the rice. Stir-fry on medium heat, stirring to separate the grains. Add 1½ tablespoons oyster sauce, and a small amount of salt and pepper. Blend in the chicken, onion, and celery. Stir in the thick soy sauce. Add extra salt and sugar if desired. To serve, garnish the chicken with the strips of fried egg and green onions.

Flavorful Fried Rice

Instead of serving fried rice immediately, try storing it in the refrigerator in a sealed container to use another day. This gives the flavors more time to blend. Just be sure to allow the fried rice to cool completely before storing.

Fried Rice with Ham

2 large eggs
Salt and pepper to taste
6 tablespoons oil for stir-frying
½ cup chopped onion
½ cup frozen peas
4 cups cold cooked rice

1 tablespoon dark soy sauce
1 tablespoon oyster sauce
1 cup cooked ham
1 green onion, minced

Serves 4

Fried rice dishes can
be prepared ahead
of time and frozen.
Thaw completely
before reheating.

1. Lightly beat the eggs and add a small amount of salt and pepper
   to taste.
2. Add 2 tablespoons oil to a preheated wok or heavy skillet and turn
   the heat on high. When oil is hot, add the egg mixture. Scramble
   gently until the eggs are almost cooked but still moist. Remove from
   the heat and let sit for 1 minute before removing from the pan.
3. Clean out the wok and add 2 tablespoons oil. When oil is hot, add
   the onion. Stir-fry for 1 minute, then add the peas. Stir-fry until the
   peas are bright green and the onion tender. Remove.
4. Wipe the wok clean and add 2 tablespoons oil. When oil is hot, add
   the rice, stirring to separate the grains. Stir-fry for 2–3 minutes, then
   add the dark soy sauce and oyster sauce. Add the ham, green peas,
   and onion. Blend in the scrambled egg. Stir in the green onion and
   serve hot.

Lumpy Leftovers

*Fried rice tastes best when you use previously cooked rice
instead of fresh, but leftover rice can get a bit lumpy. To remove
any lumps, just sprinkle a bit of cold water on the rice and break
them up with your fingers. Another trick is to add the lightly beaten
egg to the cold rice before stir-frying, instead of cooking the egg
separately. This makes the rice grains much easier to separate.*

Yangchow Fried Rice

Serves 4

This colorful dish flecked with yellow, orange, green, and pink is named for the city of Yangchow in Jiangsu province, famous for its rice dishes.

2 large eggs
2 tablespoons oyster sauce, divided
Salt and pepper to taste
4 cups cold cooked rice
1 green onion
6 tablespoons oil for stir-frying
¼ pound (4 ounces) fresh shrimp, peeled and deveined
½ cup baby carrots, halved
½ cup peas
½ teaspoon sugar
1 cup barbequed pork, cubed

1. Lightly beat the eggs. Stir in 1 tablespoon oyster sauce, and a small amount of salt and pepper to taste. Mix the egg in with the rice, stirring to separate the grains.
2. Cut the green onion into 1-inch pieces on the diagonal.
3. Add 2 tablespoons oil to a preheated wok or heavy skillet. When oil is hot, add the shrimp. Stir-fry briefly until they turn pink. Remove and drain on paper towels.
4. Clean out wok and add 2 tablespoons oil. When oil is hot, add the baby carrots. Stir-fry for 1 minute, then add the green peas. Stir-fry until the peas are bright green. Remove.
5. Wipe the wok clean and add 2 tablespoons oil. When oil is hot, add the rice and egg mixture. Stir-fry for 2–3 minutes, then add 1 tablespoon oyster sauce and the sugar. Add the barbequed pork and shrimp. Add the vegetables. Stir in the green onion and serve hot.

Pineapple Fried Rice

2 whole, fresh pineapples
2 eggs
⅛ teaspoon salt
Pepper to taste
4 cups cold cooked rice
3–4 tablespoons oil for
 stir-frying

½ cup chopped onion
½ cup peas
2 tablespoons oyster sauce
1 cup diced cooked ham

Serves 4

Serving the fried rice inside the pineapple skins adds glamour to a fairly simple dish. You can substitute cooked shrimp for the ham.

---

1. Cut the pineapples in half lengthwise, cutting through the crown. Cut out the fruit in the middle, without cutting through the skins. Turn the skins inside out to drain. Dice the pineapple fruit.

2. Lightly beat the eggs and add a small amount of salt and pepper to taste. Add the beaten eggs to the rice, stirring to separate the grains.

3. Add 2 tablespoons oil to a preheated wok or skillet. When oil is hot, add the onion. Stir-fry for 1 minute, then add the peas. Stir-fry until the peas are bright green and the onion tender. Remove.

4. Wipe the wok clean and add 2 tablespoons oil. When oil is hot, add the rice/egg mixture. Stir-fry for 2–3 minutes, then add the oyster sauce. Add the ham, peas, and onion. Stir in the diced pineapple.

5. Place 1 cup of the fried rice inside each of the pineapple half shells and serve.

Basic Congee

Serves 6–8

Feel free to adjust the proportion of chicken broth to water to suit your own tastes.

1 cup long grain rice
7 cups water

1 cup chicken stock or broth

Rinse the rice and drain. In a large saucepan, bring the rice, water, and chicken broth to a boil. Simmer, covered, for 1½ hours.

Versatile Congee

Congee does double duty as a nutritious meal and a beverage replacement. Just as the Chinese frequently serve a thin soup instead of a beverage at the main meal, a bowl of creamy congee takes the place of a beverage at the breakfast table.

Speedy Congee

Serves 4–6

Leftover fried rice comes is handy on days when there is no time to prepare fresh congee. Feel free to add other seasonings.

3 cups cold fried rice
6 cups chicken broth or water

Salt and pepper to taste

1. Make sure the fried rice is at room temperature.
2. Bring the broth or water to a boil. Add the fried rice. Bring the broth back up to a boil. Add the salt and pepper. Serve hot.

Congee with Beef

½ pound beef
2 teaspoons oyster sauce
1 cup long grain rice
6 cups water
2 cups chicken broth
2 green onions
2 tablespoons oil for stir-frying

2 slices ginger, minced
1 clove garlic, minced
2 tablespoons dark soy sauce
1 tablespoon Chinese rice wine
   or dry sherry
½ teaspoon sesame oil
Salt and pepper to taste

Serves 6–8

Serve this hearty
dish for breakfast,
or as a midday meal.
Be sure to add
bread for dipping!

⌣· 🌿 ·⌣

1. Cut the beef into thin slices. Marinate with the oyster sauce for
   30 minutes.
2. Bring the rice, water, and chicken broth to a boil. Simmer, covered,
   for 30 minutes.
3. Cut the green onions into 1-inch pieces on the diagonal.
4. Add oil to a preheated wok or skillet. When oil is hot, add the ginger
   and garlic. Stir-fry briefly until aromatic. Add the beef and stir-fry until
   it changes color and is nearly cooked through. Remove and drain on
   paper towels.
5. Add the ginger, garlic, and beef to the congee. Stir in the dark soy
   sauce and rice wine. Continue simmering for another 30 minutes, or
   until the congee has a creamy texture. Stir in the green onions.
   Drizzle with the sesame oil. Add salt to taste.

🌿 Congee—More Than a Chinese Porridge

*At its simplest, congee consists of rice cooked in water until it
has a creamy texture. However, it would be a mistake to view congee
as merely the Chinese version of porridge. Congee can be savory or
sweet; a bland, watery "soup" for a sick patient, or a hearty meal
swimming in a richly seasoned broth. It all depends on the length of
cooking time and which ingredients are added to the basic rice and
water mix. Congee is frequently accompanied by Chinese crullers: thick,
deep-fried strips of dough approximately twelve inches in length.*

Rice and Sausage Dinner

4 Chinese sausages
1 cup baby carrots
4 dried mushrooms
2 green onions
¾ cup beef broth
2 teaspoons hoisin sauce
1 teaspoon sugar

3 tablespoons oil for stir-frying
1 teaspoon minced shallot
3 cups cooked long grain rice

1. Cut the Chinese sausage into bite-sized pieces.
2. Blanch the baby carrots by plunging briefly into boiling water. Cut in half. Soak the dried mushrooms in hot water for at least 20 minutes to soften. Cut into thin slices. Cut the green onions on the diagonal into ½-inch pieces.
3. Combine the beef broth, hoisin sauce, and sugar; set aside.
4. Add 2 tablespoons oil to a preheated wok or skillet. When oil is hot, add the sausages. Stir-fry for 2–3 minutes, and remove from the wok.
5. Add 1 tablespoon oil to the wok. When oil is hot, add the shallot and stir-fry briefly until aromatic. Add the carrots, stir-fry for about 1 minute, and add the mushrooms. Make a well in the middle of the wok. Add the sauce in the middle and bring to a boil. Mix in the cooked rice. Add the sausages back to the wok. Stir in the green onions. Mix everything through and serve hot.

Hot, Sour, and Spicy Rice Noodles

¼ pound rice stick noodles
¼ cup dark soy sauce
1 teaspoon sugar
¼ teaspoon Hot Chili Oil (page 23)
¼ teaspoon Szechwan Salt and Pepper Mix (page 20)

¼ teaspoon chili paste
1 teaspoon black rice vinegar
½ cup water
1½ tablespoons oil for stir-frying
¼ cup chopped onion

Serves 4–6

Rice stick noodles come in many intriguing shapes and sizes. They can be nearly as thin as strands of human hair.

1. Soak the rice stick noodles in hot water for 15 minutes or until they are softened. Drain thoroughly.
2. Combine the dark soy sauce, sugar, Hot Chili Oil, Szechwan Salt and Pepper Mix, chili paste, black rice vinegar, and water; set aside.
3. Add oil to a preheated wok or skillet. When oil is hot, add the chopped onion. Stir-fry until it is soft and translucent.
4. Add the rice noodles and stir-fry for 2–3 minutes. Add the sauce in the middle of the wok. Mix in with the noodles and stir-fry until the noodles have absorbed all the sauce.

How to Make Toasted Szechwan Peppercorns

Toast the peppercorns on low heat in a heavy pan, shaking occasionally, until the peppercorns turn fragrant and begin to smoke. Remove and cool. Grind the peppercorns in a pepper mill or with a mortar and pestle before using.

Cellophane Noodles with Beef and Oyster Sauce

Serves 2–4

Not a fan of canned baby corn? Try substituting canned or fresh bamboo shoots instead.

½ pound flank steak
2 tablespoons soy sauce
1½ teaspoons Chinese rice wine or dry sherry, divided
1½ teaspoons sugar, divided
½ teaspoon baking soda
2-ounce bag cellophane noodles
1 can baby corn

½ cup beef broth
2 tablespoons oyster sauce
2 tablespoons dark soy sauce
1 tablespoon light soy sauce
2–4 tablespoons oil for stir-frying

1. Cut the beef into thin slices. Add the soy sauce, 1 teaspoon rice wine, ½ teaspoon sugar, and baking soda. Marinate the beef for 30 minutes.
2. Without removing the string wrapping, soak the cellophane noodles in hot water to soften. Cut the noodles along the string wrapping into thirds. Drain thoroughly. Rinse the baby corn in warm water and drain.
3. Combine the beef broth, oyster sauce, dark soy sauce, light soy sauce, ½ teaspoon rice wine, and 1 teaspoon sugar, and set aside.
4. Add 2 tablespoons oil to a preheated wok or skillet. When oil is hot, add the beef. Stir-fry until it changes color and is nearly cooked through. Remove from the wok and set aside.
5. Add more oil, if necessary. Stir-fry the baby corn for 1–2 minutes. Add the sauce to the middle of the wok and bring to a boil. Add the noodles, stirring quickly to mix in with the sauce. Add the beef. Mix everything through and serve hot.

Mad about Mein!
Mein is the Chinese word for noodles. When it comes to important staple foods, noodles rank second only to rice in the Chinese diet. Noodles are steamed, stir-fried, added to soups, and used to make dumplings. Although noodles are enjoyed throughout China, they are particularly important in the north, where a harsher climate prohibits the cultivation of rice crops.

Beef Chow Fun

4 ounces wide rice noodles
1 cup mung bean sprouts
½ cup chicken stock or broth
1 teaspoon soy sauce

2 tablespoons oil for stir-frying
1 cup cooked beef, shredded
¼ teaspoon chili paste

1. Soak the rice noodles in hot water for at least 15 minutes to soften. Drain well. Blanch the mung bean sprouts by plunging briefly into boiling water. Drain well.
2. Combine the chicken broth and soy sauce. Set aside.
3. Add oil to a preheated wok or skillet. When oil is hot, add the noodles. Stir-fry briefly, then add the sauce. Mix with the noodles and add the shredded beef. Stir in the chili paste. Add the mung bean sprouts. Mix through and serve hot.

> **Serves 4**
>
> Barbequed pork also works well in this dish. For an interesting juxtaposition of color and texture, serve with Braised Baby Bok Choy (page 256).
>
>

Noodle Pancake

8 ounces steamed egg noodles
2 teaspoons sesame oil

5 tablespoons oil

1. Cook the noodles until they are tender. Drain thoroughly and toss with the sesame oil.
2. Add 3 tablespoons oil to a preheated wok or skillet. When oil is hot, add noodles. Use a spatula to press down on the noodles and form into a pancake shape. Cook until a thin brown crust forms on the bottom—this will take at least 5 minutes. Slide the pancake out of the pan onto a plate.
3. Add 2 tablespoons oil to the wok. Turn the noodle pancake over, put back in the wok, and cook until the other side is browned. Remove from the wok. To serve, cut into quarters.

> **Serves 4**
>
> Noodle Pancake makes a nice alternative to rice in stir-fries, and tastes great topped with any Egg Foo Yung sauce (see Chapter 9).
>
>

Pork Chow Mein

Serves 4–6

The mushroom soaking liquid adds an earthy flavor to this dish. You can also use fresh mushrooms and ¼ cup water instead.

1 pound fresh egg noodles
¼ teaspoon sesame oil
1 pound pork tenderloin, cubed
1 tablespoon Chinese rice wine
¼ teaspoon salt
2½ cups shredded napa cabbage
4 large dried mushrooms
½ green or red bell pepper
⅓ cup chicken broth
⅛ cup water
⅛ cup reserved mushroom
    soaking liquid

4 teaspoons oyster sauce
⅛ teaspoon salt
4–6 tablespoons oil for stir-frying
2 garlic cloves, minced
1 carrot, diced
1 stalk celery, thinly sliced on
    the diagonal
1 cup mung bean sprouts, rinsed
    and drained
1 teaspoon cornstarch mixed
    with 4 teaspoons water
1 teaspoon sugar

1. Boil the noodles. Drain and toss with sesame oil.
2. Marinate pork in rice wine and ¼ teaspoon salt for 30 minutes.
3. Soak the dried mushrooms for at least 20 minutes to soften. Thinly slice them. Remove the seeds from the pepper and cut into cubes.
4. Combine chicken broth, water, mushroom soaking liquid, oyster sauce, and ⅛ teaspoon salt. Set aside.
5. Add 2 tablespoons oil to a preheated wok or skillet. Add the pork and stir-fry until it is nearly cooked. Remove and drain on paper towels.
6. Add 2 tablespoons oil. When oil is hot, add the noodles and stir-fry until light brown. Remove and keep warm. Clean out the wok.
7. Add 2 tablespoons oil. When oil is hot, add the garlic and stir-fry briefly until aromatic. Either stir-fry the carrot, celery, pepper, dried mushrooms, cabbage, and bean sprouts together or separately, adding one at a time and adding more oil as needed. (Move the vegetables up to the side of the wok and wait until oil is heated.)
8. Add the sauce to the middle of the wok and bring to a boil. Add the cornstarch-and-water mixture, stirring quickly to thicken. Add the sugar. Add the pork and heat through. Serve hot over the noodles.

Chicken Chow Mein

1 pound fresh egg noodles
¼ teaspoon sesame oil
1 pound boneless, skinless
  chicken breasts
10 teaspoons oyster sauce, divided
¼ teaspoon salt
½ red bell pepper
1 bunch (about 2½ cups after
  cutting) bok choy
⅓ cup chicken broth
¼ cup water

⅛ teaspoon salt
6–8 tablespoons oil for stir-frying
2 garlic cloves, minced
6–8 large mushrooms, thinly sliced
2 stalks celery, thinly sliced on
  the diagonal
1 cup mung bean sprouts, rinsed
  and drained
1 teaspoon cornstarch mixed
  with 4 teaspoons water
1 teaspoon sugar

> **Serves 4–6**
>
> Like chop suey, this is a great one-dish meal to make when it's time to clean out the vegetable section of the refrigerator.
>
>

1. Boil the noodles. Drain thoroughly and toss with sesame oil.
2. Cut the chicken breasts into thin strips. Marinate in 6 teaspoons oyster sauce and ¼ teaspoon salt for 30 minutes.
3. Remove the seeds from the red pepper and cut into thin slices. Cut the bok choy leaves across and thinly slice the stalks on the diagonal.
4. Combine chicken broth, water, 4 teaspoons oyster sauce, and ⅛ teaspoon salt. Set aside.
5. Add 2 tablespoons oil to a preheated wok or skillet. Add the chicken and stir-fry until it is nearly cooked. Drain on paper towels.
6. Add 2 tablespoons oil. Add the noodles and stir-fry until they turn light brown. Remove and keep warm. Clean out the wok.
7. Add 2 tablespoons oil. Add the garlic and stir-fry briefly until aromatic. Stir-fry the mushrooms, bok choy stalks, celery, pepper, bok choy leaves, and bean sprouts, adding one at a time and adding more oil as needed.
8. Add the sauce to the middle of the wok and bring to a boil. Add the cornstarch/water mixture, stirring quickly to thicken. Add the sugar. Add the chicken and heat through. Serve hot over the noodles.

Beef Chow Mein

1 pound wonton noodles
1 pound beef flank steak
1 tablespoon soy sauce
½ teaspoon baking soda
½ red bell pepper
½ cup snow peas
⅓ cup beef broth
¼ cup water
1 tablespoon plus 1 teaspoon
    oyster sauce
1 teaspoon sugar

⅛ teaspoon salt
4–6 tablespoons oil for
    stir-frying
2 garlic cloves, minced
½ cup carrots, thinly sliced
1 cup mung bean sprouts,
    rinsed and drained
1 teaspoon cornstarch
4 teaspoons water
½ teaspoon sesame oil

1. Boil the wonton noodles until they are soft. Drain thoroughly.
2. Cut the beef into thin strips. Marinate in the soy sauce and baking soda for 30 minutes.
3. Remove the seeds from the pepper and cut into thin slices. String the snow peas. Combine the beef broth, water, oyster sauce, sugar, and salt. Set aside.
4. Add 2 tablespoons oil to the wok. When oil is hot, add the beef. Stir-fry until it changes color and is nearly cooked. Remove and drain on paper towels.
5. Add 1–2 tablespoons oil. When oil is hot, add the wonton noodles. Stir-fry until they are golden but still soft. Remove.
6. Add 2 tablespoons oil to the wok. When oil is hot, add the garlic. Stir-fry until aromatic. Add the carrots. Stir-fry for 1 minute, then add the snow peas, red pepper, and bean sprouts. Stir-fry until the vegetables are colorful and tender.
7. Make a well in the middle of the wok. Add the sauce and bring to a boil. Add mixed cornstarch and water, stirring to thicken. Add the beef. Drizzle with sesame oil. Mix everything through and serve over the wonton noodles.

Post-Thanksgiving Turkey Chow Mein

4 cups dry chow mein noodles
4 mushrooms, sliced
1 cup bean sprouts
2 stalks celery
2 cups snow peas
4½ tablespoons oil for
   stir-frying

1 tablespoon soy sauce
½ cup cashews
2 cups cooked turkey
2 tablespoons oyster sauce
1 tablespoon cornstarch mixed
   with 4 tablespoons water

Serves 4

A great way to make use of leftover Thanksgiving turkey. Serve with Egg Drop Soup (page 57) for a nourishing fall meal.

1. Boil the chow mein noodles according to the directions on the package. Drain well. Keep warm.
2. Wash and slice the mushrooms. Parboil the bean sprouts and celery by briefly plunging into boiling water; drain thoroughly. Wash and cut the celery on the diagonal into thin slices. String the snow peas.
3. Add 2 tablespoons of oil to a preheated wok or skillet. Stir-fry the celery on medium-high heat. Add the mushrooms, bean sprouts, and soy sauce. Stir-fry, remove, and set aside.
4. Add the snow peas and fry as in the recipe for Snow Pea Stir-fry (page 233). Remove and set aside.
5. Add 1½ tablespoons oil to the wok or frying pan. Add the cashews and stir-fry on medium heat very briefly. Remove and set aside.
6. Add 1 tablespoon oil to the wok. Add the cooked turkey and the oyster sauce. Add the vegetables and mix through.
7. Make a well in the middle of the pan and add the cornstarch-and-water mixture, stirring to thicken. Mix with the other ingredients. Stir in the cashews. Serve over the chow mein noodles.

Beefy Fried Rice Noodles

Serves 4–6

For a different flavor, replace the oyster sauce in the chicken broth mixture with 1 tablespoon of hoisin sauce.

½ pound beef flank or sirloin steak
1½ teaspoons oyster sauce
⅛ teaspoon salt
¼ teaspoon baking soda
4–5 ounces medium-width rice stick noodles
1 red bell pepper
1 tablespoon oyster sauce
2 tablespoons dark soy sauce
1 teaspoon sugar
½ cup chicken stock or broth
4–5 cups oil for frying
¼ cup cornstarch
1 teaspoon finely chopped ginger
2 garlic cloves, finely chopped
1 cup mung bean sprouts, rinsed and drained

1. Cut the beef across the grain into thin strips about 2 inches long. Add the oyster sauce, salt, and baking soda. Marinate the beef for 30 minutes.
2. Soak the rice noodles in hot water for 20 minutes or until they are softened. Wash the pepper, remove the seeds, and cut into thin strips about 2 inches long.
3. Combine the oyster sauce, dark soy sauce, sugar, and chicken stock. Set aside.
4. Heat 4 cups of oil in the wok to 375°F. Lightly dust the marinated beef with the cornstarch. Deep-fry the beef in the hot oil for a few minutes, until it turns light brown. Drain on paper towels.
5. Remove all but 3 tablespoons oil from the wok or heat 3 tablespoons oil in a second wok or heavy skillet. When oil is hot, add the ginger and garlic and stir-fry until aromatic. Add the red pepper and stir-fry until it is tender and has a bright color (stir-fry in 2 batches, if necessary). Add the bean sprouts. Push the vegetables up to the side, add the sauce, and bring to a boil.
6. Turn down the heat slightly and add the noodles. Stir-fry briefly and add the beef. If necessary, add a bit of water. Mix everything through and serve hot.

Cold Szechwan Sesame Noodles

8 ounces egg noodles
Spicy Szechwan Peanut Sauce
    (page 23)
1 cucumber

½ teaspoon salt
1 tablespoon toasted sesame
    seeds

1. Prepare the egg noodles according to the instructions on the package.
2. Peel the cucumber, toss with salt, and leave for 15 minutes. Toast the sesame seeds.
3. Allow the noodles to cool. When cold, toss with the Spicy Szechwan Peanut Sauce. Sprinkle with sesame seeds. Serve over the cucumber slices.

> **Serves 4**
>
> Italian pasta can be substituted for Chinese egg noodles in this recipe. For added flair, garnish with cilantro leaves.
>
>

Deep-fried Vermicelli

4 ounces vermicelli noodles
4 cups oil for deep-frying

1. Heat oil in preheated wok or heavy saucepan to 375°F. If the noodles come with string wrappings, cut them off. Do not soak the noodles.
2. Drop one 2-ounce package of noodles into the wok. It should puff up immediately. Remove and drain on paper towels. Repeat with the other package. Cut the noodles into serving portions or serve as is.

> **Serves 6–8**
>
> Top these noodles with dishes that have a lot of sauce, such as Mongolian Beef with Vegetables (page 109).
>
>

Singapore Fried Rice Noodles

Serves 2–4

For a different taste and texture, try substituting chicken for the pork and experimenting with rice noodles of different thickness.

4 ounces rice vermicelli
½ red bell pepper
2 teaspoons mild curry powder
¼ teaspoon turmeric
½ teaspoon grated ginger
½ cup chicken stock or broth
2 tablespoons plus 1 teaspoon
   soy sauce
½ teaspoon sugar
4–5 tablespoons oil for stir-frying

2 ounces shrimp, peeled and
   deveined
1 cup mung bean sprouts,
   rinsed and drained
4 ounces barbequed pork,
   cut into very thin slices
⅛ teaspoon freshly ground
   pepper

1. Soak the rice noodles in hot water for 20 minutes or until softened. Drain thoroughly. Wash the red pepper and remove the seeds.
2. Combine the curry powder, turmeric, and ginger. Set aside. Combine the chicken broth, soy sauce, and sugar. Set aside.
3. Add 2 tablespoons oil to a preheated wok or skillet. When oil is hot, add the shrimp and stir-fry briefly until they turn pink. Remove and set aside.
4. Add 2–3 tablespoons oil. When oil is hot, add the curry powder mixture and stir-fry until aromatic. Add the red pepper and bean sprouts. Add the noodles and stir-fry for a few minutes, adding water if necessary.
5. Add the sauce in the middle of the wok. Bring to a boil. Add the barbequed pork and mix through. Add the stir-fried shrimp. Sprinkle with the freshly ground pepper and serve hot.

Dan Dan Noodles

8 ounces fresh egg noodles
2 teaspoons plus 1 tablespoon
    sesame oil, divided
3 tablespoons peanut butter
2 tablespoons dark soy sauce
1 tablespoon light soy sauce
3 tablespoons rice vinegar
4 teaspoons sugar

1 tablespoon Hot Chili Oil
    (page 23)
1½ tablespoons toasted sesame
    seeds
3 green onions, cut into 1-inch
    pieces

> **Serves 4**
>
> A mild, sweetened rice vinegar works very well in this recipe. If you want to add a vegetable, try 1 cup blanched bean sprouts.
>
>

1. Bring a pot of water to boil, and cook the noodles al dente. Drain thoroughly and toss with 2 teaspoons sesame oil. Cool.
2. Combine the peanut butter, dark soy sauce, light soy sauce, rice vinegar, sugar, 1 tablespoon sesame oil, and Hot Chili Oil. Process in a blender or food processor.
3. Mix the sauce in with the noodles. Sprinkle the toasted sesame seeds over. Garnish with the green onion.

How to Toast Sesame Seeds

Spread the sesame seeds out on a pan and cook at low heat, shaking the pan occasionally. Toast the sesame seeds until they turn a light brown. Remove from the pan, cool, and use as called for in recipes. When cooking the seeds, be sure not to overcook and let them burn.

Beef Lo Mein

Serves 4

To cook noodles al dente, boil until they are tender, but still firm and not mushy.

1 pound flank steak
2 teaspoons oyster sauce
1½ teaspoons sugar, divided
½ teaspoon baking soda
6 dried mushrooms
8 ounces fresh egg noodles
2 tablespoons dark soy sauce

1 tablespoon light soy sauce
1 teaspoon Chinese rice wine
   or dry sherry
¼ cup water
3 tablespoons oil for stir-frying
6 cabbage leaves, shredded

1. Cut the steak into thin slices, about 2 inches in length. Add the oyster sauce, ½ teaspoon sugar, and baking soda. Marinate the steak for 30 minutes.
2. Soak the dried mushrooms in hot water for at least 20 minutes to soften.
3. In a large pot of water, boil the noodles until the flour is removed but they are still firm. Drain thoroughly.
4. Cut the mushrooms into thin slices. Combine the dark soy sauce, light soy sauce, 1 teaspoon sugar, rice wine, and water, and set aside.
5. Add 2 tablespoons oil to a preheated wok or skillet. When oil is hot, add the steak. Stir-fry until it changes color and is nearly cooked through. Remove and drain on paper towels.
6. Add 1 tablespoon oil to the wok. When oil is hot, add the cabbage leaves. Stir-fry until they are bright green and tender. Season with ¼ teaspoon salt if desired. Add the mushrooms. Stir-fry briefly. Add the sauce in the middle of the wok, and bring to a boil. Turn down the heat slightly and add the beef. Add the noodles. Mix everything through and serve hot.

Chow Mein or Lo Mein?

People are often surprised to learn that the difference between these popular dishes has more to do with cooking styles than specific ingredients. Chow Mein are fried noodles cooked separately from the meat and vegetables. Lo Mein dishes feature boiled noodles that are combined with the other ingredients during the final stages of cooking.

Chicken Lo Mein

1 cup cooked chicken
8 ounces fresh egg noodles
½ cup mushrooms, fresh
   or dried
2 tablespoons oyster sauce
1 tablespoon soy sauce
1 teaspoon sugar
1 teaspoon Chinese rice wine
   or dry sherry

½ cup water
2–3 tablespoons oil for stir-frying
4 cabbage leaves, shredded
¼ teaspoon salt, optional
½ cup mung bean sprouts,
   rinsed and drained

Serves 4

Leftover Tea Smoked
Chicken (page 175)
works very well in this
recipe, imparting a
lovely smoky flavor.

---

1. Cut the cooked chicken into thin slices. In a large pot of water, boil the noodles until the flour is removed and they are tender. Drain thoroughly.
2. If using dried mushrooms, soak in hot water for at least 20 minutes to soften. Slice mushrooms.
3. Combine the oyster sauce, soy sauce, sugar, rice wine, and water, and set aside.
4. Add 2 tablespoons oil to a preheated wok or skillet. When oil is hot, add the cabbage leaves. Stir-fry until they turn bright green and are tender. Season with salt, if desired. Add 1 tablespoon oil, if necessary.
5. Add the mushrooms. Stir-fry briefly, then add the bean sprouts. Add the sauce in the middle of the wok. Bring to a boil. Turn down the heat slightly and add the chicken. Add the noodles. Mix everything through and serve hot.

Savory Shanghai Noodles

Serves 2–4

Frying the shrimp briefly in 1 cup of hot oil gives it a soft, velvety texture.

½ pound (8 ounces) fresh cooked shrimp, tails and vein removed
½ teaspoon sugar
½ teaspoon cornstarch
1 bunch spinach
¾ cup chicken broth
¼ cup water
2 tablespoons plus 2 teaspoons oyster sauce

1 teaspoon Chinese rice wine or dry sherry
1 garlic clove, finely chopped
2 slices ginger, finely chopped
½ pound fresh Shanghai noodles
½ teaspoon sesame oil
1¼ cups oil for frying

1. Rinse the shrimp in warm water and pat dry. Marinate the shrimp in the sugar and cornstarch for 15 minutes.
2. Wash the spinach and drain thoroughly. Mix together the chicken broth, water, oyster sauce, and rice wine, and set aside.
3. Add 1 cup oil to a preheated wok or skillet. When oil is hot, add the shrimp and fry briefly for 1 minute (if using raw shrimp, fry longer until the shrimp turn pink and firm up around the edges). Remove the shrimp from the wok with a slotted spoon and drain on paper towels.
4. Remove all but 2 tablespoons oil from the wok. Add the spinach and fry until it changes color. Add seasonings such as salt or soy sauce, if desired. Remove from the wok and set aside.
5. Add the garlic and ginger and stir-fry briefly until aromatic. Add the noodles. Stir-fry and toss with the sesame oil. Make a well in the middle of the wok and add the sauce. Bring to a boil. Add the spinach and the shrimp back into the wok. Mix everything through and serve hot.

Noodle Lore
The Chinese have been enjoying noodles since ancient times. Symbolizing a long life in Chinese culture, noodles occupy an important place in festive celebrations such as Chinese New Year. And birthday celebrations wouldn't be complete without a heaping bowl of longevity noodles.

Oyster Sauce Pork with Cellophane Noodles

1 pound pork
1 green onion, cut in thirds
3 tablespoons soy sauce, divided
2 stalks celery
2 tablespoons oyster sauce
1 teaspoon sugar
¼ teaspoon Chinese rice wine or dry sherry
½ cup chicken broth
1 2-ounce package cellophane noodles
4 cups oil for frying

1. Cut the pork into cubes. Marinate the pork in 1 tablespoon soy sauce and green onion for 30 minutes.
2. Blanch the celery by plunging briefly into boiling water. Drain well. Cut into thin slices along the diagonal.
3. Combine the oyster sauce, 2 tablespoons soy sauce, sugar, rice wine, and chicken broth. Set aside.
4. Add 4 cups oil to a preheated wok and heat to at least 350°F. While oil is heating, remove the string wrappings from the cellophane noodles. When oil is hot add the noodles. Deep-fry briefly until it puffs up and forms a "nest." Remove and drain on paper towels. Leave as is or cut into individual servings.
5. Drain all but 2 tablespoons oil from the wok. Add the pork and stir-fry until it changes color and is almost cooked through. Remove and drain on paper towels.
6. Add the celery and stir-fry until it turns shiny and is tender. Add the sauce to the middle of the wok and bring to a boil. Add the pork. Mix everything through. Serve over the noodles.

> **Serves 2–4**
>
> Because it resembles a bird's nest, a packet of deep-fried cellophane noodles is sometimes used to replace authentic bird's nest in mock bird's nest soup.
>
>

Cellophane Noodles

Made from mung bean starch, cellophane noodles are also called bean thread or glass noodles. After soaking they became very absorbent, picking up the flavors of the foods they are cooked with. Deep-frying without soaking first causes them to puff up immediately. Use cellophane noodles in dishes with lots of flavorful sauce.

CHAPTER 6
Beef Dishes

Basic Beef Stir-fry

½ pound beef
2 teaspoons soy sauce
1 teaspoon cornstarch
¼ teaspoon baking soda
1 tablespoon vegetable oil

2 tablespoons oil for stir-frying
1 clove garlic, smashed
1 tablespoon Chinese rice wine
  or dry sherry
½ teaspoon sugar

1. Cut the beef across the grain into thin strips. Add the soy sauce, cornstarch, and baking soda to the meat, in that order. Use your hands to mix in the cornstarch and baking soda. Marinate the meat for 30 minutes, add the vegetable oil, and marinate for another 30 minutes.
2. Add oil to a preheated wok or skillet. When oil is hot, add the garlic and stir-fry briefly until aromatic. Add the beef, laying it flat on the wok. Let the meat cook for a minute, turn over and brown on the other side, and then begin stir-frying. When it is nearly cooked through, add the rice wine and sugar. When the meat is cooked, remove from the wok and drain on paper towels.

Searing Meat

While stir-frying is normally a hands-on process, when cooking meat it's best to give the spatula a brief rest. Lay the meat out flat in the wok and brown for about thirty seconds before stir-frying.

Mongolian Beef with Vegetables

1 pound sirloin or flank steak
1 egg white
Pinch of salt
1½ teaspoons sesame oil,
    divided
1 tablespoon cornstarch
1½ tablespoons oil
2 green onions
2 garlic cloves, minced
½ teaspoon chili sauce

1 can baby corn, rinsed and
    drained
1 tablespoon Chinese rice wine
    or dry sherry
2 tablespoons hoisin sauce
1 tablespoon dark soy sauce
½ teaspoon sugar
1½ teaspoons cornstarch
2 tablespoons water
1 cup oil for frying beef

> **Serves 4**
>
> This northern Chinese favorite makes a complete meal when served with rice. For a more authentic dish, use bamboo shoots instead of baby corn.
>
>

1. Slice the beef across the grain into thin strips. Add the egg white, salt, 1 teaspoon sesame oil, and cornstarch to the beef, adding the cornstarch last. Marinate the beef for thirty minutes. Add 1½ tablespoons oil and marinate for another thirty minutes.

2. While beef is marinating, cut the green onions into thirds on the diagonal.

3. Add 1 cup oil to a preheated wok or skillet. When oil is hot, carefully slide the beef into the wok, a few pieces at a time. Fry the beef until it changes color. Remove from the wok with a slotted spoon and drain on paper towels.

4. Remove all but 2 tablespoons of oil. When oil is hot, add the garlic and chili sauce. Stir-fry briefly until the garlic is aromatic. Add the baby corn.

5. Add the beef back into the wok. Add the rice wine, hoisin sauce, dark soy sauce, and sugar. Mix the cornstarch and water, and add to the middle of the wok, stirring vigorously to thicken. Mix all the ingredients together thoroughly. Stir in the green onion. Drizzle with ½ teaspoon sesame oil and serve hot.

Mongolian Beef with Rice Noodles

Serves 4–6

Leeks are a popular vegetable in northern China, where cooks rely on hardy vegetables that can survive cold winters and a short growing season.

1 pound sirloin or flank steak
3 tablespoons dark soy sauce, divided
1 tablespoon Chinese rice wine or dry sherry
1 teaspoon sesame oil
1 tablespoon cornstarch
8 ounces rice vermicelli noodles

1 bunch leeks
2 tablespoons hoisin sauce
½ teaspoon sugar
½ teaspoon chili sauce
2 garlic cloves, minced
1½ teaspoons cornstarch
2 tablespoons water
1½ cups oil for frying

1. Slice the beef across the grain into thin slices. Add 2 tablespoons dark soy sauce, sherry, sesame oil, and cornstarch, adding the cornstarch last. Marinate the beef for 30 minutes. Soak the rice vermicelli in hot water for 15–20 minutes to soften. Drain thoroughly.
2. Wash the leek bunch, and cut into slices about 1½ inches long. Mix together the hoisin sauce, sugar, chili sauce, and 1 tablespoon dark soy sauce. Set aside.
3. Heat 1½ cups oil to 350°F in a preheated wok. When the oil is hot, add the rice vermicelli. Deep-fry until they puff up and turn crispy. Remove and drain on paper towels.
4. Remove all but 2 tablespoons oil. When oil is hot, add the garlic and stir-fry until aromatic. Add the beef and stir-fry until it changes color and is nearly cooked through. Remove and drain on paper towels.
5. Add more oil, if necessary. Add the leeks to the wok. Stir-fry for about 1 minute. Add the sauce to the middle of the wok. Mix the cornstarch and water and add to the sauce, stirring to thicken. Bring to a boil. Add the beef back into the wok and mix all the ingredients together. Serve over the rice noodles.

Beef with Peppers

1½ pounds beef, such as eye
  of round
2 tablespoons dark soy sauce
2 tablespoons Chinese rice
  wine or dry sherry, divided
1 teaspoon sesame oil
1 tablespoon cornstarch
½ red bell pepper

½ green bell pepper
½ cup canned bamboo shoots
¼ cup water
2 tablespoons soy sauce
2 teaspoons sugar
4½ tablespoons oil
2 garlic cloves, chopped
2 slices ginger, chopped

Serves 4–6

Eye of round is a good cut to use in this dish—it is one of the leanest cuts of beef and is also very tender.

1. Cut the beef in thin slices, across the grain. Mix in the dark soy sauce, 1 tablespoon rice wine, sesame oil, and cornstarch, adding the cornstarch last. Marinate the beef for 30 minutes.
2. Remove the seeds from the peppers and cut into thin strips, about 2½ inches in length. Wash the bamboo shoots.
3. Mix together the water, 1 tablespoon rice wine, soy sauce, and sugar.
4. Add 3 tablespoons oil to a preheated wok or skillet. Add the garlic and ginger and stir-fry briefly until aromatic. Add the beef and stir-fry in batches until it changes color. Remove and set aside.
5. Wipe the wok with a paper towel. Add 1½ tablespoons oil. When the oil is hot, add the red and green peppers. Stir-fry briefly and add the bamboo shoots. Add the sauce and bring to a boil. Add the beef. Mix everything through and serve hot.

Why Cut Meat Across the Grain?
The "grains" running across a piece of flank steak are muscle fibers. Since the muscle is the part of the body that does all the work, these fibers are tough. Cutting the meat across—instead of along with—the grain shortens the muscle fibers, giving the meat a more tender texture. This technique is not as important with pork and chicken, as the meat is more tender to begin with.

Beef with Tomatoes

Serves 4–6

Blanching tomatoes makes the skin easy to peel off. Serve this dish with Sweet-and-Sour Celery (page 252) for an interesting combination of flavors.

1 pound beef steak, round or flank
2 tablespoons dark soy sauce
½ teaspoon salt
⅛ teaspoon pepper or to taste
2 teaspoons cornstarch
½ teaspoon baking soda
4 large tomatoes

3–4 tablespoons oil for stir-frying
3 slices ginger, minced
½ cup beef broth
1 tablespoon oyster sauce
1 teaspoon sugar
1 tablespoon cornstarch
4 tablespoons water
¼ teaspoon sesame oil

1. Cut the beef across the grain into slices that are approximately 1½–2 inches long. Add the dark soy sauce, salt, pepper, cornstarch, and baking soda to the beef. Marinate the beef for 20 minutes.
2. Bring a large pot of water to a boil. Blanch the tomatoes. Peel off the skin and cut each into 6 equal pieces. (Be sure to remove the tomatoes from the boiling water before they soften.)
3. Add 2 tablespoons oil to a preheated wok or skillet. Add the beef. Fry until it changes color and it is nearly cooked through, turning it over once. Fry in batches if necessary. Remove the beef from the wok.
4. Wipe the wok if necessary and add 1–2 tablespoons oil. When the oil is hot, add the ginger and stir-fry briefly until aromatic. Add the tomatoes and stir-fry briefly, making sure they don't soften too much.
5. Add the beef broth, oyster sauce, and sugar, and bring to a boil. Add the cornstarch mixed with water to the middle of the wok, stirring to thicken. Add the beef back into the wok. Cover and simmer until everything is cooked through. Drizzle with the sesame oil.

Baking Soda—The Secret Tenderizer

A general rule of thumb is to use ½ teaspoon of baking soda per pound of meat. When cooking with a very tough cut of meat, add the baking soda alone first. Use your fingers to rub it over the meat. Wait 20 minutes and then rinse thoroughly to remove any baking soda flavor before adding the other marinade ingredients.

Beef with Broccoli

*¾ pound beef steak, such as
  inside round
3 teaspoons Chinese rice wine
  or dry sherry
1½ teaspoons cornstarch
½ teaspoon baking soda*

*Brown Sauce (page 19)
6–8 broccoli stalks with flowerets
¼ red onion
1½ cups oil for frying
2 garlic cloves, minced*

Serves 3–4

Serve this restaurant favorite on a bed of white rice or cooked noodles, accompanied by a few fortune cookies.

---

1. Cut the beef across the grain into thin strips about 2 inches long. Add the rice wine, cornstarch, and baking soda. Marinate the beef for 1 hour.
2. Blanch the broccoli by plunging into boiling water for about 3 minutes. Drain thoroughly. Separate the flowers and the stalks, and cut the stalks into spears along the diagonal. Chop the red onion.
3. Add 1½ cups oil to a preheated wok or skillet. When oil is hot, velvet the beef by adding it to the hot oil just until it changes color, and quickly removing from the wok. Drain the velveted beef on paper towels.
4. Remove all but 2 tablespoons oil from the wok. Add the garlic and stir-fry briefly until aromatic. Add the broccoli. Stir-fry for a minute and then add the red onion. Stir-fry the broccoli until it turns bright green and the red onion until it is soft and translucent.
5. Give the Brown Sauce a quick stir. Push the vegetables up to the sides and add the sauce into the middle of the wok. Turn up the heat and bring the sauce to a boil, stirring vigorously to thicken. Add the beef back into the wok. Mix everything through and serve hot.

Beef with Snow Peas

Serves 2–4

Feel free to follow the recipe for Mangetout and Bean Sprouts (page 237) in step 5, then add the sauce and beef and mix through.

¾ pound beef flank steak
2 teaspoons soy sauce
1 teaspoon cornstarch
¼ teaspoon baking soda
½ cup snow peas
1 cup mung bean sprouts
1 tablespoon dark soy sauce
1 tablespoon oyster sauce

1 tablespoon Chinese rice wine
  or dry sherry
1 teaspoon sugar
¼ teaspoon sesame oil
2 tablespoons water
3 tablespoons oil for stir-frying
2 garlic cloves, minced

1. Cut the beef across the grain into thin strips about 2 inches long. Add the soy sauce, cornstarch, and baking soda. Marinate the beef for 30 minutes.
2. Trim the snow peas. Blanch the bean sprouts and snow peas by plunging them briefly into boiling water. Drain well.
3. In a small bowl, combine the dark soy sauce, oyster sauce, rice wine, sugar, sesame oil, and water and set aside.
4. Add 2 tablespoons oil to a preheated wok or skillet. When oil is hot, add the beef and stir-fry until it changes color. Remove from the wok and drain on paper towels.
5. Add another tablespoon of oil to the wok. When oil is hot, add the garlic and stir-fry briefly until aromatic. Add the snow peas and bean sprouts and stir-fry briefly. Add the sauce in the middle of the wok and bring to a boil. Mix with the vegetables. Add the beef. Add 1–2 more tablespoons water if desired. Mix everything together and serve hot.

Beef and Bean Sprouts in Black Bean Sauce

½ pound beef steak
2 teaspoons soy sauce
¼ teaspoon salt
½ teaspoon sugar
1 teaspoon cornstarch
¼ teaspoon baking soda
1 cup mung bean sprouts
1 teaspoon fermented black beans

¼ teaspoon chili paste
½ cup chicken stock or broth
1 tablespoon dark soy sauce
1 teaspoon sugar
1 teaspoon red rice vinegar
3 tablespoons oil for stir-frying
1 garlic clove, minced

Serves 2–4

This dish can also be made with green jalapeno peppers—chop 3 jalapeno peppers, remove the seeds, and stir-fry with the chili paste.

---

1. Cut the beef across the grain into thin strips about 2 inches long. Add the soy sauce, salt, sugar, cornstarch, and baking soda. Marinate the beef for 30 minutes.
2. Blanch the bean sprouts by plunging very briefly into boiling water. Drain thoroughly. Soak the black beans, mash, and mix with the chili paste.
3. Mix together the chicken broth, dark soy sauce, and sugar.
4. Add 2 tablespoons oil to a preheated wok or skillet. When oil is hot, add the beef and stir-fry until it changes color and is nearly cooked through. Remove from the wok and drain on paper towels.
5. Add 1 tablespoon oil to the wok. When oil is hot, add the garlic and chili paste mixture. Stir-fry briefly until aromatic. Add the bean sprouts. Stir-fry briefly, and then add the red rice vinegar.
6. Add the sauce in the middle of the wok and bring to a boil. Add the beef. Simmer until everything is cooked through.

Do You Need to Buy a Chinese Cleaver?

Strictly speaking, no. Successful stir-frying demands food that is evenly cut, but many types of knives will do the job. Still, a Chinese cleaver has many advantages. The cleaver's wide rectangular shape makes it handy for cutting beef, pounding chicken, smashing garlic, and using its thicker-side blade to separate individual garlic cloves.

Dry Fried Beef

Serves 4

This dish tastes great combined with mustard in a sandwich or smoked in tea leaves and spices, a process described in the Tea Smoked Chicken recipe (page 175).

2 tablespoons soy sauce
1 teaspoon Chinese rice wine
  or dry sherry
½ teaspoon sugar
½ teaspoon baking soda
1 pound flank steak, shredded
5–6 tablespoons oil for frying

1. Add the soy sauce, rice wine, sugar, and baking soda to the beef. Marinate the beef for 30 minutes.
2. Add 3 tablespoons oil to a preheated wok or skillet. When oil is hot, add half the beef. Lay flat and fry for 2 minutes, then turn over and fry for another 2 minutes. Stir-fry the beef until it turns a dark brown (this will take about 8 minutes). Remove from the wok and drain on paper towels. Repeat with the remainder of the beef.

Beef Satay

Serves 6–8

For an authentic touch, thread the meat onto bamboo skewers that have been soaked in cold water for 30 minutes (to ensure that they don't burn).

½ pound beef sirloin steak
¼ cup dark soy sauce
¼ teaspoon chili paste
1 tablespoon hoisin sauce
1 teaspoon sugar
1 teaspoon orange marmalade
1 clove garlic, minced
1 slice ginger, minced

1. Cut the beef across the grain into very thin strips, about 1 inch long.
2. Combine the remaining ingredients. Marinate the beef in the refrigerator overnight or for at least 2 hours. Drain the beef, reserving the marinade.
3. Thread at least 2 slices of the marinated beef onto each skewer, weaving them in and out like an accordion. Brush with the reserved marinade.
4. Grill the beef on both sides. Serve with Hoisin Satay Sauce (page 21).

Beef Curry

½ pound beef sirloin
2 teaspoons Chinese rice wine
    or dry sherry
1 teaspoon cornstarch
¼ teaspoon baking soda
2 ounces rice stick noodles
1 tablespoon curry paste
¼ teaspoon turmeric

¼ teaspoon ground cumin
3 tablespoons oil for stir-frying
2 teaspoons minced ginger
1 teaspoon minced garlic
2 tablespoons chopped red
    onion
1 tablespoon plain yogurt

> **Serves 2–4**
>
> Yogurt helps take the edge off a hot curry—add more than 1 tablespoon, if desired.

1. Cut the beef across the grain into thin strips about 1½ inches in length. Add the rice wine, cornstarch, and baking soda (in that order). Marinate the beef for 1 hour.
2. Soak the rice noodles in hot water for 15 minutes or until they are softened. Drain thoroughly.
3. Mix together the curry paste, turmeric, and ground cumin.
4. Add 2 tablespoons oil to a preheated wok or skillet. When oil is hot, add the ginger and garlic and stir-fry briefly until aromatic. Add the beef. Stir-fry until it changes color and is nearly cooked through. Remove from the wok and drain on paper towels.
5. Add 1 tablespoon oil to the wok. When oil is hot, add the curry paste mixture and stir-fry briefly until it is aromatic. Add the onion and stir-fry until it is soft and translucent. Add the rice stick noodles and mix with the onion. Add 2 tablespoons water if necessary. Add the meat and the yogurt. Mix everything together and cook until the meat is cooked through.

Tangy Turmeric

Indian cooks have been relying on turmeric's distinctive yellow color and strong taste to lend flavor to curries since early times. It took China a bit longer to discover turmeric's possibilities. Today, turmeric is frequently found in Chinese curry recipes—a small amount mixed with curry powder or paste adds a lovely yellowish hue to the dish.

Basic Red-Cooked Beef

6 dried mushrooms
1 large daikon
2 slices ginger
1 cup light soy sauce
4 tablespoons dark soy sauce
4 tablespoons Chinese rice wine or dry sherry
4 teaspoons sugar

4 tablespoons plus 2 teaspoons brown sugar
½ teaspoon five-spice powder
2 tablespoons oil for stir-frying
2 garlic cloves, minced
1½ pounds boneless stewing beef, cut into chunks
2 cups water

1. Soak the dried mushrooms in hot water for at least 20 minutes to soften. Gently squeeze to remove any excess water, and slice. Peel the daikon and cut into ½-inch slices. Peel the ginger, if desired.
2. Combine the light soy sauce, dark soy sauce, rice wine, white sugar, brown sugar, and five-spice powder; set aside.
3. Add oil to a preheated wok or skillet. When oil is hot, add the ginger and garlic and stir-fry briefly until aromatic. Add the beef and cook until browned.
4. Add the sauce and 2 cups water. Bring to a boil, then turn down the heat and simmer. After 1 hour, add the daikon and dried mushrooms. Simmer for 30 minutes, or until the liquid is reduced.

Make Your Own Sauce for Red Cooking

In red cooking, previously browned meat is stewed in a combination of soy sauce and other ingredients. To make your own red cooking sauce, experiment with different combinations of light and dark soy sauce, rice wine, and other liquid ingredients until you find one you like. For extra flavor, add stronger seasonings such as star anise and dried tangerine peel (see Spicy Red-Cooked Beef, page 119, for ideas).

Spicy Red-Cooked Beef

6 dried mushrooms
1 large daikon
2–3 tablespoons oil for
   stir-frying
2 slices ginger
3 small garlic cloves, minced
2 pounds boneless stewing
   beef, cut into chunks
3 cups water

½ cup dark soy sauce
¼ cup light soy sauce
1 piece dried tangerine peel,
   2–3 inches wide
1 star anise
1 piece (about 1 ounce)
   yellow rock sugar

> **Serves 4–6**
>
> Star anise is a star-shaped seed pod with a strong flavor reminiscent of licorice, used to flavor meat dishes.
>
>

1. Soak the dried mushrooms in hot water for at least 20 minutes to soften. Gently squeeze to remove any excess water and slice. Peel the daikon and cut into ½-inch slices. Peel the ginger if desired.

2. Add oil to a preheated wok or skillet. When oil is hot, add the ginger and garlic and stir-fry briefly until aromatic. Add the beef and cook until browned.

3. Add the water, ¼ cup of dark soy sauce, 2 tablespoons of light soy sauce, and the tangerine peel and star anise, and bring to a boil. Reduce the heat and simmer for 45 minutes. Add the remaining dark and light soy sauce, the rock sugar, the daikon, and the dried mushrooms. Simmer for another 45 minutes, or until liquid is reduced.

Shopping for a Chinese Cleaver

When choosing a Chinese cleaver, look for one made of stainless steel or a combination of stainless and carbon steel, with a handle that attaches firmly to the blade. Try out several to find one that you're comfortable holding.

Beef with Red Onions

Serves 4–6

Red onions add a distinctive flavor to this simple dish. Serve on a bed of steamed rice.

1 pound beef steak, flank or sirloin, shredded
1 tablespoon soy sauce
½ teaspoon baking soda
1 tablespoon vegetable or peanut oil
2 green onions
3 tablespoons oil for stir-frying
1 clove garlic, minced

1 teaspoon minced ginger
1 large red onion, chopped
2 tablespoons dark soy sauce
2 teaspoons sugar
1 tablespoon Chinese rice wine or dry sherry
¼ teaspoon chili paste with garlic

1. With the beef, mix in the soy sauce and baking soda in that order, using your fingers to mix in the baking soda. Marinate the beef for 30 minutes. Add 1 tablespoon of oil and marinate the beef for another 30 minutes.
2. Cut the green onions into 1½-inch slices along the diagonal.
3. Add 2 tablespoons oil to a preheated wok or skillet. When oil is hot, add the beef. Stir-fry until it changes color and is nearly cooked through. Remove from the wok and drain on paper towels.
4. Add 1 tablespoon oil to the wok. When oil is hot, add the garlic and ginger and stir-fry briefly until aromatic. Add the red onion, and stir-fry until soft and translucent. Stir in the dark soy sauce, sugar, rice wine, and chili paste with garlic. Add the beef. Stir in the green onions. Mix everything together and cook for a few more minutes on medium heat, making sure the beef is cooked through, and serve hot.

Mu Shu Beef

½ pound beef
½ cup water
1 tablespoon dark soy sauce
1 tablespoon plus 1 teaspoon
*   hoisin sauce*
1 teaspoon sugar
1 teaspoon oyster sauce
¼ teaspoon sesame oil

2 eggs, lightly beaten
¼ teaspoon salt
3–4 tablespoons oil for stir-
*   frying*
1 slice ginger, minced
½ cup mung bean sprouts,
*   rinsed and drained*

Serves 2–3

For a more flavorful dish, try marinating the beef in oyster sauce, sugar, and cornstarch, adding the cornstarch last.

---

1. Cut the beef into thin slices. Marinate if desired.
2. Combine the water, dark soy sauce, hoisin sauce, sugar, oyster sauce, and sesame oil, and set aside.
3. Mix the eggs with ¼ teaspoon salt. Add 1 tablespoon oil to a pre-heated wok or skillet. When oil is hot, scramble the eggs and remove from the wok.
4. Add 2 more tablespoons oil. When oil is hot, add the beef and stir-fry until it changes color and is nearly cooked through. Remove from the wok and set aside.
5. Add more oil if necessary. Add the ginger and stir-fry briefly until aromatic. Add the bean sprouts. Add the sauce and bring to a boil. Add the beef and the scrambled egg. Mix everything together and serve hot.

Carrot Flowers

Although the Chinese rarely eat raw vegetables, they are a popular ingredient for garnishes. To make a quick and easy garnish, take a 3-inch-long slice of carrot and cut 4 V-shaped notches at 90° intervals. To finish, slice the carrot into thin "flowers."

Peppery Beef

1 tablespoon soy sauce
½ teaspoon Chinese rice wine
   or dry sherry
1¼ teaspoons sugar, divided
¼ teaspoon baking soda
½ pound flank steak, shredded
½ green bell pepper
½ red bell pepper
½ cup chicken stock

2 tablespoons dark soy sauce
3 tablespoons oil for stir-frying
1 clove garlic, minced
1 teaspoon minced ginger
¼ teaspoon chili paste
¼ teaspoon sesame oil
⅛ teaspoon Szechwan peppercorns, roasted and ground

1. Add the soy sauce, rice wine, ¼ teaspoon sugar, and baking soda to the beef. Marinate the beef for 30 minutes.
2. Remove the seeds from the peppers and cut into thin slices. Combine the chicken stock, dark soy sauce, and 1 teaspoon sugar and set aside.
3. Add 2 tablespoons oil to a preheated wok or skillet. When oil is hot, add the beef and stir-fry until it changes color and is nearly cooked through. Remove from the wok and drain on paper towels.
4. Add 1 tablespoon oil if necessary. Add the garlic, ginger, and chili paste. Stir-fry briefly until aromatic. Add the green peppers, stir-fry briefly, and add the red peppers. Stir-fry the peppers until they have a bright color and are tender.
5. Add the sauce to the middle of the wok and bring to a boil. Stir in the sesame oil. Add the beef. Sprinkle the Szechwan peppercorns over. Mix everything through and serve hot.

Stir-fried Orange Beef

2 teaspoons Chinese rice wine or dry sherry, divided
½ teaspoon baking soda
1 pound sirloin or flank steak, shredded
⅓ cup dried orange peel
1 green onion

2 tablespoons soy sauce
1 teaspoon sugar
¼ teaspoon chili paste
3 tablespoons oil for stir-frying
2 slices ginger, minced
1 clove garlic, minced

Serves 4–6

Leftovers can be used to make sand-wiches—purée the beef with a bit of water and spread on buttered bread.

1. Add 1 teaspoon rice wine and baking soda, using your fingers to add the baking soda, to the beef. Marinate the beef for 30 minutes.
2. Cut the dried orange peel into thin slices. Cut the green onion into 1½-inch slices on the diagonal.
3. Combine the soy sauce, sugar, chili paste, and 1 teaspoon rice wine. Set aside.
4. Add 2 tablespoons oil to a preheated wok or skillet. When oil is hot, add the beef. Stir-fry until it is nearly cooked through. Remove from the wok and drain on paper towels.
5. Add 1 tablespoon oil. Add the ginger, garlic, green onion, and dried orange peel. Stir-fry until the orange peel is aromatic. Add the sauce in the middle and bring to a boil. Add the beef back in. Mix every-thing and stir-fry until the beef is cooked through, and serve hot.

Orange Peel Cold Cure

Have a cold? Why not try an orange peel cure? For centuries, Chinese medical practitioners have recommended dried orange peel to treat everything from colds to insomnia. Whatever their medicinal value, there is no doubt that the peel contains more vitamin C than any other part of the orange.

Spicy Steamed Beef

1 pound sirloin or flank steak
1 tablespoon soy sauce
½ teaspoon baking soda
2 tablespoons dark soy sauce
½ teaspoon sugar
¼ teaspoon dried crushed chili flakes

1 tablespoon dried orange peel
1 tablespoon Toasted Szechwan Peppercorns (see sidebar on page 91)

1. Cut the beef across the grain into thin slices about 1½ inches long. Add the soy sauce and baking soda, using your fingers to mix it in the baking soda. Marinate the beef for 30 minutes.
2. Combine the dark soy sauce, sugar, and crushed chili flakes. Cut the dried orange peel into thin slices.
3. Prepare the wok for steaming. Place the beef on a heatproof plate on a bamboo steamer. Rub the roasted peppercorn mixture over the beef. Brush on half of the sauce. Place the orange peel slices around the beef.
4. Steam the beef for 20 minutes or until it is cooked through. Brush on the remainder of the sauce during steaming.

Make Your Own Orange Peel

To make dried orange peel, remove the skin from an orange. Use a paring knife to remove the white pith inside. Leave the peel to dry in the sun or dry quickly by placing in a previously warmed oven. Remove the peel before it hardens.

Beef with String Beans

1 pound flank or sirloin steak
1 tablespoon soy sauce
1 green onion, cut into 1-inch
   pieces
1 tablespoon cornstarch
1 cup string beans
¼ cup chicken stock or broth
1 tablespoon Chinese rice wine
   or dry sherry

1 teaspoon sugar
¼ teaspoon salt
3 tablespoons oil for stir-frying
1 clove garlic, minced
¼ teaspoon chili paste with
   garlic
1 teaspoon cornstarch
4 teaspoons water

Serves 4–6

When choosing
string beans, look
for younger ones
with a firm texture
and bright color.

1. Cut the beef across the grain into thin slices, about 1½ inches long. Add the soy sauce, green onion, and cornstarch, using your fingers to mix in the cornstarch. Marinate the beef for 30 minutes.
2. Trim the string beans and parboil by plunging briefly into boiling water. Drain thoroughly and cut lengthwise into thin slices.
3. Combine the chicken broth, rice wine, sugar, and salt. Set aside.
4. Add 2 tablespoons oil to a preheated wok or skillet. When oil is hot, add the beef. Stir-fry until it changes color and is nearly cooked. Remove and set aside.
5. Add 1 tablespoon oil. When oil is hot, add the garlic and the chili paste with garlic. Stir-fry briefly until aromatic. Add the string beans. Stir-fry for 3–4 minutes. Push the string beans up to the side of the wok and add the sauce in the middle. Bring to a boil. Mix the cornstarch and water and add to the sauce, stirring quickly to thicken. Add the beef. Mix everything through and cook on medium heat for a few more minutes until the beef is cooked. Serve hot.

Spicy Orange Beef

Serves 4–6

This recipe shows fiery
Szechwan cuisine at
its finest—for a less
spicy dish, leave out
the dried chili.

1 pound flank steak
4–6 cups oil for frying
2 garlic cloves, minced
3 slices ginger, minced
1 dried chili
4 tablespoons soy sauce
2 teaspoons Chinese rice wine
   or dry sherry

2 teaspoons sugar
½ teaspoon chili paste
2 medium eggs
3 tablespoons flour
2 tablespoons cornstarch
1 teaspoon dried orange peel
   or 1 small piece dried tangerine peel

1. Cut the beef across the grain into thin slices about 2 inches in length.
   Remove the seeds from the chili and chop.
2. Combine the soy sauce, rice wine, sugar, and chili paste, and set
   aside.
3. Beat the eggs and mix with the flour and cornstarch into a batter.
   Coat the beef slices with the batter, using your fingers.
4. Heat 4–5 cups of oil to 350°F. When oil is hot, add a few pieces of
   beef into the hot oil and deep-fry until they turn light brown. Remove
   with a slotted spoon and drain on paper towels. Continue with the
   rest of the beef.
5. Raise the oil temperature to 400°F. Deep-fry the beef pieces a second
   time, until they turn brown and crispy. Remove and drain.
6. Remove all but 2 tablespoons of oil from the wok or add 2 tablespoons oil to a second wok or skillet. Add the garlic, ginger, chili,
   and orange peel. Stir-fry until aromatic. Add the sauce and bring to
   a boil. Add the beef. Mix everything through and serve hot.

Ginger Beef

¾ pound flank or sirloin steak
8 tablespoons soy sauce,
    divided
4 teaspoons Chinese rice wine
    or dry sherry, divided
5½ teaspoons sugar, divided
2 teaspoons freshly squeezed
    ginger juice, divided
2 teaspoons sesame oil
Up to ¼ teaspoon chili flakes

½ cup water
3 tablespoons flour
2 tablespoons cornstarch
2 medium eggs
4–6 cups oil for frying
1 clove garlic, minced
1 slice ginger, minced
1 teaspoon cornstarch mixed
    with 4 teaspoons water

Serves 4–6

Ginger juice is easy to make—just grate the ginger and squeeze out the fresh juice.

1. Cut the beef along the grain into matchstick strips. Add 2 tablespoons soy sauce, 1 teaspoon rice wine, ½ teaspoon sugar, and 1 teaspoon ginger juice to the beef. Marinate for 30 minutes.
2. Combine 6 tablespoons soy sauce, 3 teaspoons rice wine, 5 teaspoons sugar, 1 teaspoon ginger juice, sesame oil, chili flakes, and water. Set aside.
3. Combine the flour, cornstarch, and eggs into a batter. Coat the beef in the batter, using your fingers to spread it. Add 4–5 cups oil to the wok and heat to 350°F. When oil is ready, deep-fry the beef in batches, turning occasionally, until they turn golden. Remove and drain on paper towels.
4. Raise the oil temperature to 400°F. Deep-fry the beef a second time, until it turns brown and crispy. Drain on paper towels.
5. Remove all but 2 tablespoons of oil from the wok, or add 2 table-spoons oil to a second wok or skillet. When oil is hot, add the garlic and ginger and stir-fry briefly until aromatic.
6. Add the sauce and bring to a boil. Add the cornstarch-and-water mixture, stirring quickly to thicken. Add the meat. Mix everything together and serve hot.

Dry Ginger Beef

Serves 2

For an added touch, top with a few slices of preserved red ginger before serving.

1 tablespoon soy sauce
½ teaspoon Chinese rice wine or dry sherry
¼ teaspoon sugar
¼ teaspoon baking soda
½ pound flank steak, shredded
½ red bell pepper
2 tablespoons dark soy sauce

1 tablespoon plus 1 teaspoon oyster sauce
1½ teaspoons sugar
½ cup water
4–5 tablespoons oil for frying
2 slices ginger, minced
½ cup mushrooms, sliced

1. Add the soy sauce, rice wine, sugar, and baking soda to the beef. Marinate the beef for 30 minutes.
2. Wash the red pepper, remove the seeds, and cut into thin slices.
3. Combine the dark soy sauce, oyster sauce, sugar, and water and set aside.
4. Add 3 tablespoons oil to a preheated wok or skillet. When oil is hot, add the beef. Lay flat and fry for 2 minutes, then turn over and fry for another 2 minutes. Stir-fry the beef until it turns a dark brown (this will take about 8 minutes). Remove from the wok and drain on paper towels.
5. Add 1–2 tablespoons oil to the wok. When oil is hot, add the ginger and stir-fry briefly until aromatic. Add the mushrooms and red pepper and stir-fry until tender. Add the sauce to the middle of the wok and bring to a boil. Add the beef. Mix everything through and serve hot.

Ginger Beef Origins

According to rumor, Ginger Beef originated in Alberta, the beef capital of Canada. However, it is based on an authentic Chinese dish. Authentic ginger beef is much dryer, and lacks the sweet sauce found in the Alberta version. It is frequently made with preserved red ginger.

Oriental Meatballs

½ pound ground beef
1 tablespoon dark soy sauce
1 teaspoon Chinese rice wine
    or dry sherry

1 teaspoon oyster sauce
½ teaspoon sugar
¼ teaspoon sesame oil

1. In a medium-sized bowl, mix the beef with the remaining 5 ingredients. Prepare the wok for steaming.
2. Form the beef into 6 medium-sized meatballs. Place in a heatproof bowl on a bamboo steamer in the wok and steam, covered, for about 15 minutes or until the meatballs are cooked through.

> **Yields 6 meatballs**
>
> Need a quick and easy appetizer recipe? Serve guests these tasty meatballs with Potsticker Dipping Sauce (page 28).
>
>

Beef Toast

Spicy Orange Beef (page 126)
1 cup plus 3 teaspoons water

4–6 slices bread
3 cups oil for deep-frying

1. Cool Spicy Orange Beef. Cut into thin pieces. Purée in a blender or food processor with 3 teaspoons water.
2. Cut each slice of bread into 4 equal squares. Dip into the 1 cup of water briefly and squeeze to soak out excess water. Spread the beef purée onto each square.
3. Heat oil to 375°F. When oil is ready, add 2–3 squares into the oil. Cook the top side for about 1 minute. Turn over and briefly cook the other side, until the squares turn golden brown. Drain on paper towels.

> **Serves 4**
>
> Instead of a wok or heavy skillet, smaller items like Beef Toast can be deep-fried in a medium-sized saucepan with a heavy bottom.
>
>

Beef and Lotus Root with Oyster Sauce

1 piece lotus root (about 2–3 inches)
½ pound beef
6 teaspoons oyster sauce, divided
2 teaspoons cornstarch

¼ cup chicken broth
1 teaspoon sugar
½ teaspoon sesame oil
3 tablespoons oil for stir-frying
1 slice ginger

1. Peel the lotus root. Cut into 6 thin rounds, about ¼ inch wide. Blanch the lotus root rounds briefly in boiling water.
2. Cut the beef in thin slices. Marinate in 2 teaspoons oyster sauce and the cornstarch for 30 minutes.
3. Combine 4 teaspoons oyster sauce, chicken broth, sugar, and sesame oil. Set aside.
4. Add 2 tablespoons oil to a preheated wok or skillet. When oil is hot, add the beef. Stir-fry until it changes color and is nearly cooked through. Remove and drain on paper towels.
5. Add 1 tablespoon oil. When oil is hot, add the ginger. Stir-fry briefly until aromatic. Add the lotus root. Stir-fry for 1–2 minutes. Add the sauce in the middle of the wok and bring to a boil. Add the beef. Cook for 1–2 more minutes, and serve hot.

CHAPTER 7
Pork Entrées

Ants Climbing a Tree

Serves 4

For easier handling of the noodles, don't remove the string wrapping until the noodles have been soaked and drained.

4 ounces rice vermicelli noodles
4 Chinese dried mushrooms
1 bunch spinach leaves
3 tablespoons oil for stir-frying
2 slices ginger, finely chopped
½ pound ground pork
1 tablespoon soy sauce
1 tablespoon Chinese rice wine
   or dry sherry
½ teaspoon sesame oil, divided
¼ teaspoon sugar
¼ teaspoon salt
1 tablespoon chili sauce
¼ cup chicken broth or reserved mushroom liquid
2 green onions, chopped

1. Soak the noodles in hot water for 5 minutes or until they are softened. Cut the noodles into 2-inch lengths. Soak the dried mushrooms in hot water for at least 20 minutes to soften. Reserve the soaking liquid if desired. Remove the stems from the mushrooms and cut into thin slices.
2. Wash the spinach leaves. Blanch the spinach in boiling water briefly, just until the leaves begin to wilt. Drain well and chop finely.
3. Add 2 tablespoons oil to a preheated wok or skillet. When oil is hot, add the ginger and stir-fry briefly until aromatic. Add the ground pork. Mix in the soy sauce, rice wine, and ¼ teaspoon sesame oil. Stir-fry the ground pork until it loses its pink color. Remove from the wok and set aside.
4. Wipe the wok clean with a paper towel and add 1 tablespoon oil. When the oil is hot, add the spinach. Add the sugar and salt and stir-fry briefly, for less than a minute. Add the mushrooms. Push the spinach up to the sides of the wok and add the pork. Stir in the chili sauce, and then the noodles. Add the chicken broth or reserved mushroom liquid and continue to cook until most of the liquid is absorbed. Stir in the green onions. Drizzle with ¼ teaspoon sesame oil and serve.

Lion's Head Meatball Stew

1 pound ground pork
1 tablespoon soy sauce
1 teaspoon sugar
½ teaspoon sesame oil
2 tablespoons Chinese rice
   wine or dry sherry, divided

2 bunches spinach leaves
3 tablespoons oil for stir-frying
1 cup chicken broth or stock
¼ teaspoon salt
White pepper to taste

Serves 2–4

Lion's Head Meatballs
can be made in
advance and frozen.
Bring the meatballs
back to room temper-
ature before
reheating.

1. Place the pork in a medium-sized bowl. Mix in the soy sauce, sugar, sesame oil, and 1 tablespoon rice wine. Marinate the pork for 20 minutes.
2. Wash the spinach leaves. Blanch the spinach in boiling water briefly, just until the leaves begin to wilt. Drain thoroughly.
3. Form the marinated pork into 4 large meatballs, each roughly the size of a tennis ball. (Alternately, you can make the meatballs the size of golf balls, which will give you more meatballs.)
4. Add oil to a preheated wok or skillet. Pan-fry the meatballs on medium heat for 4–5 minutes on each side, until they brown. (The meatballs will not be cooked through.) Remove and drain on paper towels.
5. While the meatballs are frying, preheat the oven to 375°F.
6. Bring the chicken broth or stock to a boil. Stir in the salt, white pepper, and 1 tablespoon rice wine. Remove from the heat.
7. Line the bottom of a casserole dish with the spinach leaves. Add the meatballs and pour the chicken stock mixture over. Bake at 375°F for 30 minutes, or until the meatballs are cooked through.

Intriguing Recipe Names

Like most cooking styles, Chinese cuisine has its share of intriguing recipe names. According to legend, Mapo Dofu, or "Pockmarked Tofu" (page 196), is named in honor of the elderly woman rumored to have invented the dish. In Ants Climbing a Tree, the tiny flecks of marinated pork are meant to resemble ants, while the fried noodles are the bark of the tree. This dish is also known as Ants Creeping up a Tree and Ants Climbing a Log.

Honey Roasted Pork

1½ pound spareribs
2 tablespoons honey
4 tablespoons hoisin sauce

4 tablespoons dark soy sauce
2 tablespoons Chinese rice wine or dry sherry

1. Separate the pork into pieces about 2 by 6 inches. Combine the honey, hoisin sauce, dark soy sauce, and rice wine. Add to the pork ribs and marinate in the refrigerator for at least 2 hours, preferably overnight.
2. Preheat oven to 375°F.
3. Drain the pork, reserving the marinade. Fill a shallow pan with boiling water and place at the bottom of the oven. Place the pork on a roasting rack, cover with half the reserved marinade and roast the pork for 15 minutes. Brush the pork with the remaining marinade and roast for another 15 minutes, or until the pork turns golden brown and is cooked. Cool.

Curry Spareribs

1 pound pork ribs
4 tablespoons soy sauce
2 tablespoons Chinese rice wine or dry sherry
2 teaspoons sugar

2 teaspoons curry paste
1 teaspoon turmeric
1 large clove garlic, chopped
2–4 cups oil for deep-frying

1. Cut the ribs into bite-sized pieces. Add the soy sauce, rice wine, sugar, curry paste, turmeric, and chopped garlic. Marinate the ribs for 30 minutes.
2. Heat the oil in the wok to 350°F. When oil is hot, deep-fry the spareribs until they turn a deep brown and rise to the surface.

Braised Spareribs in Black Bean Sauce

1–1½ pounds spareribs
1 tablespoon fermented black
   beans
1 garlic clove, minced
2 green onions
3 tablespoons hoisin sauce

3 tablespoons soy sauce
1½ teaspoons sugar
½ cup water
2 tablespoons oil for stir-frying

Serves 2–4

Savory fermented black beans nicely complement the delicate sweet flavor of pork in this recipe.

1. Wash the spareribs, pat dry, and separate. Mash the black beans with the back edge of a knife or cleaver. Mix with the garlic and a bit of water. Cut the green onions into 1-inch pieces.
2. Combine the hoisin sauce, soy sauce, sugar, and water.
3. Add oil to a preheated wok or skillet. Stir-fry the pork for 2–3 minutes. Add the fermented bean and garlic mixture and stir-fry until aromatic.
4. Add the sauce and bring to a boil. Turn down the heat, cover, and simmer for 20–25 minutes, until the spareribs are cooked. Stir in the green onions or serve as a garnish.

Fermented Black Beans

These are not the dried black beans that enliven many Mexican dishes. Instead, fermented black beans (also called salted black beans) are made with black soybeans that have been fermented in salt, garlic, and a number of spices. Fermented black beans are sold in cans and plastic bags in Asian markets. In a pinch, black bean sauce can be used as a substitute, but the dish won't have the same flavor.

Sweet-and-Sour Spareribs

1½ pounds spareribs
4 teaspoons sugar, divided
2 tablespoons plus 1 teaspoon rice vinegar, divided
2 tablespoons ketchup
2 tablespoons Worcestershire sauce
4 tablespoons soy sauce
2 tablespoons oil for stir-frying

1. Wash spareribs and pat dry. Separate into serving-sized pieces. Marinate the ribs in 1 teaspoon sugar and 1 teaspoon rice vinegar for 30 minutes.
2. Mix together 3 teaspoons sugar, 2 tablespoons rice vinegar, ketchup, Worcestershire sauce, and soy sauce, and set aside.
3. Add oil to a preheated wok or skillet. When oil is hot, add the ribs and stir-fry for about 5 minutes, until they brown.
4. Add the sauce, turn down the heat, cover, and simmer the ribs for 45 minutes to 1 hour.

Five-Spice Spareribs

1½ pounds spareribs
2 garlic cloves, smashed and peeled
3 tablespoons soy sauce
1 teaspoon sesame oil
1 tablespoon Chinese rice wine or dry sherry
2 teaspoons brown sugar
1 teaspoon Hot Chili Oil (page 23)
½ teaspoon Szechwan Salt and Pepper Mix (page 20)
½ teaspoon five-spice powder, or to taste
2 tablespoons water

1. Mix together all the ingredients except for the spareribs. Marinate the spareribs for 30 minutes. Reserve the marinade.
2. Preheat oven to 350°F. Brush half of the reserved marinade on the spareribs and roast for 15 minutes. Brush on the rest of marinade and roast the spareribs for another 15 minutes or until they are cooked.

Deep-fried Garlic Spareribs

2 pounds spareribs
1 cup brown sugar
1 cup water
3 tablespoons soy sauce
1 tablespoon dry mustard

3 garlic cloves, minced
3 eggs
1 cup flour
4–6 cups oil for deep-frying

Serves 4–6

Deep-frying the spareribs twice gives them a crispy coating and seals in the juicy flavors.

1. Cut the ribs into bite-sized pieces.
2. Combine the brown sugar, water, soy sauce, mustard, and garlic cloves. Add to the ribs and marinate for 1 hour.
3. Lightly beat the eggs and add to the flour to make a batter, adding water or more flour as needed. Use a wooden spoon to test the batter— it should drop slowly and be able to coat the back of the spoon.
4. Add the oil to a wok and heat to 350°F. While waiting for the oil to heat, coat the ribs in the batter. When oil is hot, carefully add the spareribs into the wok. Deep-fry in batches for about 5 minutes. Remove and drain on paper towels.
5. Raise the oil temperature to 400°F. Deep-fry the ribs briefly a second time, until they turn brown. Remove and drain.

Recycled Deep-frying Oil

Start deep-frying regularly, and you'll quickly find your stock of vegetable oil running low. Fortunately, deep-frying oil can be reused up to 5 times. To save the oil, simply cool and store in a sealed container. Discard the oil when it starts to smell bad, changes color, or smokes at lower temperatures.

Pork with Young Bamboo Shoots

½ pound pork tenderloin
3 teaspoons Chinese rice wine or dry sherry, divided
½ teaspoon sugar
1½ teaspoons cornstarch
8 ounces canned or fresh peeled young bamboo shoots
½ cup chicken stock or broth
1 teaspoon rice vinegar
3 tablespoons oil for stir-frying

1. Cut the pork into thin slices. Add 2 teaspoons of the rice wine, the sugar, and the cornstarch. Marinate the pork for 30 minutes.
2. Blanch the bamboo shoots in boiling water for at least 5 minutes. Drain thoroughly and chop.
3. Combine the chicken stock, 1 teaspoon rice wine, and the rice vinegar, and set aside.
4. Add 2 tablespoons oil to a preheated wok or skillet. When oil is hot, add the pork and stir-fry until it changes color and is nearly cooked. Remove and drain on paper towels.
5. Add 1 tablespoon oil to the wok. Add the bamboo shoots and stir-fry. Add the sauce in the middle of the wok and bring to a boil. Add the pork. Turn down the heat and simmer for 5 minutes. Serve hot.

Why Waste a Wok?
Don't hide your wok in the cupboard when you're not cooking Chinese food. A wok's unusual shape makes it useful for everything from mixing batter to tossing a salad. And nothing beats a wok for turning out scrambled eggs and omelets that don't stick to the bottom of the pan.

Basic Sweet-and-Sour Pork

1 pound pork loin, center cut,
   bone in
1 tablespoon soy sauce
1 tablespoon cornstarch
1 teaspoon baking soda
⅔ cup canned pineapple
   chunks
½ cup reserved pineapple juice
½ red bell pepper
½ green bell pepper
¼ pound baby carrots

⅓ cup rice vinegar
½ cup brown sugar
1 tablespoon Worcestershire
   sauce
¼ cup ketchup
¼ cup water
3 tablespoons oil for stir-frying
2 teaspoons cornstarch mixed
   with 4 teaspoons water

Serves 2–4

For extra flavor, use
2 tablespoons black
rice vinegar and
¼ cup white rice
vinegar when making
the sauce.

1. Cut away the bone from the pork and remove any fat. Cut the pork into cubes. Add the soy sauce, cornstarch, and baking soda to the pork. Marinate the pork in the refrigerator for 1½ hours.
2. Open a can of pineapple chunks and remove ⅔ cup pineapple and ½ cup juice. Blanch the peppers and carrots by plunging briefly into boiling water. Remove the seeds from the green and red peppers, and cut into cubes. Cut the carrots in half.
3. Bring the rice vinegar, brown sugar, Worcestershire sauce, ketchup, reserved pineapple juice, and water to a boil. Turn down the heat to low and keep warm.
4. Add 2 tablespoons oil to a preheated wok or skillet. When oil is hot, add the pork. Stir-fry until it changes color and is nearly cooked through. Remove from the wok and drain on paper towels.
5. Add 1 tablespoon oil. When oil is hot, add the carrots. Stir-fry for a minute and add the red and green peppers.
6. Bring the sauce back up to a boil. Add the cornstarch-and-water mixture, stirring vigorously to thicken. Mix the pineapple in with the sauce. Push the vegetables up to the sides of the wok and add the sauce in the middle. Add the pork back into the wok. Mix through and serve hot.

Deep-fried Sweet-and-Sour Pork

Serves 2–4

This is one of the most popular dishes served at Chinese restaurants. The sweet-and-sour sauce works well with pork, spareribs, and chicken.

1 pound pork loin, center cut, deboned and cubed
1 tablespoon soy sauce
3 tablespoons cornstarch, divided
1 teaspoon baking soda
½ red bell pepper
½ green bell pepper
¼ pound baby carrots
3 tablespoons flour
2 medium eggs
⅓ cup rice vinegar

½ cup brown sugar
1 tablespoon Worcestershire sauce
¼ cup ketchup
½ cup reserved pineapple juice
¼ cup water
2 teaspoons cornstarch mixed with 4 teaspoons water
4–6 cups oil for frying
⅔ cup canned pineapple chunks

1. Take the pork cubes and add the soy sauce, 1 tablespoon cornstarch, and baking soda. Marinate in the refrigerator for 1½ hours.
2. Blanch the peppers and carrots in boiling water. Deseed and cube the green and red pepper. Cut the carrots in half.
3. Combine the flour, cornstarch, and eggs into a batter. Coat the pork in the batter. Add 4–5 cups oil to the wok and heat to at least 350°F. Deep-fry the pork cubes in batches, turning occasionally, until they turn golden. Remove and drain on paper towels.
4. Increase the oil temperature to 400°F. While waiting for the oil to heat, bring the rice vinegar, brown sugar, Worcestershire sauce, ketchup, reserved pineapple juice, and water to boil in a small saucepan. Turn the heat down to low and keep the sauce warm.
5. When the oil is ready, add the pork cubes. Deep-fry a second time until they turn brown and crispy. Remove and drain on paper towels.
6. Remove all but 2 tablespoons oil from the wok. When oil is hot, add the carrots. Stir-fry for a minute and add the red and green peppers.
7. Bring the sauce back up to a boil. Add the cornstarch-and-water mixture, stirring vigorously to thicken. Add the pineapple.
8. Push the vegetables up to the sides of the wok and add the sauce in the middle. Add the pork back into the wok. Mix through and serve hot.

Twice Cooked Pork

½ pound boneless pork
½ red bell pepper
½ green bell pepper
1 clove garlic, chopped
2 slices ginger, chopped

3 tablespoons oil for stir-frying
1 teaspoon hot bean paste
2 tablespoons dark soy sauce
1 teaspoon sugar

Serves 2–4

Pork is cooked twice in this simple but popular Szechwan dish. Serve on a bed of steamed rice or noodles.

1. Boil the pork in water for 20–25 minutes. Remove and cool. Cut into thin strips.
2. Blanch the peppers by plunging briefly into boiling water. Cut into thin slices.
3. Add 3 tablespoons oil to a preheated wok or skillet. When oil is hot, add the ginger, garlic, and hot bean paste with garlic. Stir-fry briefly until the garlic and ginger are aromatic. Add the peppers and stir-fry. Mix in the dark soy sauce and sugar. Add the pork. Combine all the ingredients thoroughly and stir-fry for about 1 more minute. Serve hot.

Pork—Not the "Other White Meat"

Pork may be the "other white meat" in the West, but in China the words pork and meat are virtually synonymous. When it comes to beef, cows and oxen have traditionally been valued more as work animals than as the main source of protein at the dinner table. By contrast, economical pigs are cheaper to feed, requiring less grazing space. While beef is now widely enjoyed in northern China, it is still not uncommon for southern Chinese families to rely primarily on pork as their main source of meat.

Pork in Plum Sauce

1 pound boneless pork loin
   chops
1 tablespoon soy sauce
1 tablespoon cornstarch
1 teaspoon baking soda
2 carrots

2 slices ginger
½ cup Plum Sauce (page 19)
3 tablespoons oil for stir-frying
2 green onions, thinly sliced on
   the diagonal

1. Cut the pork into cubes. Add the soy sauce, cornstarch, and baking soda. Marinate the pork in the refrigerator for 90 minutes.
2. Peel the carrots and cut into slices about ½ inch thick. Blanch by plunging into boiling water and draining.
3. Add 2 tablespoons oil to a preheated wok or skillet. When oil is hot, add the pork. Stir-fry until it changes color and is nearly cooked through. Remove from the wok and drain on paper towels.
4. Add 1 tablespoon oil. When oil is hot, add the ginger slices and stir-fry briefly until aromatic. Add the carrots and stir-fry for about 1 minute. Add the Plum Sauce and bring to a boil.
5. Add the pork. Stir in the green onions. Mix everything through and serve hot.

Eastern and Northern China

The cuisine of eastern China features red-cooked dishes—stews that have been slowly cooked in soy sauce and seasonings. And northern China is famous for noodle-based dishes and festive specialties such as Mu Shu Pork and Peking Duck with pancakes. The influence of the Mongol warriors can be seen in dishes such as Mongolian Beef.

Pork in Bean Sauce

*1 pound pork tenderloin chops,
  boneless*
1 tablespoon oyster sauce
½ teaspoon sugar
1½ teaspoons cornstarch
2 tablespoons black bean sauce
2 tablespoons dark soy sauce
*2 teaspoons Chinese rice wine
  or dry sherry*

2 teaspoons sugar
¼ teaspoon salt
¼ cup water
¼ teaspoon sesame oil
2 tablespoons oil for stir-frying
¼ teaspoon chili paste

> **Serves 4**
>
> Serve with Glazed
> Carrots (page 234) for
> a nutritious meal with
> an interesting combi-
> nation of flavors.

1. Cut the pork into thin strips. Add the oyster sauce, sugar, and corn-starch, adding the cornstarch last. Marinate the pork for 30 minutes.
2. Combine the black bean sauce, dark soy sauce, rice wine, sugar, salt, water, and sesame oil, and set aside.
3. Add oil to a preheated wok or skillet. When oil is hot, add the chili paste and stir-fry briefly until aromatic. Add the pork. Stir-fry until it changes color and is nearly cooked through.
4. Push the pork up to the side of the wok and add the sauce in the middle. Bring to a boil. Mix the sauce with the pork. Cover and simmer for a few minutes until the pork is cooked through.

Szechwan and Cantonese Cooking

Fiery Szechwan cuisine is famous for its "mouthburners"—dishes such as Kung Pao Chicken and Mapo Tofu made with hot chilies and Toasted Szechwan Peppercorns. Reputed to represent the best of Chinese cooking, Cantonese cuisine features fresh ingredients that are subtly seasoned and not overcooked. Cantonese cooks pride them-selves on allowing the natural flavors of the ingredients to come through in dishes such as Sweet-and-Sour Pork and Lobster Cantonese.

Restaurant-Style Mu Shu Pork

½ pound boneless pork chops
3 green onions, divided
1 tablespoon soy sauce
2½ teaspoons sugar, divided
2 teaspoons cornstarch
½ teaspoon baking soda
4 dried mushrooms
½ cup reserved mushroom liquid
1 tablespoon dark soy sauce
1 tablespoon hoisin sauce

¼ teaspoon sesame oil
2 eggs
¼ teaspoon salt
3–5 tablespoons oil for stir-frying
1 slice ginger
1 cup canned bamboo shoots, rinsed
1 cup canned water chestnuts, rinsed

1. Trim any fat from the pork and cut into thin strips. Add 1 chopped green onion, soy sauce, ½ teaspoon sugar, cornstarch, and baking soda. Marinate the pork for 30 minutes.

2. Soak the dried mushrooms in hot water for at least 20 minutes to soften. Reserve the soaking liquid. Give the mushrooms a gentle squeeze to remove any excess water and thinly slice. Cut the remaining 2 green onions into 1-inch pieces.

3. Combine the reserved mushroom liquid, dark soy sauce, 2 teaspoons sugar, hoisin sauce, and sesame oil, and set aside.

4. Lightly beat the eggs and stir in ¼ teaspoon salt. Add 1 tablespoon oil to a preheated wok or skillet. When oil is hot, turn down the heat and add the eggs. Scramble quickly and remove from the wok. Wipe the wok clean if necessary.

5. Add 2 more tablespoons oil. When oil is hot, add the pork strips and stir-fry until they turn white and are nearly cooked through. Remove from the wok and set aside. Add more oil if needed. Add the ginger and green onion and stir-fry briefly. Add the mushrooms, bamboo shoots, and water chestnuts. Add the sauce and bring to a boil. Add the pork and the scrambled egg. Mix everything through and serve hot.

Traditional Mu Shu Pork

½ pound boneless pork chops
3 green onions, divided
1 tablespoon soy sauce
½ teaspoon sesame oil
2 teaspoons cornstarch
½ teaspoon baking soda
4 dried mushrooms
15 dried lily buds
4 tablespoons wood fungus
10 fresh water chestnuts
½ cup reserved mushroom liquid

2 tablespoons dark soy sauce
2 teaspoons sugar
¼ teaspoon sesame oil
2 eggs
¼ teaspoon salt
3–5 tablespoons oil for stir-frying
1 slice ginger
½ cup canned bamboo shoots, rinsed
Mandarin Pancakes (page 268)
½ cup hoisin sauce

Serves 4

For an authentic touch, use Green Onion Brushes (page 73) to brush the hoisin sauce onto the Mandarin Pancakes.

1. Trim any fat from the pork and cut into thin strips. Add 1 chopped green onion, soy sauce, sesame oil, cornstarch, and baking soda. Marinate the pork for 30 minutes.
2. Soak the dried mushrooms, dried lily buds, and wood fungus in hot water for at least 20 minutes to soften. Reserve the mushroom soaking liquid. Give the mushrooms a gentle squeeze to remove any excess water and thinly slice. Cut the remaining 2 green onions into 1-inch pieces. Peel the fresh water chestnuts and cut in half.
3. Combine the reserved mushroom liquid, dark soy sauce, sugar, and sesame oil and set aside.
4. Lightly beat the eggs and stir in ¼ teaspoon salt. Add 1 tablespoon oil to a preheated wok or skillet. When oil is hot, scramble the eggs. Remove from the wok and set aside.
5. Add 2 more tablespoons oil. When oil is hot, add the pork strips and stir-fry until they turn white and are nearly cooked through. Add the ginger and green onions and stir-fry briefly. Add the mushrooms, lily buds, wood fungus, bamboo shoots, and water chestnuts. Add the sauce and bring to a boil. Add the pork and the scrambled egg. Mix everything through.
6. To serve, brush a pancake with the hoisin sauce, add a generous helping of Mu Shu Pork, and roll up the pancake.

Pork Chop Suey

½ pound pork tenderloin
2 teaspoons Chinese rice wine or dry sherry
2 teaspoons soy sauce
2 teaspoons baking soda
2 green onions, thinly sliced on the diagonal
2 tablespoons oyster sauce
2 tablespoons chicken broth or stock
1 teaspoon sugar

4–6 tablespoons oil for stir-frying
6 fresh mushrooms, thinly sliced
1 stalk celery, thinly sliced on the diagonal
2 stalks bok choy including leaves, thinly sliced on the diagonal
1 8-ounce can bamboo shoots, drained

1. Cut the pork into thin slices. Marinate the pork with the rice wine, soy sauce, and baking soda for 30 minutes.
2. Combine the oyster sauce, chicken broth, and sugar. Set aside.
3. Add 2 tablespoons oil to a preheated wok or skillet. When oil is hot, add the pork. Stir-fry until it changes color and is nearly cooked through. Remove from the wok.
4. Add 1–2 tablespoons oil. When oil is hot, add the mushrooms and stir-fry for about 1 minute. Add the celery and the bok choy stalks, then the bamboo shoots, stir-frying each for about 1 minute in the middle of the wok before adding the next vegetable. (If the wok is too crowded, stir-fry each vegetable separately.) Add more oil as necessary, pushing the vegetables up to the side of the wok until the oil is heated. Add the bok choy leaves and the green onion.
5. Add the sauce to the middle of the wok and bring to a boil. Add the pork. Mix everything through and serve hot.

Spicy Hoisin Pork

¾ pound pork tenderloin
1 tablespoon soy sauce
2 teaspoons baking soda
1 bunch spinach
2 tablespoons hoisin sauce

1 tablespoon dark soy sauce
¼ cup water
3 tablespoons oil for stir-frying
¼ teaspoon chili paste

Serves 4

For a less spicy dish, substitute ¼ teaspoon chili sauce with garlic for the chili paste.

1. Cut the pork into thin slices. Marinate in the soy sauce and baking soda for 30 minutes.
2. Blanch the spinach briefly in boiling water and drain thoroughly.
3. Combine the hoisin sauce, dark soy sauce, and water. Set aside.
4. Add 2 tablespoons oil to a preheated wok or skillet. When oil is hot, add the pork and stir-fry until it changes color and is nearly cooked through. Remove and drain on paper towels.
5. Add 1 tablespoon oil. When oil is hot, add the chili paste and stir-fry until aromatic. Add the spinach. Stir-fry for a minute, adding sugar or soy sauce to season if desired. Add the sauce in the middle of the wok and bring to a boil. Add the pork. Turn down the heat, mix everything through, and serve hot.

How to Season a Carbon Steel Wok

It's important to properly season a wok before using it for the first time. First, wash the wok in soapy water. Dry thoroughly, then lightly coat the inside surface with vegetable oil, using a paper towel and tilting the wok to ensure even coverage. Heat the wok on low-medium heat for 10 minutes. Remove to a cool burner and wipe off the inside with a paper towel. Repeat this process several times. The wok is ready to use when the paper towel doesn't pick up any black residue.

Ham with Asian Pear

Serves 4–6

Although China's Yunnan hams are famous throughout Europe, they are hard to find in the West. Smithfield hams are a good substitute.

1½ pounds ham, thinly sliced
2 teaspoons sesame oil
2 teaspoons cornstarch
2 tablespoons soy sauce
2 tablespoons dark soy sauce
2 tablespoons honey
1 green onion
2 tablespoons oil for frying
2 Asian pears, sliced

1. Marinate the ham for 30 minutes in the sesame oil and cornstarch.
2. Combine the soy sauce, dark soy sauce, and honey. Set aside. Cut the green onion into 1-inch slices on the diagonal.
3. Add 2 tablespoons oil to a preheated wok or skillet. When oil is hot, add the sliced ham and brown briefly. Remove and drain on paper towels.
4. Prepare the wok for steaming. Place the sliced ham on a heatproof dish on a bamboo steamer. Brush half of the sauce over. Cover and steam, adding more boiling water as necessary.
5. After 25 minutes, drain the ham juices, combine with the remaining half of the sauce, and bring to a boil in a small saucepan. Arrange the pear slices with the ham. Steam the ham for another 5 minutes, or until it is cooked. Pour the cooked sauce over the ham before serving. Garnish with the green onion.

 Asian Pears

In ancient times, Chinese nobles dined on Asian pears poached in wine and honey. Today, thanks to their delicate sweetness, Asian pears are becoming a familiar sight in local supermarkets. Try them in stir-fries and salads.

Chinese Sausage and Cabbage Stir-fry

3 Chinese sausages
2 tablespoons oil for stir-frying
1 teaspoon minced shallot
6 large cabbage leaves,
   shredded
½ cup chicken broth

1 teaspoon Chinese rice wine
   or dry sherry
2 green onions, finely chopped
   on the diagonal

> **Serves 2–4**
>
> Shallot makes an interesting change from garlic and ginger in this simple recipe. Add 4 softened, dried mushrooms for a complete, one-dish meal.
>
>

1. Cut the sausage on the diagonal into bite-sized pieces.
2. Add oil to a preheated wok or skillet. When oil is hot, add the shallot and stir-fry briefly. Add the sausages. Stir-fry for about 2 minutes, then push the sausages up to the side of the wok. Add the cabbage. Stir-fry for about 2 minutes. Add the chicken broth and rice wine in the middle of the wok and bring to a boil.
3. Simmer, covered, for 3–4 minutes, stir in the green onions, and serve hot.

How to Clean a Carbon Steel Wok
Never scrub the wok with an abrasive cleanser. Instead, remove stubborn food particles with a nonmetallic scrubber. Wash the wok in soapy water. To ensure it dries completely, leave for a few minutes on the stove with the heat turned low. Add a light coating of oil before storing in the cupboard. (You can skip this last step if the wok sees a lot of use.)

CHAPTER 8

Chicken and Other Poultry

Basic Chicken Stir-fry

Serves 4–6

Simmering the chicken in broth and seasonings brings out its natural flavors. Serve with Stir-fried Bok Choy (page 235) for a quick and easy meal.

1 pound chicken meat
2 tablespoons oil for stir-frying
1 garlic clove, minced
2 thin slices ginger
½ cup chicken stock or broth

1 tablespoon Chinese rice wine
 or dry sherry
1 teaspoon sugar
¼ teaspoon salt

1. Wash the chicken meat, pat dry, and cut into cubes or thin slices.
2. Add oil to a preheated wok or skillet. When oil is hot, add the garlic and ginger. Stir-fry briefly until aromatic. Add the chicken and stir-fry until it changes color.
3. Add the chicken stock, rice wine, sugar, and salt and bring to a boil. Simmer, covered, until the chicken is cooked.

The Base of Many Chicken Recipes

Basic Chicken Stir-fry is a skeleton recipe that you can adapt according to your tastes and the ingredients you have on hand. Add a marinade and experiment with different seasonings such as chili paste. To make a one-dish meal that includes vegetables, stir-fry the chicken first and remove it from the wok. Stir-fry the vegetables and add the sauce. Add the chicken back and simmer until the meat is cooked. For longer-cooking pieces of meat such as chicken legs, increase the amount of broth and simmer the chicken for 20–30 minutes or until the meat is cooked through.

Moo Goo Gai Pan

*2 large boneless, skinless
    chicken breasts
4 tablespoons oyster sauce,
    divided
2 teaspoons cornstarch, divided
½ cup chicken stock or broth
1 teaspoon sugar*

*⅛ teaspoon white pepper
½ cup fresh mushrooms
4 tablespoons oil for stir-frying
1 clove garlic, minced
½ 8-ounce can bamboo shoots,
    rinsed*

Serves 4

The marriage of chicken and mushrooms is central to this dish, but feel free to substitute other vegetables for the bamboo shoots.

1. Wash the chicken and cut into thin slices. Mix in 2 tablespoons oyster sauce and 1 teaspoon cornstarch. Marinate the chicken for 30 minutes.
2. Mix together the chicken stock, sugar, white pepper, 2 tablespoons oyster sauce, and 1 teaspoon cornstarch. Set aside. Wipe the mushrooms clean with a damp cloth and thinly slice.
3. Add 2 tablespoons oil to a preheated wok or skillet. When oil is hot, add the garlic and stir-fry briefly until aromatic. Add the chicken and stir-fry until it changes color and is nearly cooked through. Remove the chicken from the wok and set aside.
4. Wipe the wok clean and add 2 more tablespoons oil. When the oil is hot, add the mushrooms and stir-fry for about 1 minute. Add the bamboo shoots.
5. Give the sauce a quick stir. Make a well in the middle of the wok by pushing the vegetables up to the sides. Add the sauce in the middle, stirring vigorously to thicken. Add the chicken and mix through.

Chicken Glazed in Bean Sauce

Serves 2–4

This recipe produces a tender chicken lightly glazed with savory bean sauce. For added protein, try stirring in cashews or peanuts before serving.

2 large boneless, skinless chicken breasts (12–14 ounces)
2 tablespoons Chinese rice wine or dry sherry
1 tablespoon soy sauce
2½ green onions, thinly sliced on the diagonal
½ cup chicken stock or broth

1 tablespoon dark soy sauce
1 tablespoon bean sauce
2 tablespoons brown sugar
1 clove garlic, chopped
2 tablespoons oil for stir-frying
1 teaspoon cornstarch mixed with 4 teaspoons water

1. Wash the chicken breasts, pat dry, and dice.
2. Mix together the rice wine, soy sauce, and half of a green onion. Marinate the chicken for 1 hour.
3. In a small bowl, combine the chicken stock, dark soy sauce, bean sauce, brown sugar, and garlic. Set aside.
4. Add oil to a preheated wok or skillet. When oil is hot, add the chicken and stir-fry until it is nearly cooked through. Remove from the wok and set aside.
5. Add the sauce into the wok. Add the cornstarch-and-water mixture in the middle, stirring vigorously to thicken. Add the chicken, mixing in and letting the sauce reduce until it is a glaze. Stir in the 2 sliced green onions.

Baked Oyster Sauce Chicken

1½ pounds chicken thighs
1 tablespoon dark soy sauce
2 tablespoons oyster sauce
1 tablespoon Chinese rice wine
   or dry sherry

1½ teaspoons sugar
4 tablespoons water
½ teaspoon sesame oil
2 garlic cloves, minced
1 teaspoon minced ginger

Serves 4–6

Scoring the chicken thighs makes it easier for the marinade to penetrate the meat. This dish tastes delicious served with Snow Pea Stir-fry (page 233).

1. Wash the chicken thighs and pat dry. Remove the skin and make 2 diagonal cuts on each side of the thigh.
2. Mix together the dark soy sauce, oyster sauce, rice wine, sugar, water, and sesame oil. Place the sauce in a plastic bag. Add the chicken, shaking the bag lightly to make sure the sauce coats all the chicken. Seal the bag and place in the refrigerator. Marinate the chicken for 2–3 hours, turning the bag occasionally.
3. Preheat the oven to 400°F.
4. Remove the chicken thighs from the bag, reserving the sauce. Place the chicken thighs on a baking sheet sprayed with cooking spray. Pour half of the sauce over, making sure both sides of the thighs are covered. Add the minced garlic and ginger. Bake the thighs for 15 minutes. Add the remaining half of the sauce and cook for another 15 minutes, or until the thighs are cooked.

Bagging It

Don't have a large enough bag to hold the chicken thighs? Place them on a plate and rub the marinade over, making sure to coat all the chicken. Cover with plastic wrap and refrigerate for 2–3 hours. Reserve any leftover marinade to pour over the chicken while baking.

Soy Sauce Chicken

Serves 2

For a fancier presenta-
tion, chop the chicken
legs into pieces and
place on a platter.
Pour the sauce over
the chopped chicken.

2 chicken legs
1 teaspoon five-spice powder
1 tablespoon cornstarch
½ cup soy sauce
¾ cup water
2 tablespoons Chinese rice
    wine or dry sherry

4 teaspoons brown sugar
1 large clove garlic, minced
1 slice ginger, minced
3–4 cups oil for deep-frying

1. Rinse the chicken legs and pat dry. Mix the five-spice powder and the cornstarch. Mix in with the chicken and marinate for 30 minutes.
2. In a medium bowl, mix together the soy sauce, water, rice wine, and brown sugar, and set aside.
3. Heat the oil in a wok. When the oil reaches 325°F, deep-fry the chicken legs until they are browned. Remove with a slotted spoon and drain on paper towels.
4. Drain all but 2 tablespoons oil out of the wok. Add the garlic and ginger and stir-fry briefly until aromatic. Add the sauce. Add the chicken, cover and simmer for 15–20 minutes, until the chicken is cooked.

From Marinade to Sauce
When a marinade does double duty as a sauce, it's important to ensure that it is thoroughly cooked. As an added precaution, you can bring the marinade to boil in a saucepan before adding it to the wok.

Curry Chicken Thighs

6 chicken thighs
2 green onions, divided
5 tablespoons soy sauce,
   divided
1½ tablespoons cornstarch
¼ cup chicken broth
½ cup water
¾ cup plain yogurt
1 tablespoon Chinese rice wine
   or dry sherry

1 teaspoon honey
1½ tablespoons oil for
   stir-frying
2 slices ginger, minced
1 large red onion, cut into
   wedges
1 large potato, cubed
1 tablespoon curry paste

1. Place the chicken thighs in a medium-sized bowl. Cut the green onions into 1-inch pieces on the diagonal. Mix 1 green onion, 4 tablespoons soy sauce, and cornstarch with the chicken, adding the cornstarch last. Marinate the chicken for 15 minutes.
2. Combine the chicken broth, water, yogurt, rice wine, honey, and 1 tablespoon soy sauce. Set aside.
3. Add oil to a preheated wok or skillet. When oil is hot, add the ginger and curry paste. Stir-fry briefly until aromatic. Add the chicken and stir-fry for 3 minutes. Add the onion and stir-fry for another 2 minutes, making sure to brown the chicken on both sides.
4. Give the sauce a quick stir and add it to the wok. Add the potato, reduce the heat to low or medium low, and simmer for 30 minutes or until the chicken thighs are cooked through. Stir in the remaining green onion and serve.

Hoisin Chicken

Serves 2–4

To ward off fears about bacteria, always refrigerate any dish while it is marinating.

1½ pounds chicken thighs, bone in
2 tablespoons hoisin sauce
1 tablespoon dark soy sauce
4 tablespoons water
1 teaspoon sugar

⅛ teaspoon white pepper, or to taste
1 large garlic clove, chopped

1. Wash the chicken thighs and pat dry. Remove the skin and make 2 diagonal cuts on each side of the thigh.
2. Mix together the hoisin sauce, dark soy sauce, water, sugar, white pepper, and garlic. Place the sauce in a large, zipper-lock plastic bag. Add the chicken, shaking the bag slightly to make sure the sauce coats all the chicken. Seal the bag and place in the refrigerator. Marinate the chicken for 2–3 hours, turning the bag occasionally.
3. Preheat the oven to 400°F.
4. Remove the chicken thighs from the bag, reserving the sauce. Place the thighs on a baking sheet sprayed with cooking spray. Brush on half of the sauce, making sure both sides of the thighs are covered. Bake the thighs for 15 minutes. Brush on the remainder of the sauce, and bake for another 15 minutes, or until the thighs are cooked.

Lemony Chicken Stir-fry

2 large skinless, boneless
  chicken breasts
2 tablespoons Chinese rice
  wine or dry sherry, divided
3 teaspoons soy sauce, divided
3 tablespoons plus ½ teaspoon
  freshly squeezed lemon
  juice, divided
1 teaspoon cornstarch

½ cup water
2 tablespoons brown sugar
1 teaspoon honey
3–4 tablespoons oil for stir-
  frying
1 clove garlic, minced
1 teaspoon minced ginger
1 teaspoon cornstarch mixed
  with 4 teaspoons water

> **Serves 2–4**
>
> Sweet brown sugar nicely balances tart lemon juice in this recipe. Serve with Tomato Egg Flower Soup (page 60) for an interesting flavor combination.
>
>

1. Cut the chicken into thin strips. Add 1 tablespoon rice wine, 1 teaspoon soy sauce, ½ teaspoon lemon juice, and 1 teaspoon cornstarch to the chicken, adding the cornstarch last. Marinate the chicken for 30 minutes.
2. Mix together 3 tablespoons freshly squeezed lemon juice, water, 1 tablespoon rice wine, 2 teaspoons soy sauce, brown sugar, and honey. Set aside.
3. Add 2 tablespoons oil to a preheated wok or skillet. When oil is hot, add the chicken and stir-fry until it changes color and is nearly cooked. Remove from the wok and set aside.
4. Clean out the wok with a paper towel. Preheat and add 1½ table-spoons oil. When oil is hot, add the garlic and ginger. Stir-fry briefly until aromatic. Add the sauce, bringing to a boil.
5. Give the cornstarch-and-water mixture a quick stir. Add to the sauce, stirring vigorously to thicken. Add the chicken and heat through.

Why Marinate?
Although it can seem time consuming, never forego marinating meat if a recipe calls for it. Besides lending flavor, a good mari-nade tenderizes the meat as well. It's rare to find a Chinese recipe that doesn't call for marinating meat prior to stir-frying.

Steamed Lemon Chicken

1 chicken breast
1 tablespoon minced ginger
1½ tablespoons freshly squeezed lemon juice
¼ cup water
2 teaspoons Chinese rice wine or dry sherry

1 teaspoon soy sauce
1½ teaspoons sugar
½ teaspoon black rice vinegar
1 teaspoon cornstarch

1. Place the chicken in a heatproof plate on a bamboo steamer. Add the minced ginger. Steam for 20 minutes, or until the chicken turns white and is cooked.
2. While the chicken is steaming, mix together the lemon juice, water, rice wine, soy sauce, sugar, black rice vinegar, and cornstarch. In a small saucepan, heat the sauce to boiling. Pour over the steamed chicken.

Basic Chicken Velvet

2 boneless, skinless chicken breasts
2 tablespoons rice vinegar

¼ teaspoon five-spice powder
2 teaspoons cornstarch
1 egg white

1. Using a sharp knife or a food processor, mince the chicken.
2. Mix together the rice vinegar, five-spice powder, and cornstarch. Add to the minced chicken, separating the individual chicken pieces.
3. Beat the egg white until creamy but not stiff. Fold into the chicken mixture.

Chicken Velvet Soup
Basic Chicken Velvet's delicate flavor inspired the creation of Chicken Velvet Soup (page 59). For best results, add the Basic Chicken Velvet to the boiling broth before adding seasonings and stir.

Deep-fried Chicken Velvet

½ cup chicken stock
2 tablespoons Chinese rice
    wine or dry sherry
½ teaspoon salt (or to taste)
2 leeks, cut diagonally into
    1-inch sections
1 tablespoon soy sauce

Basic Chicken Velvet (page 160)
2 teaspoons cornstarch
4 teaspoons water
4¼ cups oil for frying

Serves 2–4

Deep-fried Chicken Velvet nearly does melt in your mouth. The possibilities for pairing this dish are endless—look for contrasts in texture and color.

1. Mix together the chicken stock, rice wine, and salt. Set aside.
2. In a preheated wok, heat 4 cups oil to 350°F. While the oil is heating, use a second skillet or wok to stir-fry the leeks. Add 1–2 tablespoons of oil. When oil is hot, add the leeks. Stir-fry for about 1 minute, then add 1 tablespoon of soy sauce. Stir-fry until the leeks turn a bright green, and remove from the pan. Wipe out the pan with a paper towel if using to heat the chicken stock (see step 4).
3. When the oil for deep-frying is ready, carefully slide in the Basic Chicken Velvet pieces and deep-fry until the chicken turns white and is cooked. (This will take a minute at most.) Remove from the wok and drain on paper towels.
4. Heat the chicken broth mixture. When it is boiling, add the Basic Chicken Velvet and mix. If necessary, break up the chicken with chopsticks or a spatula. Push the chicken up to the sides of the pan. Mix the cornstarch and water and add to the middle of the pan, stirring vigorously to thicken. Mix through with the chicken. Serve the chicken with the leeks.

Chicken with Red and Green Peppers

Serves 2–4

Serve with a sweet-and-sour vegetable dish such as Sweet-and-Sour Celery (page 252) for an interesting juxtaposition of flavors.

2 boneless, skinless chicken breasts
1 tablespoon soy sauce
1 egg white
1½ teaspoons cornstarch
1 green bell pepper
1 red bell pepper
¼ cup water

1½ teaspoons sugar
1 tablespoon black bean sauce
¼ teaspoon chili paste
1 tablespoon cornstarch
3–4 tablespoons oil for stir-frying
2 garlic cloves, chopped
½ cup chopped red onion

1. Chop the chicken into 1½-inch cubes. Mix in the soy sauce, egg white, and cornstarch, being sure to add the cornstarch last. Marinate the chicken for 30 minutes.
2. Wash the green and red peppers, remove the seeds, and cut into chunks.
3. To make the sauce, mix together the water, sugar, black bean sauce, chili paste, and cornstarch, and set aside.
4. Add 2 tablespoons oil to a preheated wok or skillet. When the oil is hot, add the chopped garlic and stir-fry briefly until aromatic. Add the marinated chicken to the wok. Stir-fry until the chicken turns white and is nearly cooked through. Remove from the wok and set aside.
5. Add 2 tablespoons oil. When oil is hot, add the green pepper and onion. Stir-fry for about 1 minute, and then add the red pepper. Stir-fry until the peppers turn a bright color and the onion is softened.
6. Give the sauce a quick stir. Push the vegetables to the side of the wok and add the sauce in the middle, stirring vigorously to thicken. Mix with the vegetables. Add the chicken. Mix all the ingredients and serve hot.

Quick Red Bell Peppers
Although they are both members of the capsicum family, red peppers have a shorter cooking time than green peppers. For best results, add them at a later stage in stir-frying.

Bang Bang Chicken

*1 pound boneless, skinless
    chicken breasts
Spicy Szechwan Peanut Sauce
    (page 23)*

*1 large dried bean curd sheet
2 small cucumbers
½ teaspoon salt*

1. Boil chicken breasts in water for 15–20 minutes. Drain well.
2. Cut the bean curd sheet into 4 squares. Soak the sheet in cold water to soften. Peel the cucumbers and slice, toss with salt, and leave for 15 minutes.
3. Chop the chicken meat into thin slices. Lay the cucumber slices on a plate and top with a bean curd sheet. Top with the chicken and the sauce. Serve the remainder of the sauce in a dipping bowl so guests can help themselves.

Serves 4

To use Chinese noodles instead of bean curd sheets, cook the noodles according to instructions, drain well, and lay over the cucumber slices.

Spicy Chicken with Cashews

*2 boneless, skinless chicken
    breasts
2 tablespoons dark soy sauce
1 tablespoon Chinese rice wine
    or dry sherry*

*1 teaspoon sugar
¼ teaspoon sesame oil
¼ teaspoon chili paste
3 tablespoons oil for stir-frying
½ cup cashews*

1. Cut the chicken into 1-inch cubes. Mix together the dark soy sauce, rice wine, sugar, sesame oil, and chili paste, and set aside.
2. Add 2 tablespoons oil to a preheated wok or skillet. Stir-fry the chicken until it is nearly cooked through. Remove, and drain on paper towels.
3. Wipe the wok clean with a paper towel and add 1 tablespoon of oil. Stir-fry the cashews very briefly, until they are golden.
4. Add the sauce to the wok and bring to a boil. Turn down the heat and add the chicken back into the wok. Mix through and serve hot.

Serves 2–4

Native to Brazil, cashews made their way east via seventeenth-century Portuguese explorers and are now commonly featured in Asian dishes.

General Tso's Chicken

Serves 4

To serve a vegetable with this dish, stir-fry while you are waiting for the oil to heat up for deep-frying.

1 pound dark chicken meat
2 tablespoons soy sauce
3 teaspoons Chinese rice wine
   or dry sherry, divided
⅛ teaspoon white pepper
1 tablespoon cornstarch
4 tablespoons dark soy sauce
2 teaspoons sugar
½ teaspoon sesame oil
6 dried red chilies
4–6 cups oil for deep-frying
1 large clove garlic, minced
1 teaspoon minced ginger
2 green onions, thinly sliced

1. Cut the chicken into cubes. Mix in the soy sauce, 2 teaspoons of the rice wine, white pepper, and the cornstarch, adding the cornstarch last. Marinate the chicken for 30 minutes.

2. Combine the dark soy sauce, sugar, sesame oil, and 1 teaspoon rice wine. Set aside. Cut the red chilies in half and remove the seeds. Chop and set aside.

3. Heat the oil to 350°F. When the oil is hot, add the chicken cubes and deep-fry until they are lightly browned. Remove from the wok and drain on paper towels.

4. Raise the temperature of the wok to 400°F. Deep-fry the chicken a second time briefly, until the chicken turns golden brown. Remove from the wok and drain on paper towels.

5. Drain the wok, leaving 2 tablespoons of oil for stir-frying. When the oil is hot, add the garlic, ginger, and green onions. Stir-fry briefly until aromatic. Add the chilies and cook for 1 minute. Add the sauce in the middle of the wok and bring to a boil. Add the chicken and mix through.

Food Fit for a General

General Tso's Chicken is named after a famous military leader who helped quash China's Taipeng rebellion in the mid-1800s. How the dish came to be named after General Tso is lost to history, although he was rumored to have a penchant for fiery foods.

Quick and Easy Orange Chicken

*2 large boneless, skinless chicken
    breasts, about 7 ounces each
2 tablespoons Chinese rice
    wine or dry sherry
1 egg white
5 teaspoons cornstarch, divided
¼ cup water
5 teaspoons freshly squeezed
    orange juice
1 tablespoon soy sauce*

*1½ teaspoons brown sugar
¼ teaspoon chili paste
¼ teaspoon sesame oil
2 tablespoons oil for stir-frying
1 teaspoon minced ginger
1 clove garlic, minced*

Serves 4

Serve with rice and a
steamed vegetable for
a quick and easy dish
on busy weeknights.

1. Cut the chicken into 1-inch cubes. Mix in the rice wine, egg white,
   and 3 teaspoons cornstarch, adding the cornstarch last. Marinate the
   chicken for 15 minutes.
2. Mix together the water, orange juice, soy sauce, brown sugar, chili
   paste, sesame oil, and 2 teaspoons cornstarch.
3. Add oil to a preheated wok or skillet. When the oil is ready, add the
   ginger and garlic. Stir-fry briefly until aromatic.
4. Add the chicken and stir-fry until the chicken changes color and is
   nearly cooked through.
5. Give the sauce a quick stir. Push the chicken up the sides of the wok
   and add the sauce, stirring vigorously to thicken. Mix the sauce with
   the chicken and cook the chicken for another minute.

Kung Pao Stir-fry

Serves 2–4

This healthier version of Kung Pao Chicken uses less oil but still contains protein-rich peanuts.

2 boneless, skinless chicken breasts
1 tablespoon soy sauce
2 tablespoons Chinese rice wine or dry sherry, divided
1 tablespoon cornstarch
2 tablespoons dark soy sauce
1 teaspoon sugar
¼ teaspoon sesame oil
4 tablespoons oil for stir-frying
1 clove garlic, minced
¼ teaspoon chili paste
½ cup unsalted, roasted peanuts

1. Cut the chicken into 1-inch cubes. Add the soy sauce, 1 tablespoon rice wine, and the cornstarch to the chicken, adding the cornstarch last. Marinate the chicken for 30 minutes.
2. Mix together the dark soy sauce, 1 tablespoon rice wine, sugar, and sesame oil.
3. Add 2 tablespoons oil to a preheated wok or skillet. When oil is hot, add the chicken cubes and stir-fry until they turn golden. Remove the chicken from the wok and drain on paper towels.
4. Add 2 tablespoons oil. When oil is hot, add the garlic clove and chili paste. Stir-fry briefly until aromatic. Add the peanuts and stir-fry very briefly, taking care not to burn.
5. Add the sauce to the wok and bring to a boil. Turn down the heat and add the chicken. Mix everything and simmer for a few minutes until the chicken is cooked through.

Sweet-and-Sour Chicken

1½ cups chicken meat
¾ cup pineapple juice
2 tablespoons rice vinegar
1 teaspoon black rice vinegar
1 tablespoon soy sauce
½ green bell pepper
½ red bell pepper
2 tablespoons oil for stir-frying

2 tablespoons plus 1 teaspoon sugar
¼ cup pineapple chunks
1 tablespoon cornstarch mixed with 4 tablespoons water

Serves 4

This is a variation on traditional Chinese Pineapple Chicken, where the chicken is deep-fried in batter before mixing with the sauce.

1. Cut the chicken meat into bite-sized pieces. Mix together the pineapple juice, rice vinegar, black rice vinegar, and soy sauce, and set aside. Cut the green and red peppers into bite-sized cubes.
2. Add oil to a preheated wok or skillet. When oil is hot, add the chicken. Stir-fry until it changes color and is nearly cooked through.
3. In a medium saucepan, bring the pineapple juice mixture to a boil. Stir in the sugar, stirring to dissolve. Add the green and red peppers and the pineapple chunks. Bring back to a boil and add the corn-starch-and-water mixture, stirring quickly to thicken.
4. Pour the sauce over the stir-fried chicken and heat through.

Or Make It Pineapple-Orange Chicken

To transform the sweet-and-sour sauce into a pineapple-orange sauce, just decrease the amount of pineapple juice to ½ cup and add 1 tablespoon plus 1 teaspoon of orange juice. Include or leave out the peppers and pineapple chunks as desired.

Sesame Hoisin Surprise

3 boneless, skinless chicken breasts
2 tablespoons soy sauce
1 tablespoon Chinese rice wine or dry sherry
3 tablespoons cornstarch, divided
1 cup water
2 teaspoons hoisin sauce
2 tablespoons brown sugar
4 teaspoons dark soy sauce
Up to 2 teaspoons chili paste
2 teaspoons vegetable oil
2 garlic cloves, minced
2 tablespoons oil for stir-frying
1 green onion, thinly sliced
2 tablespoons toasted sesame seeds

1. Cut the chicken into 1-inch cubes. Mix in the soy sauce, rice wine, and 1 tablespoon cornstarch, adding the cornstarch last. Marinate the chicken for 30 minutes.

2. In a small saucepan, bring the water, hoisin sauce, brown sugar, dark soy sauce, chili paste, vegetable oil, garlic cloves, and 2 tablespoons cornstarch to a boil. Turn down the heat to low and keep warm while stir-frying the chicken.

3. Add the oil to a preheated wok or skillet. When oil is hot, add the marinated chicken pieces and stir-fry until they change color and are nearly cooked through. Remove the chicken from the wok and set aside.

4. As you finish stir-frying the chicken, bring the sauce back up to a boil. Mix in the green onion. Pour the sauce over the chicken and mix through. Garnish with the toasted sesame seeds.

Garlic Chicken

4 boneless, skinless, chicken
  breasts
2 egg whites
¼ teaspoon salt
2 teaspoons cornstarch
2 tablespoons oil for stir-frying
3 large garlic cloves, chopped
½ tablespoon chili paste

¼ cup soy sauce
2 tablespoons Chinese rice
  wine or dry sherry
½ teaspoon sesame oil
2 green onions, cut into
  1½-inch pieces
1 tomato, cut into wedges

> **Serves 4**
>
> This dish is a garlic lover's delight. To increase its potent aroma, add more cloves or mince them instead of chopping.
>
>

1. Wash the chicken, pat dry, and cut into cubes. Add the egg whites, salt, and cornstarch, adding the cornstarch last. Marinate the chicken for 1 hour.

2. Bring a large pot of water to a very low boil. Add the chicken, stirring to separate the pieces, and remove as soon as it is just turning white (about 60–90 seconds). Drain immediately.

3. Add oil to a preheated wok or skillet. When oil is hot, add the garlic and chili paste and stir-fry until the garlic is aromatic. Add the chicken and stir-fry briefly. Add the soy sauce and rice wine. Bring to a boil and cook for a few minutes until everything is heated through. Stir in the green onions and drizzle with the sesame oil. Serve on a bed of white rice, garnished with the tomato wedges.

Water-Poached Chicken

Poaching poultry in water gives it a soft and tender texture. For best results keep the water at a low simmer and not strongly bubbling. It helps to have a colander set up before you poach the chicken, since it should be drained immediately. On its own, the whitish color of water-poached chicken can be a little disconcerting. This technique works best when you have a darker cut of meat or plan to cook the chicken in a dark-colored sauce.

Chicken with Walnuts

2 boneless, skinless chicken breasts
1 egg white
¼ teaspoon salt
2 teaspoons cornstarch
1½ tablespoons dark soy sauce
3 tablespoons oyster sauce
1½ tablespoons Chinese rice wine or dry sherry
2¼ teaspoons sugar
⅓ cup water
½ cup walnut halves
1 garlic clove, smashed
1 teaspoon cornstarch mixed with 4 teaspoons water
1¼ cups oil for frying

1. Cut the chicken into 1-inch cubes. Mix in the egg white, salt, and cornstarch, adding the cornstarch last. Marinate the chicken for 30 minutes.
2. Combine the dark soy sauce, oyster sauce, rice wine, sugar, and water, and set aside.
3. Boil the walnuts in water for at least 5 minutes. Drain and dry.
4. Add 1 cup oil to a preheated wok or skillet. When oil is hot, add the chicken cubes. Velvet the chicken cubes by submerging them in the hot oil just until they change color. Remove immediately and drain on paper towels.
5. Remove all but 1 tablespoon oil. When oil is hot, add the garlic and stir-fry until aromatic. Add the walnuts and stir-fry for about 1 minute. Push up to the side of the wok and add the sauce in the middle. Bring to a boil.
6. Give the cornstarch-and-water mixture a quick stir. Add in the middle of the wok, stirring quickly to thicken. Add the chicken. Mix everything together. Cover and simmer for a few minutes until the chicken is cooked through.

Chengdu Chicken

4 boneless, skinless chicken
   breasts
2 stalks celery
3 teaspoons red or black rice
   vinegar
1 teaspoon sugar
¾ teaspoon salt, divided
½ cup hot water

1 teaspoon Chinese rice wine
   or dry sherry
3 tablespoons oil for stir-frying
1 tablespoon chopped ginger
2 garlic cloves, chopped
2 tablespoons hot bean sauce
2 teaspoons cornstarch
¼ cup water

Serves 4

Chengdu Chicken is
named after Chengdu,
the capital city of
Szechuan province in
western China.

1. Rinse the chicken breasts and cut into cubes. Cut the celery into
   1-inch slices on the diagonal. Blanch or parboil the celery in a pot
   of boiling water for 2–3 minutes.
2. Combine the rice vinegar, sugar, ½ teaspoon salt, hot water, and rice
   wine. Set aside.
3. Add 1 tablespoon oil to a preheated wok or skillet. When the oil is
   hot, add the celery. Stir-fry briefly and add ¼ teaspoon salt. Stir-fry
   until the celery changes color and is tender but still firm. Remove
   from the wok.
4. Wipe the wok clean with a paper towel. Add 2 tablespoons oil. When
   the oil is hot, add the ginger and garlic and stir-fry briefly until aromatic. Add the chicken cubes. Stir-fry for 2–3 minutes, then add the
   hot bean sauce. Stir-fry until the chicken changes color and is nearly
   cooked through.
5. Add the sauce and bring to a boil. Mix the cornstarch and water and
   add to the middle of the wok, stirring vigorously to thicken. Add the
   celery. Mix everything through and serve hot.

Mango Chicken

Serves 4

Turmeric is a distant relative of ginger. In this recipe it gives the chicken a nice yellow color.

4 boneless, skinless chicken breasts

1 egg white

1 tablespoon Chinese rice wine or dry sherry

¼ teaspoon salt

2 teaspoons cornstarch

2 tablespoons rice vinegar

2 tablespoons plus 1 teaspoon brown sugar

1 can mango slices with reserved juice

1 tablespoon minced ginger

1 teaspoon curry paste

½ teaspoon turmeric

1 cup oil for frying

1. Cut the chicken into cubes. Mix in the egg white, rice wine, salt, and cornstarch. Marinate the chicken for 30 minutes.
2. In a small saucepan, bring the rice vinegar, brown sugar, and ¾ cup of reserved mango juice to a boil. Keep warm on low heat.
3. Add 1 cup oil to a preheated wok or skillet. When the oil is hot, velvet the chicken by cooking very briefly in the hot oil, until it changes color and is nearly cooked through (about 30 seconds). Use tongs or cooking chopsticks to separate the individual pieces of chicken while it is cooking.
4. Remove all but 2 tablespoons oil from the wok. (Wipe out the wok with a paper towel if necessary.) When oil is hot, add the ginger, curry paste, and turmeric. Stir-fry for about 1 minute until aromatic. Add the chicken and mix with the curry paste.
5. Add the sauce and bring to a boil. Stir in the mango slices. Mix all the ingredients and serve hot.

 Velveting Meat

Velveting meat is a handy trick restaurants use to tenderize meat such as chicken, pork, or beef. Why does it work? The initial contact with hot oil shocks the muscles, causing them to relax. The muscles remain relaxed when they are stir- or deep-fried according to the recipe instructions. The result is a piece of meat that is both firm and juicy.

Quick and Easy Curry Chicken

2 boneless, skinless chicken
   breasts
2 green onions, minced
1 heaping teaspoon minced
   ginger
1 clove garlic, minced

1 tablespoon mild curry powder,
   or to taste
Stir-fried Water Chestnuts and
   Bamboo Shoots (page 232)
¼ cup chicken broth
4 tablespoons oil, or as needed

Serves 2

Worried your curry powder is too strong? Add 1–2 teaspoons while stir-frying the ginger and garlic, and then add more with the chicken, if desired.

1. Wash the chicken breasts, pat dry, and cut into cubes. Cut the green onions into thin slices.

2. Add 2 tablespoons oil to a preheated wok or skillet. When oil is hot, add the ginger, garlic, and curry powder and stir-fry until there is a strong odor of curry. Add the chicken and stir-fry for about 5 minutes, until the chicken is well mixed with the curry powder. Remove and set aside.

3. Add the Stir-fried Water Chestnuts and Bamboo Shoots to the wok. If making from scratch, follow the directions in the recipe. If previously made, bring to a boil. Add oil as required.

4. Add the chicken back into the wok. Add the chicken broth. Bring to a boil, cover and simmer until the dish is cooked through. Stir in the green onions or add as a garnish.

Curry—More Than a Powder

Although we tend to think of curry as a spice or blend of spices, the word has its origins in the Tamil word kahri, a spicy sauce. We have a British official to thank for the association of curry with a dry powder. The story is that, when leaving India, the official ordered his servant to prepare a compilation of spices so that he could enjoy his favorite Indian dishes upon returning home to Britain. Freshly made curry powder is preferable to commercially prepared brands. Still, in today's busy world it's not always possible to find time for chopping herbs and grinding fresh spices. Although this recipe uses a mild curry powder, the hotter Madras curry powders generally work best in Chinese dishes.

Princess Chicken

1 pound light chicken meat
6 tablespoons soy sauce, divided
4 teaspoons Chinese rice wine or dry sherry, divided
1 tablespoon cornstarch
2 teaspoons sugar
¼ teaspoon sesame oil

6 dried red chilies
3 tablespoons oil for stir-frying
1 large clove garlic, minced
1 teaspoon minced ginger
2 green onions, thinly sliced

1. Cut the chicken into cubes. Mix in 2 tablespoons soy sauce, 3 teaspoons rice wine, and the cornstarch, adding the cornstarch last. Marinate the chicken for 30 minutes.
2. Combine the 4 tablespoons soy sauce, 1 teaspoon rice wine, sugar, and the sesame oil, and set aside. Cut the red chilies in half and remove the seeds. Chop and set aside.
3. Add 2 tablespoons oil to a preheated wok or skillet. When the oil is hot, add the chicken cubes and stir-fry until they are nearly cooked through. Remove from the wok and drain on paper towels.
4. Add 1 tablespoon oil to the wok. When the oil is hot, add the garlic, ginger, and green onions. Stir-fry briefly until aromatic. Add the chilies and cook for 1 minute. Add the sauce in the middle of the wok and bring to a boil. Add the chicken and mix through.

Tea Smoked Chicken

3-pound fryer chicken
2 tablespoons dark soy sauce
1 teaspoon sugar
1½ teaspoons Chinese rice
wine or dry sherry
½ green onion, minced

3 tablespoons black tea leaves
½ cup brown sugar
¼ teaspoon Szechwan Salt and
Pepper Mix (page 20)
½ cup uncooked rice

<table><tr><td>Serves 6</td></tr></table>

For a different flavor, try simmering the chicken prior to steaming in the black tea leaves.

1. Wash the chicken and pat dry. Mix together the dark soy sauce, sugar, rice wine, and green onion. Rub over the chicken and marinate for 1 hour. Mix together the tea leaves, brown sugar, Szechwan Salt and Pepper Mix, and rice. Set aside.
2. Prepare a bamboo steamer and steam the chicken for about 45 minutes, until it is cooked.
3. Cover the bottom of the wok and the inside of the wok with several layers of aluminum foil. Place the smoking spices at the bottom of the wok. Place a cake rack inside the wok and place the chicken on the rack. Turn the heat up. When smoke appears in a few places (about 10–15 minutes), cover the chicken with the lid and adjust the heat so that the stream of smoke remains steady. Continue smoking until the chicken turns a deep brown (about 15 minutes).

Tea-Smoked Food

There is no need to purchase a wood smoker to make Chinese favorites such as tea smoked duck or chicken. Along with steaming and stir-frying, the versatile wok also functions as a smoker. Chinese cooks make a further departure from traditional smoking methods by using smoking solely to impart flavor to the food, not to cook it. (The food to be cooked is usually steamed or simmered first.) The smoking ingredient of choice in Chinese cooking is tea leaves; black are most popular, although green tea leaves are also used. Other spices and seasonings that may be added to the smoking mix include star anise, and brown or white sugar.

Deep-fried Chicken

Serves 2–4

This tastes delicious dipped in Quick and Easy Sweet-and-Sour Sauce (page 22) or Sweet-and-Sour Worcestershire Sauce (page 21).

2 boneless, skinless chicken breasts
2 teaspoons Chinese rice wine or dry sherry
½ green onion, cut into 1-inch pieces
2 teaspoons soy sauce
2 thin slices ginger
1½ cups oil for frying

1. Cut the chicken into 1-inch cubes. Add the rice wine, green onion, soy sauce, and ginger. Marinate the chicken for 30 minutes.
2. Add oil to a preheated wok or skillet. When oil is hot, add the chicken cubes. Fry until they are browned and evenly cooked (about 4–5 minutes). Remove with a slotted spoon and drain on paper towels.

Deep-fried Breaded Chicken

Serves 2–4

This is an elegant appetizer when served with Hot Mustard Dip (page 18) and garnished with sprigs of cilantro.

2 boneless, skinless chicken breasts
2 teaspoons Chinese rice wine
½ green onion, cut into 1-inch pieces
2 teaspoons soy sauce
2 thin slices ginger
6 tablespoons breadcrumbs
½ teaspoon Szechwan peppercorns, roasted and ground
1 egg, lightly beaten
1½ cups oil for frying

1. Cut the chicken into 1-inch cubes. Add the rice wine, green onion, soy sauce, and ginger. Marinate the chicken for 30 minutes.
2. Process the breadcrumbs and add the peppercorns.
3. Add oil to a preheated wok or skillet. When oil is heating, dip the chicken in the egg and dredge in the breadcrumbs.
4. When oil is hot, add the chicken and fry until it is evenly cooked (about 4–5 minutes). Remove and drain on paper towels.

Mu Shu Chicken

*½ pound boneless, skinless
    chicken legs or thighs*
1 tablespoon soy sauce
2½ teaspoons sugar, divided
2 teaspoons cornstarch
*4 water chestnuts, fresh if
    possible*
2 green onions

½ cup water
1 tablespoon dark soy sauce
1 tablespoon hoisin sauce
¼ teaspoon sesame oil
2 eggs
¼ teaspoon salt
3–4 tablespoons oil for stir-frying
1 slice ginger, minced

Serves 4–6

While Mu Shu Pork is a
popular restaurant
dish, the basic recipe
can be adjusted to use
with chicken, beef,
and even vegetables.

1. Cut the chicken into thin slices. Add the soy sauce, 2 teaspoons sugar, and cornstarch, adding the cornstarch last. Marinate the chicken for 30 minutes.
2. If using fresh water chestnuts, peel and cut in half. If using canned, rinse with warm water to remove any "tinny" taste, drain well, and cut in half. Cut the green onions into 1-inch pieces on the diagonal.
3. Combine the water, dark soy sauce, hoisin sauce, ½ teaspoon sugar, and sesame oil, and set aside.
4. Lightly beat the eggs and stir in ¼ teaspoon salt. Add 1 tablespoon oil to a preheated wok or skillet. When oil is hot, turn up the heat and scramble the eggs. Scramble quickly and remove from the wok.
5. Add 2 more tablespoons oil to the wok. When oil is hot, add the chicken and stir-fry until it changes color and is nearly cooked through. Remove from the wok and set aside.
6. Add more oil if needed. Add the ginger and green onions and stir-fry until aromatic. Add the water chestnuts. Make a well in the middle of the wok, add the sauce and bring to a boil. Add the chicken and scrambled egg. Mix through and serve hot.

Sesame Chicken

3 whole boneless chicken breasts
2 tablespoons soy sauce
1 tablespoon Chinese rice wine or dry sherry
⅛ teaspoon sesame oil
2 tablespoons flour
¼ teaspoon baking powder
¼ teaspoon baking soda
2 tablespoons water
6 tablespoons cornstarch, divided
1 teaspoon vegetable oil

½ cup water
1 cup chicken stock or broth
2 tablespoons dark soy sauce
½ cup vinegar
2 teaspoons chili sauce with garlic
1 large clove garlic, minced
1 teaspoon rice vinegar
¾ cup sugar
2 tablespoons sesame seeds
4–6 cups oil for deep-frying

1. Cut the chicken into cubes. Mix in the soy sauce, rice wine, sesame oil, flour, baking powder, baking soda, water, 2 tablespoons cornstarch, and vegetable oil. Marinate the chicken for 30 minutes.
2. In a medium bowl, combine ½ cup water, chicken stock, dark soy sauce, vinegar, chili sauce with garlic, garlic clove, rice vinegar, sugar, and 4 tablespoons cornstarch. Set aside.
3. Heat oil in wok to 350°F. Add the marinated chicken and deep-fry until golden brown. Remove from the wok with a slotted spoon and drain on paper towels.
4. Raise the oil temperature in the wok to 400°F. Deep-fry the chicken a second time, until it turns golden brown. Remove and drain.
5. Give the sauce a quick stir. Bring to a boil in a medium-sized saucepan. Pour over the deep-fried chicken. Garnish with the sesame seeds.

Double Deep-frying
Deep-frying meat twice is another technique Chinese restaurant chefs have in their cooking repertoire. Besides adding a crispier coating, the second frying seals in the meat's juices. Replacing egg in the batter with vegetable oil helps increase the crispiness.

Spicy Braised Chicken Wings

12 chicken wings
¼ cup chicken broth
½ cup plain yogurt
1 tablespoon Chinese rice wine
  or dry sherry
1 tablespoon soy sauce
1 teaspoon honey
1 tablespoon curry paste
4 cups oil for deep-frying

1. Chop the chicken wings into pieces. In a large saucepan, blanch the chicken wing pieces in boiling water for 2 minutes. Drain.
2. Combine the chicken broth, yogurt, rice wine, soy sauce, honey, and curry paste. Set aside.
3. Heat oil for deep-frying. When the oil reaches 350°F, carefully slide the chicken wing pieces into the wok. Deep-fry until they turn light brown. Remove with a slotted spoon and drain on paper towels.
4. Bring the sauce to a boil in a skillet or wok. Add the chicken pieces, cover, and simmer for 10–15 minutes, or until the chicken is cooked through.

Serves 4–6

Madras, a hot curry paste made with turmeric, chili, cumin, and coriander, works well in this recipe.

Sweet-and-Sour Chicken Wings

5 chicken wings
Sweet-and-Sour Sauce with
  Ketchup (page 22)

1. Cut the wing tip off the wings. Blanch the wings in boiling water for 2 minutes and drain.
2. Brush the chicken wings with the Sweet-and-Sour Sauce with Ketchup, making sure both sides are covered. Reserve any leftover sauce. Marinate the chicken wings for 1 hour.
3. Preheat the oven to 400°F. Place the wings on a baking sheet. Brush the chicken with half the leftover sauce and bake the chicken wings for 30 minutes. Turn over and brush with the remainder of the leftover sauce and bake for another 30 minutes. Remove from the stove and cool.

Serves 5

Unused wing tips are perfect for making soup stock. Serve the sweet-and-sour wings with watercress soup for an interesting combination of flavors.

Oyster Sauce Chicken Wings

16 chicken wings
⅓ cup soy sauce
1 tablespoon dark soy sauce
3 tablespoons oyster sauce
1 tablespoon Chinese rice wine
  or dry sherry
2 teaspoons sugar

2 tablespoons water
2 teaspoons sesame oil
3 garlic cloves, minced

1. Rinse the chicken wings and pat dry. Combine the soy sauce, dark soy sauce, oyster sauce, rice wine, sugar, water, and sesame oil. Place the sauce in a plastic bag. Add the chicken, shaking the bag lightly to make sure the sauce coats all the chicken. Seal the bag and place in the refrigerator. Marinate the chicken for 2–3 hours, turning the bag occasionally.
2. Preheat the oven to 350°F.
3. Remove the chicken wings from the bag, reserving the sauce. Place the wings on a baking sheet sprayed with cooking spray. Pour ½ the sauce over. Add the minced garlic. Bake the wings for 20 minutes. Add the remaining half of the sauce and cook for another 15 minutes, or until the wings are cooked.

How to Reduce Splattering During Deep-frying
Make sure the food to be deep-fried is at room temperature. If deep-frying foods are coated in a sauce or batter, use a slotted spoon to drain off any excess before adding the food to the wok.

Stuffed Chicken Wings

10 chicken wings
2 Chinese dried mushrooms
½ 8-ounce can bamboo shoots, drained
½ cup ground pork
½ tablespoon soy sauce
½ tablespoon Chinese rice wine or dry sherry
¼ teaspoon sesame oil
½ teaspoon sugar
Salt and pepper to taste

Serves 10

Serve this appetizer on a bed of lettuce leaves garnished with cilantro, with a dipping sauce.

1. Wash the chicken wings and pat dry. Cut through the middle section and discard the drummette. Take a paring knife and, starting with the end of the midsection that was attached to the drummette, carefully scrape the meat away from the 2 bones in the middle section, taking care not to cut the skin. When the meat is scraped away, pull and remove the 2 bones in the midsection. This will give you a pouch to stuff.
2. Soak the dried mushrooms in hot water for at least 20 minutes to soften. Give the mushrooms a gentle squeeze to remove any excess water. Cut into thin slices. Julienne the bamboo shoots.
3. Place the pork in a medium bowl. Use your hands to mix the soy sauce, rice wine, sesame oil, sugar, and salt and pepper in with the pork.
4. Take a small ball of pork and place inside the chicken skin. Add 2 slices of bamboo and 2 slices of sliced mushrooms. Continue with the remainder of the chicken wings.
5. Steam the chicken wings on a heatproof plate on a bamboo steamer in the wok for about 20 minutes, or until the pork is cooked through.

Drunken Chicken Wings

8–10 chicken wings
¼ teaspoon salt
Pepper to taste
1 green onion, chopped

2 slices ginger
6 cups dry white wine to
    cover

1. In a large pot, bring 8 cups of water to a boil. While waiting for the water to boil, chop the chicken wings through the middle so that you have a drummette and the midsection. Chop off and discard the wing tips.
2. Cook the chicken wings in the boiling water for 5 minutes.
3. Add the salt, pepper, green onion, and ginger. Cover and simmer the chicken for 45 minutes. Cool.
4. Place the chicken wings in a sealed container and cover with the wine. Refrigerate for at least 12 hours before serving.

Out of Chicken Wings?

You can also make this dish using a whole chicken. Increase the amount of seasonings if desired. When ready to serve, place the whole chicken on a platter and garnish with sprigs of cilantro or Green Onion Brushes (page 73). Carve up the chicken in front of guests.

Turkey with Water Chestnuts

1½ pounds turkey breast
2 tablespoons hoisin sauce
2 tablesoons soy sauce
3 tablespoons water
3 teaspoons brown sugar
3 tablespoons oil for stir-frying

2 garlic cloves, minced
2 slices ginger, minced
1 can water chestnuts, rinsed
¼ teaspoon salt

> **Serves 4**
>
> For extra flavor, add ¼ teaspoon of chili paste to the sauce. Serve with a spicy dish such as Cold Szechwan Sesame Noodles (page 99).
>
>

1. Rinse the turkey. Remove the skin and the breastbone. Chop into 1½-inch cubes.
2. Combine the hoisin sauce, soy sauce, water, and brown sugar in a bowl and set aside.
3. Add oil to a preheated wok or skillet. When the oil is hot, add the garlic and ginger and stir-fry briefly until aromatic. Add the turkey and stir-fry in batches on medium to medium-high heat for about 4–5 minutes, until the meat is tender. Remove from the wok and set aside.
4. Add 1 tablespoon oil. When oil is hot, add the water chestnuts to the wok and stir-fry for about 1 minute. Add the salt and stir-fry until they turn light brown. Push the water chestnuts up to the sides of the wok. Add the sauce in the middle of the wok and bring to a boil. Add the turkey cubes and stir-fry for another couple of minutes, until all the ingredients are mixed together.

Peking Duck

1 5-pound duck
8 cups water
3 tablespoons honey
1½ tablespoons rice vinegar

1 tablespoon Chinese rice wine or dry sherry

1. Thaw the duck and remove the inner organs. Rinse through with cold water, and pat dry.
2. Take a long piece of string and tie a knot at the end of each of the duck's legs to form a loop. (This will make it easy to hang the duck from a hook or nail.)
3. Bring the water to a boil in a large pot or a wok. Stir in the honey, rice vinegar, and rice wine. Turn down the heat and simmer the sauce, covered, for about 20 minutes, stirring occasionally.
4. Ladle the honey and water mixture over the skin of the duck several times, making sure the skin is completely coated. Dry the duck by hanging in a cool place for at least 4 hours, keeping a pan underneath to catch any drippings.
5. While the duck is drying, preheat the oven to 375°F. Fill the bottom of a roasting pan with water (this prevents the fat from splattering when you remove the duck from the oven). Place the duck on the roasting pan, breast side up. Roast for 30 minutes, turn over and roast for 30 minutes on the other side, and then turn and roast a final 10 minutes on the breast side, or until the duck is cooked. Cool and carve into thin slices. Serve on Mandarin Pancakes (page 268) brushed with hoisin sauce.

Stir-fried Duck with Pineapple

1 pound duck breast
1 tablespoon hoisin sauce
1 teaspoon Chinese rice wine
   or dry sherry
⅔ cup pineapple juice
2½ tablespoons black rice
   vinegar

1 teaspoon sugar
½ cup pineapple chunks
2 tablespoons oil for stir-frying
1 tablespoon minced ginger

Serves 2–4

For a balanced meal,
serve with Stir-fried
Baby Bok Choy (page
241) on a bed of
wild rice.

1. Cut the duck breast meat into thin slices approximately 2 inches in length. Marinate the duck in the hoisin sauce and rice wine for 30 minutes.
2. In a small saucepan, bring the pineapple juice, black rice vinegar, and sugar to a boil. Stir in the pineapple chunks. Keep warm on low heat.
3. Add oil to a preheated wok or skillet. When oil is hot, add the ginger. Stir-fry briefly until aromatic. Add the duck and stir-fry for 2–3 minutes.
4. Add the pineapple juice mixture. Heat through and serve.

Clay Pot Cooking

Used since ancient times, clay pot cooking features prominently in Shanghai cuisine. One advantage of clay pot cooking is that the food can be transported straight from stove to dinner table, with the clay pot doing double duty as cooking vessel and serving dish. In contrast to terra cotta pots, clay pots are unglazed on the inside, which is why they are also called sand pots. The main danger with clay pot dishes is unintentional cracking—be sure to follow the manu-facturer's instructions very carefully.

CHAPTER 9
Tofu and Eggs

Deep-fried Tofu

1 block firm tofu
¼ cup cornstarch

4–5 cups oil for deep-frying

1. Drain the tofu and cut into cubes. Coat with the cornstarch.
2. Add oil to a preheated wok and heat to 350°F. When oil is hot, add the tofu squares and deep-fry until they turn golden. Drain on paper towels.

How to Drain Tofu

Cut the tofu into smaller pieces. To drain, place the tofu on a paper towel on a plate. Cover with paper towels and place a weight on top of the tofu, such as a bowl or a book. Drain for 20 minutes. If possible, the easiest method for draining tofu is to position the plate so that it is tilting over the sink, allowing the water to flow out naturally.

Tofu Shake

1 banana, sliced
1 cup canned mandarin
 oranges with juice
1 cup soft or silken tofu

2 tablespoons honey
1 teaspoon cinnamon

Process all the ingredients in a food processor or blender. Chill and serve.

Slow Fried Tofu

1 block firm tofu
4–5 cups oil for deep-frying

1. Drain the tofu and cut into cubes.
2. Add oil to a preheated wok and heat to 350°F. When oil is hot, add the tofu.
3. Deep-fry until the cubes turn a golden brown. (This will take about 10 minutes.) Drain the deep-fried tofu on paper towels.

Soft and Firm Tofu

Soft tofu is also known as silken tofu. It is used mainly in desserts—its soft texture doesn't hold up well when fried. Soft tofu contains less protein than firm tofu but has a creamy texture that makes it perfect for shakes and puddings.

Thicker and denser than soft tofu, firm tofu can hold its shape in soups and stir-fried and deep-fried dishes. It can even be used in recipes normally requiring the extra-firm texture of pressed tofu when it is pressed and drained for 2 hours or more. Firm tofu should always be drained for at least 20 minutes before using.

Serves 4–6

Although it takes longer to cook, tofu retains more of its texture when it is deep-fried without a starch coating.

Fermented Bean Curd with Spinach

5 cups spinach leaves
4 cubes fermented bean curd
 with chilies
A pinch of five-spice powder
 (less than ⅛ teaspoon)

2 tablespoons oil for stir-frying
2 garlic cloves, minced
½ teaspoon sugar

1. Blanch the spinach by plunging the leaves briefly into boiling water. Drain thoroughly.
2. Mash the fermented tofu cubes and mix in the five-spice powder.
3. Add oil to a preheated wok or skillet. When the oil is hot, add the garlic and stir-fry briefly until aromatic. Add the spinach and stir-fry for 1–2 minutes. Add the sugar. Add the mashed bean curd in the middle of the wok and mix with the spinach. Cook through and serve hot.

Fermented Bean Curd

These small cubes of bean curd preserved in rice and spicy seasonings have a pungent aroma reminiscent of strong cheese. Sold in glass jars in Asian markets, fermented bean curd marries well with other savory foods such as garlic and salted black beans. Usually 1 or 2 cubes is all that is needed.

Stewed Tofu

1 pound beef
4 dried mushrooms
8 ounces pressed tofu
1 cup light soy sauce
¼ cup dark soy sauce
¼ cup Chinese rice wine or
*   dry sherry*
4 teaspoons white sugar

¼ cup brown sugar
2 tablespoons oil for stir-frying
2 slices ginger
2 garlic cloves, minced
2 cups water
1 star anise

Serves 4–6

Experiment with adding favorite spices to come up with your own version of red-cooked tofu.

---

1. Cut the beef into thin slices. Soak the dried mushrooms in hot water for at least 20 minutes to soften. Gently squeeze to remove any excess water and slice.

2. Cut the tofu into ½-inch cubes. Combine the light soy sauce, dark soy sauce, rice wine, white sugar, and brown sugar, and set aside.

3. Add oil to a preheated wok or skillet. When oil is hot, add the ginger slices and garlic and stir-fry briefly until aromatic. Add the beef and cook until browned. Before the beef has finished cooking, add the tofu cubes and fry briefly.

4. Add the sauce and 2 cups water. Add the star anise. Bring to a boil, then turn down the heat and simmer. After 1 hour, add the dried mushrooms. Simmer for another 30 minutes, or until the liquid is reduced. If desired, remove the star anise before serving.

Bean Curd with Bean Sauce and Noodles

Serves 4

Slow Fried Tofu (page 189) works well in this recipe. You can substitute other fresh noodles for the Peking noodles.

8 ounces fresh Peking-style
   noodles
1 12-ounce block firm tofu
3 large stalks bok choy
2 green onions
1/3 cup dark soy sauce
2 tablespoons black bean sauce
2 teaspoons Chinese rice wine
   or dry sherry
2 teaspoons black rice vinegar
2 teaspoons sugar

1/4 teaspoon salt
1/4 teaspoon chili paste with
   garlic
1 teaspoon Hot Chili Oil
   (page 23)
1/4 teaspoon sesame oil
1/2 cup water
2 tablespoons oil for stir-frying
2 slices ginger, minced
2 garlic cloves, minced
1/4 of a red onion, chopped

1. Cook the noodles in boiling water until they are tender. Drain thoroughly. Drain the tofu and cut into cubes.
2. Parboil the bok choy by plunging briefly into boiling water and draining thoroughly. Separate the stalks and leaves. Cut the green onions on the diagonal into 1-inch slices.
3. Combine the dark soy sauce, black bean sauce, rice wine, black rice vinegar, sugar, salt, chili paste with garlic, Hot Chili Oil, sesame oil, and water. Set aside.
4. Add oil to a preheated wok or skillet. When oil is hot, add the ginger, garlic, and green onions. Stir-fry briefly until aromatic. Add the red onion and stir-fry briefly. Push up to the sides and add the bok choy stalks. Add the leaves and stir-fry until the bok choy is a bright green and the onion tender. If desired, season with 1/4 teaspoon salt and 1/4 teaspoon sugar.
5. Add the sauce in the middle of the wok and bring to a boil. Add the tofu. Simmer for a few minutes to allow the tofu to absorb the sauce. Add the noodles. Mix everything through and serve hot.

Tofu Stuffed with Shrimp

½ pound firm tofu
2 ounces cooked shrimp,
    peeled and deveined
⅛ teaspoon salt
Pepper to taste
¼ teaspoon cornstarch
½ cup chicken broth
½ teaspoon Chinese rice wine
    or dry sherry

¼ cup water
2 tablespoons oyster sauce
2 tablespoons oil for stir-frying
1 green onion, cut into 1-inch
    pieces

Serves 4

This nutritious dish is
packed with protein.
Serve with a salad for
a complete meal.

1. Drain the tofu. Wash the shrimp and pat dry with paper towels.
   Marinate the shrimp in the salt, pepper, and cornstarch for 15 minutes.
2. Holding the cleaver parallel to the cutting board, cut the tofu in half
   lengthwise. Cut each half into 2 triangles, then cut each triangle into
   2 more triangles. You should now have 8 triangles.
3. Cut a slit lengthwise on one side of the tofu. Stuff ¼–½ teaspoon of
   the shrimp into the slit.
4. Add oil to a preheated wok or skillet. When oil is hot, add the tofu.
   Brown the tofu for about 3–4 minutes, turning it over at least once
   and making sure it doesn't stick to the bottom of the wok. If you have
   leftover shrimp, add it during the last minute of cooking.
5. Add the chicken broth, rice wine, water, and oyster sauce to the
   middle of the wok. Bring to a boil. Turn down the heat, cover, and
   simmer for 5–6 minutes. Stir in the green onion. Serve hot.

Why Drain Tofu?

*Think of a block of tofu as a large white sponge. Just as
you'd want to drain excess water out of a sponge prior to use,
draining the tofu enhances its ability to absorb the flavors of the
food it is cooked with.*

Pressed Bean Curd with Preserved Szechwan Vegetable

Serves 2–4

Find preserved Szechwan vegetable a little too salty? Try soaking it in warm water for 15 minutes prior to stir-frying, or substitute blanched spinach leaves.

7 ounces (2 blocks) pressed bean curd

¼ cup preserved Szechwan vegetable

½ cup chicken stock or broth

1 teaspoon Chinese rice wine or dry sherry

½ teaspoon sugar

½ teaspoon soy sauce

4–5 cups oil for frying

1. Heat at least 4 cups oil in a preheated wok to 350°F. While waiting for the oil to heat, cut the pressed bean curd into 1-inch cubes. Chop the Szechwan vegetable into cubes. Combine the chicken stock and rice wine and set aside.

2. When oil is hot, add the bean curd cubes, and deep-fry until they turn light brown. Remove from the wok with a slotted spoon and set aside.

3. Remove all but 2 tablespoons oil from the wok. Add the preserved Szechwan vegetable. Stir-fry for 1–2 minutes, then push up to the side of the wok. Add the chicken broth mixture in the middle of the wok and bring to a boil. Mix in the sugar and the soy sauce. Add the pressed bean curd. Mix everything together, simmer for a few minutes, and serve hot.

For Salt Lovers

Who said vegetables are bland? Preserved Szechwan vegetable is famous for its salty taste. The round green vegetable with the reddish trim is one of the ingredients that gives Szechwan cuisine its distinctive flavor. Preserved Szechwan vegetable is sold in cans in Asian markets. Stored in a covered jar after opening, it should last for several months. Pickled first in salt and then in chili paste, it can be a bit overpowering, so use sparingly at first.

Twice Cooked Tofu

½ pound firm tofu
2 tablespoons hoisin sauce
2 tablespoons water
½ teaspoon sugar
1 teaspoon ground Toasted
 Szechwan Peppercorns (see
 sidebar on page 91)

1 tablespoon cornstarch
3 cups oil for deep-frying

Serves 4

These tofu cubes make a flavorful addition to stir-fries, cooked noodles, and salad. Cooked Szechwan peppercorns give them an intriguing aroma reminiscent of cinnamon.

1. Preheat oven to 325°F.
2. Drain tofu and cut into ½-inch cubes. Place the tofu cubes on a baking dish.
3. Combine the hoisin sauce, water, and sugar in a small bowl. Spread half the mixture over the tofu cubes. Sprinkle with the Toasted Szechwan Peppercorns. Bake for 15 minutes. Spread the remaining sauce over the tofu and bake for another 15 minutes or until the tofu is browned and cooked.
4. Add oil to a preheated wok and heat to 350°F. While oil is heating, coat the tofu cubes in the cornstarch.
5. When oil is hot, carefully add the tofu cubes into the wok. Deep-fry until browned (this will take 1–2 minutes). Remove and drain on paper towels.

Mapo Dofu (Pockmarked Tofu)

Serves 4

Out of Szechwan peppercorns? Sprinkle the tofu with a bit of freshly ground black pepper.

¾ pound firm tofu
½ pound ground pork
3 tablespoons soy sauce, divided
1½ teaspoons sugar, divided
1½ teaspoons cornstarch
2 stalks bok choy with leaves
1 green onion, chopped
⅔ cup chicken broth
⅓ cup water
1 teaspoon Chinese rice wine
 or dry sherry

½ teaspoon sesame oil
2 tablespoons oil for stir-frying
2 slices ginger, minced
2 garlic cloves, minced
¼ teaspoon chili paste
2 teaspoons cornstarch
4 teaspoons water
1 teaspoon ground Toasted
 Szechwan Peppercorns
 (see sidebar on page 91)

1. Drain the tofu and cut into ½-inch cubes.
2. Place ground pork in a medium bowl. Add 1 tablespoon soy sauce, ½ teaspoon sugar, and cornstarch, adding the cornstarch last. Marinate the pork for 30 minutes.
3. Wash the bok choy and drain thoroughly. Separate the stalks and leaves. Cut into 1-inch pieces. Chop the green onion into 1-inch pieces on the diagonal.
4. Combine the chicken broth, water, 2 tablespoons soy sauce, 1 teaspoon sugar, rice wine, and sesame oil. Set aside.
5. Add oil to a preheated wok or skillet. When oil is hot, add the ginger, garlic, green onion, and chili paste, and stir-fry until aromatic. Add the ground pork. Cook until it changes color, then push up to the side and add the bok choy. Stir-fry until the bok choy turns bright green and tender.
6. Add the sauce to the middle of the wok and bring to a boil. Give the cornstarch-and-water mixture a quick stir and add to the sauce, stirring quickly to thicken. Turn down the heat slightly and add the tofu. Sprinkle the Toasted Szechwan Peppercorns over the tofu. Mix everything through and cook for five more minutes. Serve hot.

Braised Tofu with Three Vegetables

4 dried mushrooms
1/4 cup reserved mushroom
    soaking liquid
2/3 cup fresh mushrooms
1/2 cup chicken broth
1 1/2 tablespoons oyster sauce
1 teaspoon Chinese rice wine
    or dry sherry

2 tablespoons oil for stir-frying
1 garlic clove, minced
1 cup baby carrots, halved
2 teaspoons cornstarch mixed
    with 4 teaspoons water
3/4 pound pressed tofu, cut into
    1/2-inch cubes

Serves 2–4

This recipe can easily
be doubled to serve
as a main dish for
4 people.

1. Soak the dried mushrooms in hot water for at least 20 minutes. Reserve 1/4 cup of the soaking liquid. Slice the dried and fresh mushrooms.
2. Combine the reserved mushroom liquid, chicken broth, oyster sauce, and rice wine. Set aside.
3. Add oil to a preheated wok or skillet. When oil is hot, add the garlic and stir-fry briefly until aromatic. Add the carrots. Stir-fry for 1 minute, then add the mushrooms and stir-fry.
4. Add the sauce and bring to a boil. Give the cornstarch-and-water mixture a stir and add to the sauce, stirring quickly to thicken.
5. Add the tofu cubes. Mix everything together, turn down the heat, and simmer for 5–6 minutes. Serve hot.

Pressed Tofu

With most of the moisture removed, pressed tofu is one of the few types of bean curd that doesn't require draining or soaking before cooking. Its firm texture means it holds its shape, making it an excellent choice for braising and grilling. For a different flavor, try boiling pressed tofu in your favorite tea with sugar.

Pork Filled Tofu Triangles

Serves 8

For variety, try adding fresh shrimp marinated in rice wine to the pork stuffing mixture.

½ pound firm tofu
¼ pound ground pork
⅛ teaspoon salt
Pepper to taste
½ teaspoon Chinese rice wine
   or dry sherry
½ cup chicken broth

¼ cup water
2 tablespoons oyster sauce
2 tablespoons oil for stir-frying
1 green onion, cut into 1-inch
   pieces

1. Drain the tofu. Place the ground pork in a medium bowl. Add the salt, pepper, and rice wine. Marinate the pork for 15 minutes.
2. Holding the cleaver parallel to the cutting board, cut the tofu in half lengthwise. Cut each half into 2 triangles, then cut each triangle into 2 more triangles. You should now have 8 triangles.
3. Cut a slit lengthwise along one of the edges of each tofu triangle. Stuff a heaping ¼ teaspoon of the ground pork into the slit.
4. Add oil to a preheated wok or skillet. When oil is hot, add the tofu. If you have leftover ground pork, add it also. Brown the tofu for about 3–4 minutes, turning it over at least once and making sure it doesn't stick to the bottom of the wok.
5. Add the chicken broth, water, and oyster sauce to the middle of the wok. Bring to a boil. Turn the heat down, cover, and simmer for 5–6 minutes. Stir in the green onion. Serve hot.

Tofu Pudding

⅔ pound (1⅓ cups) soft tofu
8 Chinese dates
1 large banana, sliced

2 tablespoons honey
½ teaspoon powdered ginger

1. Drain the tofu. Soak the Chinese dates in water for 30 minutes or until softened. Cut in half, removing the pit.
2. Process half of the block of tofu in a blender or food processor until smooth. Add the other half and process. Add the banana, honey, dates, and powdered ginger. Process until smooth.
3. Pour into small bowls and chill for 1 hour.

> **Serves 4**
>
> Out of Chinese dates? Try substituting pitted prunes. This pudding makes a great evening snack, as Chinese dates are rumored to help cure insomnia.
>
>

Tea Eggs

6 hard-boiled eggs, cooled
½ cup brewed black tea
1 dried tangerine peel

1 cinnamon stick
3½ cups water

1. Tap each egg very gently with the back of a spoon, until tiny lines form. Try not to actually crack the eggs.
2. Add eggs, black tea, tangerine peel, and cinnamon stick to 3½ cups water and bring to a boil. Simmer, covered, for 2 hours. Turn off the heat, and let the eggs sit in the liquid for a few more hours before serving.
3. To serve, remove the shell and cut into quarters.

> **Serves 6**
>
> This snack puts a new spin on plain hard-boiled eggs. Watch for the "fault" lines traveling down the cooked egg.
>
>

🌿 Cracked Egg
Don't worry if you crack the egg—the effect of the marbled lines crisscrossing the cooked egg should still be visible.

Egg Foo Yung with Shrimp

Serves 4

This is a great dish for a weekend brunch or days when you want to make something special.

½ cup mung bean sprouts
4 snow peas
¼ red bell pepper
2–4 tablespoons oil
1 oyster mushroom cap, thinly sliced
1–2 button mushrooms, thinly sliced
6 eggs

¼ teaspoon salt
⅛ teaspoon pepper
1 tablespoon oyster sauce
½ teaspoon sugar
1 green onion, cut into 1-inch pieces
6 ounces cooked shrimp, peeled and deveined

1. Blanch the bean sprouts and snow peas by plunging them briefly into boiling water and quickly removing. Drain well.
2. Remove the seeds from the red pepper and cut into thin slices about 1 inch long. Chop the snow peas.
3. Add ½ tablespoon oil to a preheated wok or skillet. When oil is hot, sauté the oyster mushroom slices briefly, just until they collapse. (You can sauté the button mushrooms as well or leave them raw.) Remove from the wok and set aside.
4. Lightly beat the eggs. Stir in the salt, pepper, oyster sauce, and sugar. Mix in the vegetables and the cooked shrimp.
5. Add 2 tablespoons oil to a preheated wok or skillet. When the oil is hot, add a quarter of the egg mixture. Cook until the bottom is cooked, then turn over and cook the other side. Continue with the remainder of the egg mixture, adding more oil if necessary, making 4 omelets. Enjoy as is, or serve with Egg Foo Yung Hoisin Sauce (page 204).

Egg Foo Yung Without the Sauce

Although they taste fine on their own, egg foo yung dishes are normally meant to be accompanied by a savory sauce. If not serving a sauce, consider adding small amounts of powerful seasonings such as chili paste or hoisin sauce to the egg mixture.

Veggie Egg Foo Yung

½ red bell pepper
1 cup mung bean sprouts
6 eggs
¼ teaspoon salt
⅛ teaspoon pepper
1 teaspoon Chinese rice wine
  or dry sherry
½ teaspoon sugar

4 mushrooms, thinly sliced
1 green onion, thinly sliced
1 cube fermented bean curd,
  mashed
2–4 tablespoons oil

Serves 4

In this Chinese version of an omelet, the fillings are mixed with the egg prior to cooking, not added in the pan.

1. Remove the seeds from the red pepper and cut into chunks. Blanch the bean sprouts by plunging them briefly into boiling water, and drain.
2. Lightly beat the eggs. Stir in the salt, pepper, rice wine, and sugar. Add the vegetables and mashed bean curd. Mix well.
3. Add 2 tablespoons oil to a preheated wok or skillet. When the oil is hot, add a quarter of the egg mixture. Cook until the bottom is cooked, then turn the omelet over and cook the other side. Continue with the remainder of the mixture, making 4 omelets. Serve with an egg foo yung sauce or soy sauce.

Raw or Cooked?
Lightly cooking vegetables by blanching or sautéing prior to combining with the egg mixture helps coax out their natural flavors. However, if you prefer a crisper texture and higher nutrient content, feel free to skip this step. Another option is to top the egg foo yung with an assortment of raw veggies such as bean sprouts and red and green bell peppers.

Egg Foo Yung with Pork

Serves 6

Barbecued or roast pork works well in this recipe. Be sure to remove any bones before adding the pork to the egg mixture.

¼ red bell pepper
⅔ cup mung bean sprouts
1 stalk celery
1 cup cooked pork, cut into
    small pieces
4–6 tablespoons oil for stir-frying
½ teaspoon salt, divided

6 eggs
⅛ teaspoon pepper
1 teaspoon Chinese rice wine
    or dry sherry
4 button mushroom caps,
    thinly sliced

1. Remove the seeds from the red pepper and cut into thin slices about 1 inch long. Blanch the bean sprouts by plunging briefly into boiling water. Blanch the celery by plunging into the boiling water and boiling for 2–3 minutes. Drain the blanched vegetables thoroughly. Cut the celery into thin slices on the diagonal.
2. Add 2 teaspoons oil to a preheated wok or skillet. When the oil is hot, add the celery and stir-fry on medium high heat. Add ¼ teaspoon salt. Remove the cooked celery from the wok.
3. Lightly beat the eggs. Stir in the pepper, ¼ teaspoon salt, and the rice wine. Add the pork and vegetables, mixing well.
4. Add 2 tablespoons oil to a preheated wok or skillet. When the oil is hot, add one-sixth of the egg mixture. Cook until the bottom is cooked, then turn over and cook the other side. Continue with the remainder of the egg mixture, making 6 omelets. Add more oil while cooking as necessary. Serve with an egg foo yung sauce or soy sauce.

Egg Foo Yung with Chinese Sausage

¼ red bell pepper
½ cup bean sprouts
3 Chinese sausages, cut into
    small pieces
4–6 tablespoons oil for stir-
    frying
1 cabbage leaf, shredded

½ teaspoon salt, divided
6 eggs
⅛ teaspoon pepper
1 teaspoon Chinese rice wine
    or dry sherry
4 button mushroom caps,
    thinly sliced

Serves 6

This Chinese version of eggs and sausages uses Chinese sausage, which is leaner and contains less fat than many pork sausages.

1. Remove the seeds from the red pepper and cut into thin slices about 1 inch long. Blanch the bean sprouts by plunging briefly into boiling water. Drain thoroughly.
2. Add 2 tablespoons oil to a preheated wok or skillet. When the oil is hot, add the cabbage and stir-fry on medium-high heat. Add ¼ teaspoon salt. Remove from the wok.
3. Lightly beat the eggs. Stir in the pepper, ¼ teaspoon salt, and the rice wine. Add the sausage and vegetables, mixing well.
4. Add 2 tablespoons oil to a preheated wok or skillet. When the oil is hot, add ⅙ of the egg mixture. Cook until the bottom is cooked, then turn over and cook the other side. Continue with the remainder of the egg mixture, making 6 omelets. Add more oil while cooking as necessary. Serve with an egg foo yung sauce or soy sauce.

Egg Foo Yung Hoisin Sauce

Yields ⅓ cup

This savory combination of oyster and hoisin sauce makes a nice accompaniment to Egg Foo Yung with Shrimp (page 200).

1 tablespoon oyster sauce
2 teaspoons hoisin sauce
1 teaspoon Chinese rice wine
  or dry sherry

2 tablespoons water
1 teaspoon cornstarch mixed
  with 4 teaspoons water

Bring the oyster sauce, hoisin sauce, rice wine, and water to a boil. Add the cornstarch-and-water mixture and stir vigorously to thicken. Serve with egg foo yung.

Egg Foo Yung Sauce with Beef Broth

Yields ½ cup

This robust sauce goes well with omelet dishes containing meat, such as Egg Foo Yung with Pork (page 202).

½ cup beef broth
1 teaspoon sugar
¼ teaspoon sesame oil

1 tablespoon cornstarch mixed
  with 4 tablespoons water

1. Bring the beef broth, sugar, and sesame oil to a boil.
2. Add the cornstarch-and-water mixture, stirring vigorously. Serve with egg foo yung.

Egg Foo Yung Chicken Sauce

½ cup chicken broth or stock
1 tablespoon soy sauce
1 tablespoon Chinese rice wine
   or dry sherry
¼ teaspoon sesame oil

A pinch of freshly ground
   black pepper

Combine all the ingredients and bring to a boil. Serve with egg
foo yung.

> **Yields ½ cup**
>
> For a thicker sauce, add 1 teaspoon corn-starch mixed with 4 teaspoons water. Pour the sauce over the egg foo yung or serve separately.

Basic Scrambled Eggs

4 large eggs, lightly beaten
¼ cup chicken broth or stock
½ teaspoon Chinese rice wine
   or dry sherry
Up to ⅛ teaspoon salt

Pepper to taste
1½ green onions, thinly sliced
   on the diagonal
2 tablespoons oil for frying

1. Take the beaten eggs and stir in the chicken broth, rice wine, salt, pepper, and green onions.
2. Add the oil to a preheated wok or heavy skillet and turn the heat on high. When oil is hot, add the egg mixture. Scramble gently until the eggs are almost cooked but still moist. Remove from the heat and let sit for a minute before serving.

> **Serves 3–4**
>
> Long cooking chop-sticks are perfect for lightly beating the eggs and scrambling them during cooking.

Scrambled Eggs with Sausage

4 large eggs, lightly beaten
¼ cup beef broth
Salt and pepper to taste
½ teaspoon sugar
1 green onion, thinly sliced on
   the diagonal

2 tablespoons oil for stir-frying
2 Chinese sausages, cut into
   small pieces

1. Take the beaten eggs and stir in the beef broth, salt, pepper, sugar, and green onion.
2. Add 1 tablespoon oil to a preheated wok or skillet. When the oil is hot, add the sausages. Stir-fry until they are cooked and drain on paper towels.
3. Add 1 tablespoon oil and turn the heat on high. When oil is hot, add the egg mixture. Scramble gently for about 30 seconds, then add the sausages. Continue scrambling until the eggs are almost cooked but still moist. Remove from the heat and let sit for a minute before serving.

Red Eggs and Ginger

The Chinese celebrate a baby's one-month birthday by holding a Red Egg and Ginger Party. Like any birthday party, guests bring gifts for the baby. Meanwhile, the proud parents hand out dyed red eggs. In Chinese culture, red symbolizes happiness, while eggs are a symbol of fertility.

Scrambled Eggs with Shrimp

4 ounces shrimp, peeled and
  deveined
4 large eggs, lightly beaten
¼ cup chicken broth or stock
Up to ⅛ teaspoon salt
Pepper to taste

½ teaspoon Chinese rice wine
  or dry sherry
1 teaspoon oyster sauce
1 green onion, thinly sliced on
  the diagonal
2 tablespoons oil for frying

Serves 4

If you wish, marinate
the shrimp in rice wine
or dry sherry and a bit
of cornstarch before
stir-frying.

1. Wash the shrimp and pat dry. Take beaten eggs and stir in the
   chicken broth, salt, pepper, rice wine, oyster sauce, and green onion.
2. Add 1 tablespoon oil to a preheated wok or skillet. When the oil is
   hot, add the shrimp. Stir-fry briefly, until they turn pink. Remove and
   drain.
3. Add 1 tablespoon oil and turn the heat on high. When oil is hot, add
   the egg mixture. Scramble gently for about 1 minute, then add the
   shrimp. Continue scrambling until the eggs are almost cooked but still
   moist. Remove from the heat and let sit for a minute before serving.

Thousand-Year-Old Eggs

*Of course, they're not really 1,000 years old. A better name for
the dark, strongly flavored eggs found in Asian markets is preserved
eggs. Duck eggs are preserved in a mixture of pine ash, clay or
mud, and salt for about 100 days. Refrigerated, thousand-year-old
eggs will last for months, but they do need to be rinsed thoroughly
before eating.*

CHAPTER 10

Fish and Other Seafood

Shrimply Delicious Pork Balls

Yields 12–14 balls

This dish can be pre-pared up to the deep-frying stage and frozen until ready to use. Thaw before deep-frying.

3½ ounces fresh shrimp,
    shells on
¾ pound ground pork
¾ teaspoon grated ginger
2 teaspoons finely minced
    green onion
2 teaspoons finely chopped
    water chestnut
1¼ teaspoons Chinese rice
    wine or dry sherry

⅛ teaspoon salt
Pepper to taste
1 egg
1 teaspoon cornstarch
4–6 cups oil for deep-frying

1. Remove the shells from the shrimp and devein. Mince the shrimp into a fine paste.
2. Add the ground pork to the shrimp. Mix in the ginger, green onion, water chestnut, rice wine, salt, pepper, egg, and cornstarch.
3. Heat oil in a preheated wok to at least 350°F. While oil is heating, shape the shrimp and pork mixture into round balls approximately the size of golf balls.
4. When oil is ready, deep-fry the shrimp-and-pork balls, a few at a time, until they are golden brown. (Make sure the pork is cooked but don't overcook.) Remove from the wok with a slotted spoon and drain on paper towels.

Butter Prawns

2 cups fresh tiger prawns
½ teaspoon Chinese rice wine
   or dry sherry
¼ teaspoon salt
1 teaspoon cornstarch
½ cup chicken broth
1 tablespoon plus 1 teaspoon
   oyster sauce

½ teaspoon sugar
2 tablespoons oil for stir-frying
1 tablespoon butter
1 small garlic clove, minced
½ teaspoon chili sauce with
   garlic

Serves 4–6

Butter prawns taste delicious served with steamed rice, stir-fried noodles, or on toasted French bread.

1. Shell and devein the prawns. Rinse in warm water and pat dry with paper towels. Marinate the prawns in the rice wine, salt, and cornstarch for 15 minutes.
2. Combine the chicken broth, oyster sauce, and sugar, and set aside.
3. Add oil to a preheated wok or skillet. When oil is hot, add the prawns and stir-fry briefly, until they turn pink. Remove and drain on paper towels.
4. Add the butter, garlic, and chili sauce with garlic. Stir-fry briefly, then add the prawns. Stir-fry for about a minute, mixing the prawns in with the butter, then add the sauce. Bring the sauce to a boil. Mix the sauce with the prawns and serve hot.

How to Devein a Prawn
Deveining a prawn or shrimp removes the gray, threadlike intestinal track running along its back. To devein, peel the prawn or shrimp. Take a sharp knife and cut a slit down the back. Remove the vein.

Spicy Fish Fry

½ pound fish fillets
½ cup chicken broth
1 teaspoon brown sugar
1 teaspoon black rice vinegar
1 green onion

3 tablespoons oil for stir-frying
½ tablespoon minced ginger
¼ teaspoon chili paste
1 cup fresh mushrooms, sliced

1. Wash the fish fillets and pat dry. Cut into slices approximately 2 inches by ½ inch.
2. Combine the chicken broth, brown sugar, and black rice vinegar. Set aside. Cut the green onion into 1-inch slices on the diagonal.
3. Add 2 tablespoons oil to a preheated wok or skillet. When oil is hot, add the fish pieces. Stir-fry until browned. Remove from the wok and drain on paper towels.
4. Add 1 tablespoon oil to the wok. Add the ginger and chili paste and stir-fry until aromatic. Add the mushrooms. Stir-fry until tender, then push up to the sides of the wok. Add the sauce in the middle of the wok and bring to a boil. Add the fish and stir in the green onion. Mix through and serve hot.

Fish Tales

Fish plays an important role in Chinese celebrations. It is common to serve a whole fish on special occasions, as it symbolizes wealth and abundance. If entertaining, the head is pointed toward the guest of honor.

Stir-fried Fish Fillets

½ pound fish fillets
1 teaspoon Chinese rice wine
   or dry sherry
1 tablespoon soy sauce
2 green onions, divided
2 tablespoons oil for stir-frying

½ cup chicken broth
2 tablespoons oyster sauce
2 teaspoons brown sugar
¼ teaspoon sesame oil
½ tablespoon minced ginger

> **Serves 2–4**
>
> Cod fillets work well in this dish. Serve with rice and stir-fried vegetables for a healthy, protein-packed meal.
>
>

1. Wash the fish fillets and pat dry with paper towels. Marinate in the rice wine, soy sauce, and 1 sliced green onion for 30 minutes.
2. Combine the chicken broth, oyster sauce, brown sugar, and sesame oil. Set aside. Cut the remaining green onion into 1-inch pieces.
3. Add oil to a preheated wok or skillet. When oil is hot, add the ginger. Stir-fry briefly until aromatic. Add the fish fillets and cook until they are browned on both sides (2–3 minutes on each side).
4. Add the sauce in the middle of the wok and bring to a boil. Stir in the green onion. Reduce the heat, cover, and simmer for about 10 minutes. Serve hot.

Lumpy Brown Sugar

One of the less attractive features of brown sugar is its tendency to form lumps. This happens when the sugar loses moisture and hardens. There are several ways to remove lumps. First, if the sugar is being used in a hot sauce, simply melt it to remove the lumps before adding to the sauce. Stir constantly while the sugar is melting in the saucepan. If the recipe calls for dry sugar, use a strainer to squeeze out the lumps. Several techniques exist for adding the moisture back into the sugar, but these normally take several days.

Honey Walnut Shrimp

Yields 2 cups

The sweet flavor of coconut milk nicely balances the tart lemon in this popular restaurant dish.

½ cup chopped walnut pieces
¼ cup sugar
½ pound shrimp
1 egg, lightly beaten
4 tablespoons cornstarch
1½ tablespoons honey
3 tablespoons mayonnaise

3¾ teaspoons freshly squeezed lemon juice
3 tablespoons coconut milk
3 cups oil for deep-frying

1. Earlier in the day, boil the walnut pieces for 5 minutes. Drain well. Spread the sugar on a piece of wax paper. Roll the walnut pieces in the sugar and allow to dry.
2. Peel and devein the shrimp. Wash and pat dry with paper towels.
3. Heat oil to 375°F. While waiting for oil to heat, mix the egg with the cornstarch to form a batter. Dip the shrimp in the egg batter. Deep-fry the shrimp until they turn golden brown. Remove from the wok with a slotted spoon and drain on paper towels. Cool.
4. Combine the honey, mayonnaise, lemon juice, and coconut milk. Mix in with the shrimp. Serve on a platter with the sugared walnuts arranged around the shrimp.

Prawns versus Shrimp

If you think a prawn and a shrimp look nearly identical, you're right. One type of prawn is merely an oversized shrimp. (The word prawn is also given to another type of crustacean related to the lobster.) Prawns can be substituted for shrimp in most recipes—just be sure to adjust for differences in volume where necessary.

Kung Pao Shrimp

1 pound shrimp, peeled and deveined
½ cup chicken broth
2 tablespoons Chinese rice wine or dry sherry
2 teaspoons soy sauce

2½–3 tablespoons oil for stir-frying
2 slices ginger, minced
¼ teaspoon chili paste
½ cup peanuts

Serves 4

This simple dish makes an excellent appetizer as well as main course. Like Kung Pao Chicken, it can also be made with cashews instead of peanuts.

1. Wash the shrimp and pat dry with paper towels. Combine the chicken broth, rice wine, and soy sauce, and set aside.
2. Add 1½ tablespoons oil to a preheated wok or skillet. When oil is hot, add the shrimp. Stir-fry very briefly, just until they change color. Remove and set aside.
3. Add 1 tablespoon oil to the wok. When oil is hot, add the ginger and chili paste. Stir-fry briefly until aromatic. Add the peanuts. Stir-fry for about 1 minute until they turn golden but are not burnt.
4. Push the peanuts up to the side of the wok. Add the sauce to the middle of the wok and bring to a boil. Add the shrimp back into the wok. Mix everything together and serve hot.

Storing Ginger

Ginger will keep for several days when stored in a paper bag that is kept in the vegetable crisper section of the refrigerator. For longer storage, place the ginger in a sealed container, fill with Chinese rice wine or a good pale, dry sherry, and store in the refrigerator. As the ginger flavor fades, you will have the flavor of the sherry to compensate.

Shrimp Paste

½ pound (8 ounces) shrimp, peeled and deveined
1 tablespoon plus 1 teaspoon vegetable shortening
½ teaspoon grated ginger
2 teaspoons minced green onion
2 teaspoons finely minced water chestnut
½ teaspoon Chinese rice wine or dry sherry
⅛ teaspoon salt
Pepper to taste
1 medium egg
1 tablespoon plus 1 teaspoon cornstarch

1. Rinse the shrimp in warm water and pat dry with paper towels. Purée the shrimp and the vegetable shortening in a food processor or blender. Add the ginger, green onion, water chestnut, rice wine, salt, and pepper. Purée.
2. Lightly beat the egg. Mix in the shrimp and vegetable mixture. Add the cornstarch, using your hands to mix it in. The shrimp paste is now ready.

Traditional Shrimp Toast

12–15 slices of white bread, crusts removed
Shrimp Paste
4–6 cups oil for deep-frying

1. Add oil to a preheated wok and heat to 350°F. While oil is heating, cut each slice of bread into 4 triangles. Spread up to ½ teaspoon of shrimp paste on each bread piece.
2. When oil is hot, carefully add the bread into the wok. Cook for 2 minutes on one side, then turn over and cook for 2 minutes on the other side. Remove and drain on paper towels. Serve immediately.

Quick and Easy Shrimp Toast

7 ounces shrimp
½ teaspoon grated ginger
2 teaspoons finely minced
   green onion
2 teaspoons finely chopped
   water chestnut
½ teaspoon Chinese rice wine
   or dry sherry

⅛ teaspoon salt
Pepper to taste
1 egg
1 teaspoon cornstarch
8 slices bread
¼ cup water
4–6 cups oil for deep-frying

> **Serves 4**
>
> This recipe makes a quick and easy lunch or snack. For a more formal dish, try Traditional Shrimp Toast (page 216) or Crispy Fried Shrimp Toast (page 218).
>
>

1. Remove the shells from the shrimp and devein. Mince the shrimp into a fine paste.
2. Mix in the ginger, green onion, water chestnut, rice wine, salt, pepper, egg, and cornstarch.
3. Add the oil to a preheated wok and heat to at least 350°F. While oil is heating, break each slice of bread into 4 equal squares. Dip briefly into the water, remove, and use your fingers to squeeze out excess water.
4. Spread a heaping teaspoon of the shrimp mixture onto each square of bread. When oil is hot, slide a few of the squares into the hot oil. Fry one side until it turns brown (about 1 minute), then turn over and brown the other side. Remove from the wok with a slotted spoon and drain on paper towels. Continue with the remainder of the bread squares.

Crispy Fried Shrimp Toast

Yields 25 appetizers

This recipe can also be made with prawns. For added flavor, serve with a bowl of dipping sauce such as Speedy Sweet Chili Sauce (page 26).

¾ cup flour
1 teaspoon baking powder
½ teaspoon sugar
¼ teaspoon salt
2 tablespoons vegetable oil
¾ cup water

6 slices white bread, crusts removed
Shrimp Paste (page 216)
4–6 cups oil for deep-frying

1. Sift together the flour and baking powder. Stir in the sugar, salt, and vegetable oil. Slowly stir in the water, adding more or less as needed to make a batter.
2. Add oil to a preheated wok and heat to 360°F. While oil is heating, cut each slice of bread into 4 triangles. Spread ½ teaspoon of shrimp paste on each side of the triangle.
3. When ready to cook, use your fingers to coat the bread with the batter. Carefully add the bread into the wok, a few slices at a time. Cook on one side for 2 minutes, then turn over and cook the other side for 2 minutes or until the batter has turned golden brown. Remove and drain on paper towels.

Quick and Easy Shrimp Paste
To make shrimp paste, finely mince the shrimp, then hold the cleaver parallel to the cutting board and use it to drag the shrimp along the board.

Butterfly Prawns

10 large tiger prawns
1 large egg
½ teaspoon Szechwan pepper-
corns, roasted and ground

5 tablespoons breadcrumbs
3–4 cups oil for deep-frying

1. Remove the shells from the prawns, but leave the tails intact. Rinse the prawns in warm water. Pat dry with paper towels.
2. Lightly beat the egg. In a separate bowl, mix the Szechwan peppercorns with the breadcrumbs.
3. Add oil to a preheated wok and heat to at least 350°F. To prepare prawns for deep-frying, grab by the tail and dip into the beaten egg, then coat with the breadcrumbs.
4. When oil is hot, deep-fry the prawns until they turn golden brown (about 1 minute). Remove and drain on paper towels. Serve warm.

> **Yields 10 prawns**
>
> This dish tastes delicious with stir-fried spinach or Chinese greens. For added flavor, serve with a dipping sauce.
>
>

Fried Prawn Crackers

1 package prawn crackers
4–6 cups oil for deep-frying

Heat oil to 350°F, and deep-fry the crackers. They will puff up within seconds. Remove immediately and drain on paper towels.

> **Serves 6**
>
> These delicate crackers make a tasty appetizer or snack. Be sure to remove them from the hot oil as soon as they puff up.
>
>

Sweet-and-Sour Shrimp

Serves 2–4

The delicate sweet flavor of pineapple goes well with shrimp. Serve with Basic Scented Rice (page 80).

20 large fresh shrimp, peeled and deveined
1/2 green bell pepper
1/2 red bell pepper
1/3 cup rice vinegar
1/4 cup brown sugar
2 tablespoons ketchup
1 tablespoon soy sauce
1/2 cup water
2 teaspoons cornstarch mixed with 4 teaspoons water
1/2 cup pineapple chunks
2 tablespoons oil for stir-frying

1. Rinse the shrimp in warm water and pat dry with paper towels. Wash the peppers, remove the seeds, and cut into cubes.
2. In a small saucepan, combine the rice vinegar, brown sugar, ketchup, soy sauce, and water, and bring to a boil.
3. Stir in the cornstarch-and-water mixture, stirring vigorously to thicken. Add the pineapple and peppers. Turn the heat to low and keep the sauce warm while stir-frying the shrimp.
4. Add oil to a preheated wok or skillet. When oil is hot, add the shrimp. Stir-fry briefly until they are cooked. Remove from the wok.
5. Pour the sauce over the shrimp and serve hot.

Daily Rice Bowl

Rice is so important in southern China that the phrase for eating includes the word "rice." And instead of saying hello, people greet each other by asking, "Have you eaten yet?"

Lobster Cantonese

1 teaspoon fermented black
    beans
1 clove garlic, minced
¾ cup chicken broth
2 tablespoons Chinese rice
    wine or dry sherry, divided
1 tablespoon soy sauce
2 tablespoons oil for stir-frying
¼ pound ground pork

3 slices ginger, minced
1 green onion, thinly sliced
1 tablespoon cornstarch mixed
    with 4 tablespoons water
2 lobster tails, cut into ½-inch
    pieces
1 teaspoon sugar
1 egg, lightly beaten

> **Serves 2**
>
> The secret to preparing this popular Cantonese dish is not to overcook the lobster tails.
>
>

1. Soak the beans in warm water and rinse. Mash, chop finely, and mix with the garlic clove.
2. Combine the chicken broth, 1 tablespoon rice wine, and soy sauce. Set aside.
3. Add oil to a preheated wok or skillet. When oil is hot, add the garlic and black bean mixture. Stir-fry briefly until aromatic. Add the pork and stir-fry for several minutes, until cooked through.
4. Push the ingredients up to the side of the wok. Add the ginger and green onion in the middle. Stir-fry briefly. Add the sauce and bring to a boil. Give the cornstarch-and-water mixture a quick stir and add, stirring quickly to thicken.
5. Add the lobster, the sugar, and 1 tablespoon rice wine. Stir-fry for about 2 minutes, then stream in the egg. Mix together and serve.

Preparing Fermented Black Beans
Soak the beans until they are softened. Mash the beans by flattening them under the blade of a knife or cleaver, and then mince or chop as called for in the recipe.

Pepper-Salt Shrimp or Prawns

1 pound fresh shrimp or prawns, peeled and deveined
2 egg whites
¼ cup cornstarch

2 tablespoons Szechwan Salt and Pepper Mix (page 20)
1–2 cups oil for deep-frying

1. Wash and pat dry the shrimp or prawns with paper towels.
2. Heat oil in a preheated wok to 375°F. While oil is heating, mix the egg whites with cornstarch to form a smooth batter.
3. Lightly coat the shrimp with the Szechwan Salt and Pepper Mix. Dip into the batter. Place a few shrimp at a time into the wok. Deep-fry until they turn golden brown (about 3 minutes). Remove and drain on paper towels.

Deep-fried Fish

½ pound fish fillets
1 egg white
2 teaspoons soy sauce

1 tablespoon cornstarch
4 cups oil for deep-frying

1. Wash fish and pat dry. Cut into bite-sized squares. Add the egg white, soy sauce, and cornstarch, adding the cornstarch last. Marinate the fish for 30 minutes.
2. Heat oil in a preheated wok to 375°F. When oil is hot, add the fish. Fry until golden brown. Remove and drain on paper towels.

Hot and Sour Prawns

2 cups fresh tiger prawns
½ teaspoon Chinese rice wine
   or dry sherry
¼ teaspoon salt
1 teaspoon cornstarch
½ cup water
2 tablespoons black rice vinegar

½–1 teaspoon Hot Chili Oil
   (page 23)
1½ teaspoons Worcestershire
   sauce
2 teaspoons cornstarch mixed
   with 4 teaspoons water
2 tablespoons oil for stir-frying

> **Serves 4–6**
>
> This hot dish is a great way to enliven plain stir-fried or boiled noodles or steamed rice.
>
>

1. Shell and devein the prawns. Rinse in warm water and pat dry with paper towels. Marinate the prawns in the rice wine, salt, and cornstarch for 15 minutes.
2. In a small saucepan, bring the water, black rice vinegar, Hot Chili Oil, and Worcestershire sauce to a boil. Add the cornstarch-and-water mixture, stirring quickly to thicken. Turn the heat to low and keep warm.
3. Add oil to a preheated wok or skillet. When oil is hot, add the prawns and stir-fry briefly, until they turn pink. Push up to the side and add the sauce in the middle of the wok. Mix the prawns with the sauce. Serve hot.

Yin and Yang Harmony

The philosophy of yin and yang permeates every aspect of Chinese culture, including the kitchens of its cooks. Yin and yang represent all the forces in the universe. Things that are feminine, cold, dark, or submissive are said to be yin in nature, while masculinity, heat, light, and dominance are yang forces. Chinese physicians frequently treat illness as an imbalance between yin and yang in the body. For example, since heartburn is thought to come from consuming too many spicy yang foods, a physician might prescribe a soup featuring yin ingredients like walnuts as a tonic.

Sweet-and-Sour Fish

1 pound fish fillets
2 teaspoons Chinese rice wine
   or dry sherry
2 tablespoons soy sauce
½ cup rice vinegar
½ cup brown sugar
½ cup water
3 tablespoons tomato paste
3–4 tablespoons oil for stir-
   frying

2 slices ginger, minced
1 cup mushrooms, thinly sliced
1 stalk celery, thinly sliced on
   the diagonal
⅓ cup canned bamboo shoots,
   shredded
1 teaspoon cornstarch
4 teaspoons water
1 green onion, thinly sliced on
   the diagonal

1. Wash fish fillets and pat dry. Cut into pieces approximately 2 inches by ½ inch. Marinate in the rice wine and soy sauce for 30 minutes.
2. Combine the rice vinegar, brown sugar, water, and tomato paste. Set aside.
3. Add 2 tablespoons oil to a preheated wok or skillet. When oil is hot, add the fish and stir-fry until it is nicely browned all over. Remove and drain on paper towels.
4. Add 1 tablespoon oil to the wok. Add the ginger and stir-fry briefly until aromatic. Add the mushrooms. Stir-fry for a minute, then add the celery and the bamboo shoots. Stir-fry until tender, adding salt or sugar to season if desired.
5. Push the vegetables up to the side of the wok and add the sauce in the middle. Bring to a boil. Mix the cornstarch and water, and add to the wok, stirring quickly to thicken. Add the fish and stir in the green onion. Cook for a few more minutes and serve hot.

Prawns with Mangetout (Snow Peas)

20 fresh prawns
1 teaspoon sugar
1 teaspoon cornstarch
1 cup (about 25) snow peas
½ cup mung bean sprouts
2 tablespoons oil for stir-frying

1 slice ginger, finely chopped
1½ teaspoons Chinese rice
  wine or dry sherry

Serves 2–4
Serve on a bed of steamed rice mixed with green onion, garnished with slices of orange.

1. Shell and devein the prawns. Rinse in warm water and pat dry with paper towels. Marinate in the sugar and cornstarch for 15 minutes.
2. Wash and string the snow peas. Blanch the snow peas and bean sprouts by plunging briefly into boiling water. Drain thoroughly.
3. Add oil to a preheated wok or skillet. When oil is hot, add the ginger and stir-fry briefly until aromatic. Add the prawns and stir-fry briefly until they turn a pinkish-red color.
4. Add the snow peas to the wok. Stir-fry briefly, then add the bean sprouts. Splash with the 1½ teaspoons rice wine. Serve hot.

Mung Bean Sprouts

While raw mung bean sprouts are a popular salad topping in the West, the Chinese prefer their sprouts cooked. Mung bean sprouts feature prominently in stir-fries and appetizers. When choosing mung bean sprouts, look for ones that are plump and don't have any brown coloring. If using within a few days, store the sprouts with a few drops of water in a plastic bag in the refrigerator. They can also be frozen for use later in stir-fries, although the texture won't be as crisp.

Spicy Shrimp with Hot Shanghai Noodles

Serves 4

Adding the hot bean sauce after the noodles helps reduce its strength. Use sparingly at first, and add more to taste if desired.

10 ounces cooked shrimp
¼ teaspoon five-spice powder
½ teaspoon cornstarch
2 stalks bok choy
4 tablespoons oil for stir-frying
2 leaves cabbage, shredded
1 teaspoon soy sauce

2 garlic cloves, finely chopped
2 slices ginger, finely chopped
¾ pound fresh Shanghai
   noodles
1 tablespoon hot bean sauce,
   or to taste

1. Rinse the shrimp in warm water and pat dry. Marinate the shrimp in the five-spice powder and cornstarch for at least 15 minutes.
2. Wash the bok choy and drain thoroughly. Separate the stalks and leaves. Cut across the leaves and cut the stalks into 1-inch pieces on the diagonal.
3. Add 2 tablespoons oil to a preheated wok or skillet. When oil is hot, add the shrimp and stir-fry briefly until it changes color. Push the shrimp up to the side and add the bok choy stalks and cabbage. Stir-fry briefly, then add the bok choy leaves. Add 1 teaspoon soy sauce, and stir-fry until the vegetables turn a bright color and are tender. Remove from the wok and set aside.
4. Add 2 tablespoons oil to the wok or skillet. When oil is hot, add the garlic and ginger. Stir-fry briefly until aromatic. Add the noodles. Stir-fry briefly, then mix in the hot bean sauce. If necessary, add 2 tablespoons water. Add the shrimp and vegetables. Mix everything through and serve hot.

Sweet-and-Sour Fish with Lychees

1 pound fish fillets
2 egg whites
4 teaspoons soy sauce
2 tablespoons cornstarch
1 cup lychees, drained
½ cup rice vinegar
½ cup brown sugar

½ cup water
3 tablespoons tomato paste
1 tablespoon minced ginger
1 green onion, thinly sliced
1 teaspoon cornstarch mixed
    with 4 teaspoons water
4 cups oil for frying

Serves 4–6

The Chinese consider the heart-shaped lychee to be a symbol of romance. Its sweet flavor goes very well with a sweet-and-sour sauce.

1. Wash the fish and pat dry with paper towels. Cut into thin slices.
2. Add the egg whites, soy sauce, and cornstarch, adding the cornstarch last. Marinate the fish for 30 minutes. Cut the lychees in half if desired.
3. Bring the rice vinegar, brown sugar, water, and tomato paste to boil in a small saucepan. Stir in the lychees. Keep warm.
4. Heat oil in a preheated wok to 375°F. When oil is hot, add the fish. Deep-fry until golden brown. Remove and drain on paper towels.
5. Remove all but 2 tablespoons oil from the wok. Add the ginger and stir-fry briefly until aromatic. Add the green onion. Add the sauce and bring to a boil. Give the cornstarch-and-water mixture a quick stir. Add, stirring to thicken. Reduce the heat. Add the fish. Mix through and serve hot.

Lychee Lore

Native to southern China, lychees hold a special place in Chinese food culture. Successions of Emperors prized the small, heart-shaped fruit for its sweet flavor. An exiled Chinese poet is reputed to have consoled himself by consuming 300 lychees daily. Nutritionally, lychees are low in calories and a good source of vitamin C. Fresh lychees come into season during the summer months; they are available canned in syrup year-round. Both are sold in Asian markets.

Shrimp with Lobster Sauce

Serves 4

For a fancier presentation, butterfly the shrimp by removing the shell but leaving the tail intact. Prepare the sauce separately and pour over the shrimp.

½ pound medium shrimp
1 teaspoon fermented black beans
1 clove garlic, minced
¾ cup chicken broth
2 tablespoons Chinese rice wine or dry sherry, divided
1 tablespoon soy sauce

¼ pound ground pork
4 tablespoons oil for stir-frying
1 tablespoon cornstarch
4 tablespoons water
1 teaspoon sugar
1 egg, lightly beaten

1. Shell and devein shrimp.
2. Add 2 tablespoons oil to a preheated wok or skillet. When oil is hot, add the shrimp. Stir-fry until they turn pink and are nearly cooked. Remove from the wok and drain on paper towels.
3. To prepare the lobster sauce: Soak the fermented black beans in warm water and rinse. Mash, chop finely, and mix with the garlic clove. Combine the chicken broth, 1 tablespoon rice wine, and soy sauce. Set aside.
4. Add 1–2 tablespoons oil. When oil is hot, add the garlic and black bean mixture. Stir-fry briefly until aromatic. Add the pork and stir-fry for several minutes, until cooked through.
5. Push the ingredients up to the side of the wok. Add the sauce and bring to a boil. Mix cornstarch and water and add to the wok, stirring quickly to thicken.
6. Mix in the sugar, and 1 tablespoon rice wine. Stream in the egg. Add the shrimp. Mix together and serve hot.

Shrimp with Lobster Sauce
The name of this dish can be confusing, since it doesn't contain any lobster. It derives its name from the dried black beans that lend a savory flavor to the sauce. Fermented black beans are also a key ingredient in Lobster Cantonese (page 221).

Quick and Easy Salt and Pepper Squid

1 pound cleaned squid
2 teaspoons Szechwan Salt
*   and Pepper Mix (page 20)*
¼ cup cornstarch
2 tablespoons soy sauce
1 tablespoon Chinese rice wine
*   or dry sherry*
1 teaspoon sugar

½ teaspoon sesame oil
½ teaspoon Hot Chili Oil
*   (page 23)*
1 clove garlic, minced
2 slices ginger, minced
2–3 cups oil for frying

> **Serves 4**
>
> The trick to this dish is not to overcook the seafood. When cooked too long, squid turns rubbery.

1. Cut the cleaned squid into 1-inch pieces.
2. In a bowl, mix the Szechwan Salt and Pepper Mix in with the cornstarch. In a separate bowl, combine the soy sauce, rice wine, sugar, sesame oil, and Hot Chili Oil. Set aside.
3. Add oil to a preheated wok or skillet. While oil is heating, dip the squid pieces in the Szechwan Salt and Pepper and cornstarch mixture.
4. When oil is hot, add the squid pieces, a few at a time. Deep-fry for about 2 minutes, until they change color. Remove and drain on paper towels.
5. Remove all but 2 tablespoons oil from the wok. Add the ginger and garlic, and stir-fry briefly until aromatic. Add the sauce in the middle of the wok and bring to a boil. Add the squid and cook very briefly. Mix through and serve hot.

Stir-fried Water Chestnuts and Bamboo Shoots

2 tablespoons oil for stir-frying
1 teaspoon minced ginger
1 8-ounce can bamboo shoots, rinsed and drained
¼ teaspoon salt
1 can water chestnuts, rinsed and drained
½ cup chicken broth

1 tablespoon soy sauce
1 teaspoon sugar
1 green onion, cut into 1½-inch pieces

1. Cut the water chestnuts in half.
2. Add the oil to a preheated wok or skillet. When the oil is hot, add the ginger. Stir-fry briefly until aromatic. Add the bamboo shoots. Stir-fry for 1–2 minutes, and add the salt. Mix in and add the water chestnuts. Stir-fry for 1–2 more minutes, and then add the chicken broth, soy sauce, and sugar.
3. Bring the broth to a boil, and then turn down the heat and simmer for a few more minutes, until everything is nicely cooked through. Stir in the green onion and serve.

Stir-frying in Order

Stir-fry vegetables according to density, adding the thickest vegetables to the wok first, so that they cook longest. If you're uncertain about the correct order, just stir-fry all the vegetables separately and add back into the wok during the final stages of cooking.

Snow Pea Stir-fry

2 cups snow peas
1½ tablespoons oil for stir-
    frying

¾ teaspoon sugar
1½ tablespoons Chinese rice
    wine or dry sherry

Serves 4

Serve as a side dish
with Lemony Chicken
Stir-fry (page 159),
or use where snow
peas are called
for in recipes.

1. Wash and string the snow peas. In a frying pan or preheated wok, add the oil.
2. When oil is hot, begin stir-frying the snow peas. Add the sugar and rice wine.
3. Stir-fry until the snow peas turn a bright green and are hot.

Parsnips with Creamy Sauce

1 tablespoon cornstarch
6 tablespoons water, divided
1½ tablespoons oil for stir-
    frying
3 parsnips, sliced on the
    diagonal

1 teaspoon brown sugar
⅛ teaspoon salt, or to taste
½ cup milk

Serves 3–4

While milk isn't nor-
mally used in Chinese
cooking, it is found in
this variation on a
popular northern
Chinese dish.

1. In a small bowl, mix the cornstarch with 2 tablespoons water.
2. Add oil to a preheated wok or skillet. When oil is hot, add the parsnips. Stir-fry for about 1 minute. Add 4 tablespoons water, brown sugar, and salt. Cover and cook on medium heat for about another 5 minutes.
3. Give the cornstarch-and-water mixture a quick stir and add it to the milk. Push the parsnips up the side of the wok and add the cornstarch and milk mixture in the middle. Turn up the heat and stir rapidly to thicken.

Glazed Carrots

2 tablespoons oil for stir-frying
4 large carrots, julienned
4 teaspoons soy sauce

1/2 teaspoon brown sugar
1/2 cup chicken broth or water

1. Add oil to a preheated wok or frying pan. When oil is hot, add the carrots. Stir-fry for 2–3 minutes. Add the soy sauce.
2. Add the brown sugar and broth. Turn the heat down to medium-low and simmer, covered for about 5 or 6 minutes, until the carrots are tender.

Stir-fried Spinach

18 spinach leaves
1 tablespoon oil for stir-frying

1/4 teaspoon sugar
1/4 teaspoon salt

1. Wash the spinach leaves. Blanch the spinach in boiling water briefly, just until the leaves begin to wilt. Drain well.
2. Add oil to a preheated wok or skillet. When the oil is hot, add the spinach. Add the sugar and salt and stir-fry briefly, for less than a minute. Serve hot.

Stir-fried Bok Choy

1 bok choy
2 tablespoons oil for stir-frying
¼ teaspoon salt
1½ tablespoons water

Serves 2–4

Serve on the side, or use to enliven a basic meat dish such as Basic Chicken Stir-fry (page 152).

1. Separate each stalk and leaves. Cut the stalks diagonally into 1-inch pieces. Cut the leaves crosswise into 1-inch pieces.
2. Add the oil to a preheated wok or skillet. When oil is hot, add the bok choy stalks. Stir-fry for about 1 minute and then add the leaves. Add salt, sprinkle the water over, and cover and cook on medium heat, until the bok choy is tender but still firm and not mushy.

Better Bok Choy
For best results, always separate bok choy stalks from the leaves prior to stir-frying, as the thick stalks take longer to cook.

Stir-fried Bean Sprouts

1 tablespoon oil for stir-frying
1 cup mung bean sprouts, rinsed and drained
1 tablespoon red rice vinegar
½ teaspoon sugar
¼ teaspoon salt

Serves 4

Tart red rice vinegar contrasts nicely with sweet mung bean sprouts in this quick and easy stir-fry.

1. Add the oil to a frying pan or preheated wok. When the oil is hot, add the bean sprouts and stir-fry rapidly for less than a minute.
2. Add the rice vinegar, sugar, and salt. Stir-fry for another few seconds and serve hot.

Spruced Up Sprouts
Silver sprouts are bean sprouts that have been trimmed at the ends, or "topped and tailed." It gives the sprouts a nicer appearance, but unless you're entertaining it isn't really worth the extra effort.

Sweet-and-Sour Chinese Greens

Serves 4

Both bok choy and napa cabbage can be found in the produce section of most supermarkets.

½ pound bok choy
½ pound napa cabbage
2 tablespoons oil for stir-frying
¼ teaspoon salt

2¼ teaspoons sugar, divided
¼ cup water
3 tablespoons black rice vinegar

1. Separate the bok choy stalks and leaves. Cut the stalk diagonally into 1-inch pieces. Cut the leaves crosswise into 1-inch pieces. Cut the cabbage leaves by piling the leaves on top of each other and cutting lengthwise and then crosswise into 1-inch pieces.
2. Add oil to a preheated wok or skillet. When oil is hot, add the bok choy stalks. Stir-fry for a minute, then add the bok choy leaves and the cabbage. Stir-fry for another minute. Add the salt, ¼ teaspoon sugar, and the water. Cover and cook for 2–3 minutes on medium heat, until the vegetables are tender but still firm.
3. Remove the cover and add the black rice vinegar and 2 teaspoons sugar. Mix thoroughly with the bok choy and cabbage.

Substituting Vinegar
To replace the rice vinegar in this recipe with white distilled vinegar, use 3 tablespoons of distilled vinegar to 2 teaspoons of brown sugar. Increase the amount of brown sugar if the vinegar flavor is a little too overpowering.

Steamed Broccoli

1 pound broccoli
2 tablespoons light soy sauce
1 tablespoon rice wine or dry sherry
1 teaspoon minced ginger

1 tablespoon finely chopped green onion, the green part only
¼ teaspoon sesame oil

1. Wash the broccoli and drain. Break off the flowerets and cut in half. Cut the spears on the diagonal into thin slices. Steam the broccoli until tender.
2. Mix together the other ingredients and pour over the broccoli.

Serves 4

Looking for an alternative to beef and broccoli with oyster sauce? Try this side dish with a beef stir-fry. Experiment with substituting seasonal vegetables.

Mangetout and Bean Sprouts

1 cup mangetout (snow peas)
1 cup mung bean sprouts, rinsed and drained
1½ tablespoons oil for stir-frying

¾ teaspoon sugar
1 tablespoon Chinese rice wine or dry sherry

1. String the snow peas. Blanch both the vegetables by plunging them briefly into boiling water and quickly removing. Drain well.
2. Add the oil to a preheated wok or skillet. When the oil is hot, begin stir-frying the snow peas. Stir-fry for a minute and add the bean sprouts. Add the sugar and rice wine. Stir-fry until the snow peas turn a bright green and are hot.

Serves 4

Blanching vegetables prior to stir-frying helps them retain their vivid colors and reduces the cooking time.

Mushrooms and Bamboo Shoots

8 dried mushrooms
½ cup reserved mushroom
    soaking liquid
1 8-ounce can bamboo shoots,
    rinsed and drained
2 tablespoons dark soy sauce

2 teaspoons sugar
2 tablespoons oil for stir-frying
1 tablespoon cornstarch mixed
    with 4 tablespoons water

1. Soak the mushrooms in hot water for 20 minutes to soften or reconstitute. Reserve the soaking liquid. Give the reconstituted mushrooms a gentle squeeze to remove excess water and thinly slice.
2. Cut the bamboo shoots in half, so they are approximately 1 inch in length. Mix together the dark soy sauce and sugar and set aside.
3. Add the oil to a preheated wok or heavy skillet. When oil is hot, add the bamboo shoots. Stir-fry for a minute and add the mushrooms.
4. Add the dark soy sauce and sugar, and the reserved mushroom liquid. Turn the heat down to low, cover, and simmer the vegetables for 10 minutes.
5. Give the cornstarch-and-water mixture a quick stir. Turn the heat up and push the vegetables up to the side of the wok. Add the cornstarch/water in the middle, stirring quickly to thicken. Mix through and serve hot.

Don't Discard the Soaking Liquid

The soaking liquid from reconstituted (softened) ingredients like dried mushrooms and wood fungus makes a flavorful substitute for water in recipes. Before using, strain the water to remove any gritty particles. Vegetarians can use the reconstituted liquid in place of chicken broth.

Mushrooms and Cabbage

4 dried mushrooms
1 8-ounce can bamboo shoots,
   drained, rinsed and drained
2 cabbage leaves
2 tablespoons light soy sauce
1 tablespoon dark soy sauce

3 teaspoons sugar
2 tablespoons oil for stir-frying
6 fresh mushrooms, sliced
½ cup water
1 tablespoon cornstarch
4 tablespoons water

Serves 2

The combination of fresh and dried mushrooms gives this dish a more elegant appearance. Feel free to use either napa or other types of cabbage.

1. Soak the dried mushrooms in hot water for 20 minutes to reconstitute. Reserve the soaking liquid. Give the reconstituted mushrooms a gentle squeeze to remove excess water and thinly slice.
2. Cut the bamboo shoots in half, so they are approximately 1 inch in length. Blanch the cabbage leaves by plunging briefly into boiling water. Drain thoroughly and shred.
3. Mix together the light soy sauce, dark soy sauce, and sugar. Set aside.
4. Add the oil to a preheated wok or heavy skillet. When oil is hot, add the bamboo shoots and stir-fry. Add the mushrooms and stir-fry. Add the cabbage leaves.
5. Add the soy sauce and sugar mixture, and the reserved mushroom liquid. Add the water. Turn the heat down to low, cover, and simmer the vegetables for 10 minutes.
6. Mix cornstarch and water. Turn the heat up and push the vegetables up to the side of the wok. Give the cornstarch/water mixture a quick stir and add in the middle, stirring quickly to thicken. Mix through and serve hot.

Stir-fried Spinach with Roasted Garlic

Serves 4

Roasted garlic lends a sweet flavor. Ideally, the garlic should be removed from the oven and begin cooling just before you start stir-frying.

3 garlic cloves
¼ cup chicken stock
18 fresh spinach leaves
1 tablespoon oil for stir-frying

1 tablespoon soy sauce
½ teaspoon sugar

1. Begin preparing the garlic 1 hour ahead of time. Preheat the oven to 350°F. Peel the garlic and drizzle with the chicken stock. Bake 1 hour or until the cloves are golden. Cool. Press down on cloves to release the garlic (it should come out easily).
2. Wash the spinach and trim the ends. Make sure the spinach is well drained.
3. Add oil to a preheated wok or skillet. When the oil is hot, add the spinach leaves. Stir-fry for about a minute, then add the soy sauce and sugar. Continue stir-frying until the spinach turns a bright green. Serve with the garlic.

Too Much Garlic

Garlic's pungent aroma nicely complements the strong flavor of spinach, but it can overpower more delicate vegetables such as mushrooms. When in doubt, use ginger instead.

Stir-fried Baby Bok Choy

4 bunches baby bok choy
  (1 bunch per person)
2 tablespoons oil for stir-frying
2 garlic cloves, chopped

1 tablespoon rice vinegar
1 teaspoon sugar
¼ teaspoon salt
1 teaspoon sesame oil

1. Rinse the baby bok choy and drain well.
2. Add oil to a preheated wok or skillet. When oil is hot, add garlic and stir-fry until aromatic. Add the baby bok choy, and stir-fry briefly.
3. Add the rice vinegar, sugar, and salt. Cook for about another minute. Drizzle the sesame oil over and serve.

Serves 4

For best results, wash bok choy and mung bean sprouts earlier in the day so that they have plenty of time to drain before stir-frying.

Pickled Carrots

1½ cups (12 ounces) baby
  carrots
⅓ cup rice vinegar

⅓ cup sugar
¼ teaspoon salt
2 cups water

1. Wash the baby carrots. Place them in a glass jar. In a medium saucepan, bring the remaining 4 ingredients to a boil, stirring to dissolve the sugar.
2. Pour the liquid over the carrots, seal the jar, and refrigerate for at least 2 days.

Yields 1½ cups

Pickled vegetables are very popular in Cantonese cuisine; look for them on the menu the next time you dine at a Cantonese restaurant.

Broccoli with Oyster Sauce

1 pound broccoli
2 tablespoons oil for stir-frying
3 teaspoons oyster sauce
2 teaspoons sugar
¼ cup water

1 teaspoon cornstarch
4 teaspoons water

1. Break off the broccoli flowerets and cut in half. Cut the spears on the diagonal into thin slices.
2. Add oil to a skillet or a preheated wok. When oil is hot, add the broccoli, adding the spears first and then the flowerets.
3. Add the oyster sauce, sugar, and ¼ cup water. Cover and cook about 3 minutes, or until the broccoli turns a brilliant green.
4. Mix the cornstarch and water. Uncover the wok, make a well in the middle, and add the cornstarch/water mixture, stirring quickly to thicken. Mix through.

Colorless Vegetables

Covering and cooking firm green vegetables in a bit of water will help make them more tender. Do not lift the wok lid to check on covered green vegetables more than once during cooking. If you do, the vegetable will turn yellow.

Braised Ridged Gourd with Mushrooms

1 ridged gourd (also called
   angled luffa)
3 tablespoons oil for stir-frying
1 clove garlic, minced
5 mushrooms, sliced
¼ teaspoon salt
¼ cup chicken broth

2 tablespoons Chinese rice
   wine or dry sherry
2 teaspoons soy sauce
1 teaspoon brown sugar
1 teaspoon cornstarch
4 teaspoons water

> **Serves 4**
>
> Like tofu, this gourd acts like a sponge, soaking up the flavors of the food it is cooked with.
>
>

1. Peel the gourd, leaving a few strips of green if desired to add a bit of color. Cut diagonally into thin slices.
2. Add oil to a preheated wok or skillet. When the oil is hot, add the garlic clove. When the garlic is aromatic, add the ridged gourd, and stir-fry for about a minute. Add the mushrooms and the salt.
3. Add the chicken broth and stir-fry for another minute. Add the rice wine, soy sauce, and brown sugar.
4. Mix the cornstarch and water and add to the middle of the wok, stirring quickly to thicken. Mix through.

Too Much Cornstarch

If the mixture of cornstarch and water in a recipe produces a soggier sauce than you would like, try reducing the amount of cornstarch while keeping the ratio of cornstarch to water constant. For example, instead of 1 tablespoon of cornstarch mixed with 4 tablespoons of water, use ½ tablespoon cornstarch and 2 tablespoons water.

Braised Chinese Broccoli (Gai Lan) in Oyster Sauce

Serves 4

Chinese broccoli or gai lan has an attractive appearance and an earthy flavor—plus, it's rich in vitamins A and C.

½ pound Chinese broccoli (gai lan)
1 tablespoon plus 1 teaspoon oyster sauce
2 teaspoons soy sauce
½ teaspoon sugar
¼ cup water
2 tablespoons oil for stir-frying
2 slices ginger
1 teaspoon tapioca starch
4 teaspoons water

1. Blanch the gai lan by plunging briefly into boiling water, until the stalks turn a bright green. Drain thoroughly. Separate the stalks and leaves. Cut the leaves across, and cut the stalks thinly on the diagonal.
2. Combine the oyster sauce, soy sauce, sugar, and water. Set aside.
3. Add oil to a preheated wok or skillet. When oil is hot, add the ginger slices. Stir-fry briefly until aromatic. Add the gai lan stalks. Stir-fry for a minute, then add the leaves. Stir-fry until the leaves turn a bright green. Add the oyster sauce mixture. Turn down the heat and cook, covered, for 4–5 minutes.
4. Mix the tapioca starch and water and add to the middle of the wok, stirring to thicken. Mix with the gai lan and serve hot.

Revamping Recipes

Want to adjust a recipe to suit your family's tastes? The easiest method is simply to double a recipe (it helps to have a second wok or frying pan ready to handle the extra volume). Often, the proportion of meat to vegetables in a Chinese recipe can be a little low for Western tastes. To add more meat, simply increase the amount of marinade, and stir-fry or deep-fry the meat in batches. Be prepared to increase the amount of sauce as well. Again, a second wok or frying pan may be needed when the meat is brought together with the vegetables and sauce in the final stages of cooking.

Stir-fried Young Bamboo Shoots

4 pieces (1 cup) peeled young
    bamboo shoots
1 green onion
1½ tablespoons oil for stir-
    frying
1 tablespoon soy sauce

1 teaspoon Chinese rice wine
    or dry sherry
1 teaspoon rice vinegar

> **Serves 4**
>
> Blanching fresh young bamboo shoots lessens their acidic flavor. Serve with a sweet dish such as Sweet-and-Sour Spareribs (page 136).
>
>

1. Blanch the bamboo shoots in boiling water for at least 5 minutes. Drain thoroughly and chop into 1-inch pieces. Cut the green onion on the diagonal into 1-inch slices.
2. Add oil to a preheated wok or skillet. When oil is hot, add the bamboo shoots. Stir-fry for about 2 minutes, then add the soy sauce, rice wine, and rice vinegar. Stir in the green onion. Simmer for 5 more minutes. Chill.

Vegetable Nomenclature
Don't let the use of common Cantonese names prevent you from sampling the colorful profusion of vegetables found in Asian markets. Anything with "choi" or "choy" in the name is a type of cabbage, while "gwa" or "gua" refers to a melon. If you're still confused, just ask; the clerks will be happy to help!

Ridged Gourd with Red Pepper

1 ridged gourd
1 red bell pepper
2 tablespoons oil for stir-frying
1 slice ginger
½ cup chicken broth

2 tablespoons Chinese rice
  wine or dry sherry
1 tablespoon soy sauce
1 teaspoon sugar

1. Peel the gourd, leaving a few strips of green if desired to add a bit of color. Cut diagonally into thin slices. Cut the pepper in half, remove the seeds, and cut into thin strips.
2. Add oil to a preheated wok or skillet. When the oil is hot, add the ginger slice and stir-fry until aromatic. Add the ridged gourd, and stir-fry for about a minute. Add the red pepper and stir-fry until it is bright red.
3. Add the chicken broth and bring back to a boil. Add the rice wine, soy sauce, and sugar. Serve hot.

Southern Stir-fry

Because it resembles okra in taste and texture, ridged gourd is sometimes called Chinese okra. Ridged gourd makes an interesting substitute for okra in dishes of the American south, while okra can replace ridged gourd (also known as silk squash) in stir-fries.

Stuffed Red Peppers

1 red bell pepper
1 cup ground pork
1 tablespoon brown bean sauce
2 tablespoons soy sauce,
   divided
½ teaspoon sugar

1 teaspoon Chinese rice wine
   or dry sherry
1 green onion, minced
1 clove garlic, chopped

1. Preheat the oven to 300°F.
2. Wash the red pepper; cut off the top and set it aside. Remove the seeds.
3. In a medium-sized bowl, use your hands to mix the ground pork with the brown bean sauce, 1 tablespoon soy sauce, sugar, and rice wine. Add the green onion and chopped garlic.
4. Stuff the red pepper with the ground pork mixture. Add 1 tablespoon soy sauce on top and replace the lid. Place in a heatproof dish in the oven, and bake until the pork is cooked through, about 45–55 minutes.

Picking Peppers

While Szechwan cooks favor fiery chili peppers, bell peppers also make a frequent appearance in Chinese dishes. Like their hotter cousin, sweet bell peppers are a New World fruit, discovered by Christopher Columbus during his trips to the Americas. The intrepid explorer took them back to his homeland, where they eventually spread throughout Europe and Asia. The round shape of bell peppers makes them perfect for stuffing. Be sure to remove all seeds and membranes before filling.

Vegetable Chop Suey

Serves 4

Don't have any bok choy on hand? You can use broccoli instead of bok choy and green beans instead of snow peas.

½ cup water chestnuts
1 green bell pepper
1 red bell pepper
1 bunch bok choy
½ pound snow peas
4 tablespoons oil for stir-frying
¼ teaspoon salt
1½ tablespoons water
½ teaspoon minced ginger
½ teaspoon minced garlic

½ red onion, chopped
1 cup fresh mushrooms
1 teaspoon sugar
1 carrot, thinly sliced on the diagonal
½ cup mung bean sprouts, rinsed and drained
1 tablespoon cornstarch
4 tablespoons water
2 tablespoons oyster sauce

1. Clean the mushrooms with a damp towel and slice. If using fresh water chestnuts, wash and peel. If using canned, rinse in warm water and slice.
2. Cut the green and red bell peppers in half, remove the seeds, and cut into thin strips. For the bok choy, separate each stalk and leaves. Cut the stalk diagonally and cut the leaves across. Wash and string the snow peas.
3. Add 2 tablespoons oil to a preheated wok or frying pan. When oil is ready, add the bok choy stalks. Cook for about 1 minute, then add the leaves. Add the salt, and sprinkle with water. Cover and cook on medium heat until the bok choy is tender but still firm. Remove and set aside.
4. Wipe out the wok with a paper towel and add 2 tablespoons of oil. When oil is ready, add the ginger and garlic and stir-fry until aromatic. Add the red onion and stir-fry. Remove from the wok and set aside. Add the green and red peppers and the snow peas. Stir-fry for about a minute, then add the mushrooms and 1 teaspoon of sugar and continue stir-frying. Remove from the wok and set aside. Add the water chestnuts and carrot. Stir-fry for a minute, then add the bean sprouts.
5. Mix cornstarch and water, then stir in the oyster sauce. Add the removed vegetables back into the wok and mix. Make a well in the center and gradually add the cornstarch/oyster sauce mixture, stirring to thicken. Bring to a boil, remove from the heat, and serve hot.

Stir-fried Potatoes

1 pound potatoes
3 tablespoons chicken broth
1½ tablespoons Chinese rice wine or dry sherry
1½ teaspoons sugar

1½ teaspoons cornstarch mixed with 2 tablespoons water
2 tablespoons oil for stir-frying
1 slice ginger
¼ teaspoon salt

Serves 4

This Chinese dish proves that you don't need to douse a potato with sour cream and chives to add flavor.

1. Wash the potatoes, peel, and julienne. Bring a large pot of water to a boil and boil the potatoes until they are cooked but still a bit firm (about 15 minutes). Drain well.
2. Add the chicken broth, rice wine, and sugar to the cornstarch-and-water mixture, stirring. Set aside.
3. Add oil to a preheated wok or a frying pan. When oil is hot, add the slice of ginger and stir-fry until it is aromatic. Add the potatoes, stir-frying in batches if necessary. Add the salt. Continue stir-frying until the potatoes are tender, about 4–5 minutes. Taste and add more salt if desired.
4. Stir the broth mixture. Make a well in the middle of the wok by pushing the potatoes up to the side. Add the broth mixture in the middle, stirring vigorously to thicken. Mix with the potatoes.

Three Vegetable Stir-fry

4 ounces snow peas
1½ tablespoons oil for stir-frying
1 can baby corn, rinsed and drained
6 shiitake mushrooms, sliced

1 tablespoon dark soy sauce
½ teaspoon sugar
½ teaspoon salt

1. Wash and string the snow peas.
2. Add oil to a preheated wok or frying pan. Add the baby corn and stir-fry briefly, then add the snow peas. Stir-fry until the snow peas turn a bright green. Push them up to the side and stir-fry the mushrooms. Add the dark soy sauce, sugar, and salt. Mix through.

Lucky Recipes

The Chinese love to create vegetable and dessert recipes with 3, 5, or 8 main ingredients, as these are considered to be lucky numbers. The number 8 is particularly auspicious, symbolizing sudden prosperity and good fortune. The next time you're dining at a Chinese restaurant, look for recipes with these numbers in their name.

Peppers with Potato Stuffing

4 green bell peppers
2 tablespoons chicken broth
2 tablespoons soy sauce
1 teaspoon sugar

4 tablespoons water
¼ teaspoon chili paste
Stir-fried Potatoes (page 249)

1. Preheat oven to 300°F.
2. Wash the green peppers. Cut off the tops and save. Remove the seeds. In a medium bowl, mix together the chicken broth, soy sauce, sugar, water, and chili paste. Add the stir-fried potatoes and toss.
3. Stuff each pepper with the potato mixture and drizzle a bit of the sauce over the top. If any sauce is remaining, add that into each pepper. Place the stuffed peppers in a 9" × 9" baking dish. Bake for 45 minutes or until peppers are tender.

Serves 4

Potato and peppers make a great combination. Substitute red peppers for added color and an intriguing mix of spicy and sweet.

Spicy Eggplant Stir-fry

1 eggplant
3 tablespoons oil for stir-frying
2 tablespoons red rice vinegar
½ teaspoon brown sugar

2 tablespoons soy sauce
1 tablespoon chopped garlic
½ teaspoon chili paste
¼ teaspoon sesame oil

1. Wash the eggplant, cut off the ends, and slice diagonally into 1-inch pieces.
2. Add oil to a preheated wok or skillet. When the oil is hot, add the eggplant slices, stir-frying in batches if necessary. Stir-fry for about 2–3 minutes.
3. Add the red rice vinegar, brown sugar, soy sauce, garlic, and chili paste, and mix through. Drizzle the sesame oil over and give a final stir.

Serves 4

This dish can be made with truncheon-shaped Chinese eggplant or the thicker eggplant commonly available in local supermarkets.

Sweet-and-Sour Celery

Serves 4–6

Blanching the celery before stir-frying gives it a brilliant green color. For an intriguing mix of flavors, serve with a savory dish.

4 stalks celery
2 tablespoons oil for stir-frying
¼ teaspoon salt
3 tablespoons rice vinegar
2 tablespoons sugar
¼ teaspoon cinnamon

1. Bring a large pot of water to a boil. Wash the celery and cut into 1-inch slices on the diagonal. Blanch by plunging into boiling water and boiling for 2–3 minutes.
2. Add oil to a preheated wok or skillet. When the oil is hot, begin stir-frying the celery. Add the salt.
3. Stir in the rice vinegar, sugar, and cinnamon. Remove the celery from the wok and pour any remaining sauce over.

Cutting Green Vegetables
Unless the instructions state differently, cut green vegetables like celery, bok choy spears, and green onions on the diagonal. This gives maximum heat exposure and ensures even cooking.

Bitter Melon Stir-fry

2 bitter melons
1 teaspoon salt
2 tablespoons oil for stir-frying
1 clove garlic, chopped
2 tablespoons hoisin sauce

4 tablespoons water
1 tablespoon Chinese rice wine
  or dry sherry
½ teaspoon brown sugar

> **Serves 4–6**
>
> Even with degorging, bitter melon has an acrid, almost chalky taste. Feel free to substitute another gourd such as angled luffa.
>
>

1. Wash the bitter melons, cut in half, and remove the seeds inside the pods. Slice thinly on the diagonal.
2. To degorge the bitter melons, place the slices in a bowl and toss with salt. Leave for 15 minutes and place on paper towels to drain out excess water.
3. Bring a large pot of water to a boil. Boil the bitter melons for 3 minutes. Drain well.
4. Add oil to a preheated wok or skillet. Add the garlic and stir-fry briefly until aromatic. Add the bitter melon and stir-fry for 2–3 minutes. Add the hoisin sauce, water, rice wine, and brown sugar. Mix through and serve hot.

A Remarkable Melon
Bitter melon is one of those foods that people either love or hate. Native to China, it works best with pungent ingredients such as chilies and black bean sauce that can hold their own against its strong flavor. To reduce the bitterness, try degorging or steaming.

Szechwan Eggplant with Black Rice Vinegar

Serves 4

In order not to waste any oil, strain the oil from stir-frying the eggplant so that it can be used again.

5 tablespoons oil for stir-frying
2 Chinese eggplants, chopped
   into tiny pieces
2 teaspoons soy sauce
½ teaspoon black rice vinegar
½ teaspoon sugar
1 teaspoon dark soy sauce
¼ teaspoon salt
1 tablespoon chopped ginger

1 garlic clove, chopped
1 teaspoon hot bean sauce
¼ cup chicken stock or broth
¼ teaspoon sesame oil
2 green onions, chopped into
   thirds

1. Mix together the soy sauce, black rice vinegar, sugar, dark soy sauce, and salt. Set aside.
2. Add 4 tablespoons oil to a preheated wok or skillet. When oil is hot, add the eggplant. Stir-fry about 5 minutes, until the eggplant is soft. Gently press the eggplant with a spatula to remove any excess oil. Remove from the wok.
3. Remove the oil from the wok, and wipe the wok clean with a paper towel. Add 1 tablespoon of oil back into the wok. When the oil is hot, add the ginger, garlic, and hot bean sauce and stir-fry briefly. Add the sauce and the chicken stock. Bring to a boil. Add the eggplant back to the wok, and stir-fry until the sauce is nearly gone.
4. Add the sesame oil and green onions. Give the dish a final stir.

Steamed Carrots with Oyster Sauce

2 cups baby carrots
2 tablespoons oyster sauce
¼ cup water
1 teaspoon Chinese rice wine
   or dry sherry

1½ tablespoons oil for stir-
   frying
2 teaspoons minced ginger
½ teaspoon sugar

> **Serves 4**
>
> Oyster sauce is frequently married to broccoli in restaurant dishes, but there are numerous other possibilities—like baby carrots.

1. Steam the carrots until tender. Drain well.
2. Mix together the oyster sauce, water, and rice wine. Set aside.
3. Add oil to a preheated wok or skillet. When oil is ready, add the ginger and stir-fry until it is aromatic.
4. Add the steamed baby carrots. Stir-fry for about 1 minute, until the carrots turn a bright orange color. Add the oyster sauce mixture, and the sugar. Bring the sauce to a boil and stir-fry for another minute, mixing the sauce thoroughly with the vegetables.

Substituting Vegetables

When it comes to making substitutions, the names of Chinese vegetables can be misleading. Although bok choy and choy sum are both types of cabbage, choy sum's delicate pale green leaves bear little resemblance to hardy bok choy. When you need to make a substitution, pay attention to the vegetable's texture and color.

Stuffed Eggplant

Serves 4

Large western egg-plant works best in this dish. Freeze any leftover ground pork to use in dishes such as Lion's Head Meatball Stew (page 133).

4 eggplants
2 eggs, lightly beaten
2 tablespoons soy sauce
¼ teaspoon white pepper

2 tablespoons Chinese rice wine or dry sherry
2 pounds ground pork

1. Preheat the oven to 350°F.
2. Wash the eggplants. Cut in half lengthwise and scoop out as much of the middle as possible without splitting the eggplant. Discard the pulp.
3. Mix the beaten egg, soy sauce, white pepper, and rice wine in with the pork, using your hands. Marinate the pork for 15 minutes.
4. Take a quarter of the pork mixture and stuff it into each eggplant. If possible, cover with the top half of the eggplant.
5. Place the stuffed eggplants in a baking dish. Bake at 350°F for 30 minutes or until the eggplants are cooked.

Braised Baby Bok Choy

Serves 4

Also called Shanghai bok choy, baby bok choy has a sweeter flavor and is more tender than regular bok choy.

4 bunches baby bok choy
½ cup chicken stock or broth
½ cup water
1 teaspoon sugar

1½ teaspoons rice vinegar
2 tablespoons oil for stir-frying
2 garlic cloves, finely chopped
½ teaspoon sesame oil

1. Wash and drain the baby bok choy. Cut off the roots and separate the stalks and leaves.
2. Combine the chicken stock, water, sugar, and rice vinegar.
3. Add oil to a preheated wok or skillet. When oil is ready, add the garlic. Stir-fry until aromatic.
4. Add the bok choy stalks and stir-fry until they turn a bright green. While stir-frying the stalks, add the leaves.
5. Add the chicken broth mixture. Turn down the heat and simmer, covered, for 5 minutes. Turn off the heat and drizzle with the sesame oil.

Mu Shu Vegetables

2 bok choy stalks
½ red bell pepper
¼ cup water
¼ cup chicken broth
1 tablespoon dark soy sauce
1 teaspoon sugar

2 eggs, lightly beaten
¼ teaspoon salt
3 tablespoons oil for stir-frying
4 fresh mushrooms, sliced
½ teaspoon sesame oil

Serves 4

The combination of eggs and vegetables makes this a nutritious, quick, and easy meal for busy weekdays.

1. Separate the bok choy stalks and leaves. Cut the stalks diagonally into 1-inch pieces. Cut the leaves crosswise into 1-inch pieces. Remove the seeds from the pepper and cut into thin strips.
2. Combine the water, chicken broth, dark soy sauce, and sugar. Set aside.
3. Stir ¼ teaspoon salt in to the eggs. Add 1 tablespoon oil to a pre-heated wok or skillet. When oil is hot, scramble the eggs. Remove from the wok and set aside.
4. Clean out the wok and add 2 tablespoons oil. When oil is hot, add the bok choy stalks. Stir-fry for about 1 minute, then add the mushrooms and red pepper. Stir-fry briefly and add the bok choy leaves. Add the sauce in the middle of the wok. Bring to a boil. Stir in the scrambled egg. Drizzle the sesame oil over. Mix through and serve hot.

Wrap It Up!

Meat and vegetables cooked in the mu shu style make a great filling for tortilla wraps. To make, adjust the above recipe by draining out some of the sauce so that the filling isn't too wet. Lay the wrap in front of you and add ½ cup of filling to the bottom. Fold over the right side of the wrap. Fold the bottom of the wrap over the food, and continue rolling up the wrap. For added variety, try the flavored wraps, such as spinach, pesto, or garlic.

CHAPTER 12

Desserts and Snacks

Almond Cookies

Yields 30–35 cookies

Delicately flavored
with a hint of almond,
these cookies make a
satisfying light after-
noon snack or finale
to a dim sum brunch.

2 cups flour
½ teaspoon baking powder
½ teaspoon baking soda
½ cup margarine or butter, as
    preferred
½ cup shortening

¾ cup white sugar
2 eggs
2 teaspoons almond extract
¼ pound whole, blanched
    almonds (1 for each cookie)
1 egg, lightly beaten

1. Preheat oven to 325°F.
2. In a large bowl, sift the flour, baking powder, and baking soda. In a medium bowl, use an electric mixer to beat the butter or margarine, shortening, and sugar. Add the eggs and almond extract and beat until well blended. Add to the flour mixture, stirring.
3. Knead the dough into a roll or log. If you find 1 long roll too difficult to work with, split the dough into 2 equal pieces.
4. Cut the dough into 30–35 pieces. (If desired, lightly score the dough before cutting to get an idea of the correct size.) Roll each piece into a ball and place on a lightly greased cookie tray, approximately 2 inches apart. Place an almond in the center of each cookie and press down lightly.
5. Brush each cookie lightly with beaten egg before baking. Bake at 325°F for 15 minutes or until golden brown. Cool and store in a sealed container.

Fortune Cookie Origins

Although a Chinese restaurant meal wouldn't seem complete without them, the fortune cookie is an American creation. Restaurant chefs in both Los Angeles and San Francisco lay claim to having invented the popular baked cookie containing a special message. Today, fortune cookies are catching on in China as well.

Egg Custard Tarts

2 cups flour
¾ teaspoon salt
⅔ cup lard
½ teaspoon vanilla extract
3 tablespoons hot water

2 large eggs
½ cup evaporated milk
½ cup milk
¼ cup sugar

Yields 18 tarts

Egg tarts are a popular dim sum treat. Make sure that the tart pans are well greased so that the pastry does not stick.

1. Preheat oven to 300°F.
2. To make the dough: In a large bowl, sift together the flour and salt. Cut in the lard, and then use your fingers to mix in. When it is mealy and has the consistency of breadcrumbs, add the vanilla extract and hot water and mix together to form a dough. Add another tablespoon of water if necessary. Cut the dough into thirds.
3. On a lightly floured surface, roll each piece of dough out until it is ⅛ inch thick. Cut 6 circles that are each 3 inches in diameter, so that you have a total of 18 circles.
4. Place the circles into greased tart pans or muffin tins, carefully shaping the sides so that they reach the rim.
5. To make the egg custard filling: Lightly beat the eggs, and stir in the evaporated milk, milk, and sugar. Add up to 2 tablespoons of the custard into each tart shell, so that it nicely fills the shell but does not overflow.
6. Bake at 300°F for about 25 minutes or until the custard is cooked through and a knife stuck in the middle comes out clean.

Almond Fruit Gelatin

Serves 4–6

Colorful fresh fruits like strawberries or peaches make a nice contrast to the almond gelatin in this elegant, easy-to-make dessert.

1½ packages Knox unflavored
   gelatin
1 cup cold water
3 tablespoons sugar
1 cup boiling water

1 cup evaporated milk
2 teaspoons almond extract
1 cup fresh fruit slices

1. Pour the gelatin over the cold water and wait about 3 minutes for it to soften.
2. In a separate bowl, add the sugar to the boiling water, stirring to dissolve. Add the evaporated milk to the sugar and water mixture. Wait a few minutes for the mixture to cool slightly and stir in the almond extract.
3. Add the evaporated milk mixture to the gelatin and water. Stir well and pour into a shallow pan or a serving mold. Chill until firm.
4. Cut into diamond shapes and place on a serving tray. Garnish with the fresh fruit slices.

Aromatic Almonds
Cooks have been exploiting almond's rich flavor since biblical times. In China of days past, peddlers traveled from door to door selling almond tea, a sweet concoction made with almonds ground into a paste. Today, almonds are featured in desserts and some restaurant dishes.

Mango Pudding

2 cups canned mango pieces
½ cup boiling water
2 packages Knox unflavored
  gelatin
¾ cup sugar
1 cup evaporated milk
1 cup syrup from the canned
  mango

1. In a food processor, purée the mango pieces. Reserve the syrup and set aside.
2. In a large bowl, pour the boiling water over the gelatin and stir for about 2 minutes until it is dissolved.
3. In a medium saucepan, bring the sugar, evaporated milk, and mango syrup to a boil, stirring. Remove from the heat and add the puréed mango. Add to the bowl of gelatin, stirring.
4. Pour the mixture into a dish or individual serving bowls. Chill until set.

Serves 6

The delicate flavor of Mango Pudding sets it apart from thicker, heavier puddings. Traditionally, agar-agar would have been used in place of gelatin crystals.

Almond Float

Almond Fruit Gelatin (page 262)
2 cups water
½ cup brown sugar
1 teaspoon almond extract
Canned pineapple and man-
  darin orange slices

1. To make the syrup: In a medium saucepan, add 2 cups of water and ½ cup brown sugar. Heat to boiling, stirring to dissolve the sugar. When the sugar is dissolved, cool. Add 1 teaspoon almond extract and chill.
2. When ready to serve, cut the almond gelatin into ½-inch cubes and place in a large serving bowl. Cover with the chilled sugar water. Add mandarin and pineapple slices along with as much of the canned syrup as desired. Add enough so that the almond gelatin "floats" in the liquid.

Serves 6

For a more tropical flavor, substitute canned lychees and jackfruit for the mandarin orange and pineapple slices.

Poached Asian Pears

1½ cups cranberry juice
3 cups water
2 slices ginger

¾ tablespoon pumpkin spice
4 Asian pears, cored and
 halved

1. In a large pot, add the cranberry juice, water, and ginger slices. Add the pumpkin pie spice, placing in a cheesecloth bag if desired. Bring to a boil.
2. Add the pears. Simmer, turning occasionally, until they are tender and can be pierced easily with a fork (depending on the firmness of the pear, this can take 30–35 minutes). Serve warm.

Poached Pears with Lemon

3 cups water
1½ cups cranberry juice
¾ cup sugar
1 cinnamon stick

1 teaspoon freshly squeezed
 lemon juice
4 Asian pears, cored and
 halved

1. In a large pot, bring all the ingredients except the pears to a boil.
2. Add the pears. Simmer, turning occasionally until they are tender and can be easily pierced with a fork. Remove the pears with a slotted spoon and place in individual serving dishes.
3. Continue to simmer the syrup until it thickens and lightly coats the back of a spoon. Pour the sauce over the pears. Serve warm or chilled.

Steamed Apples

4 apples
4 tablespoons honey

1 teaspoon cinnamon
1 ½ tablespoons raisins

1. Slice off the top of each apple and set aside to serve as the lid. Core the apples.
2. Mix together the honey, cinnamon, and raisins. Spoon a quarter of the mixture into each apple and replace the lids.
3. Steam the apples until they are soft but not mushy. Serve warm.

Steamed Fruit

When steaming fruit, it's important to remove the fruit from the pot immediately, so that it doesn't continue cooking in the hot liquid and become mushy.

> **Serves 4**
>
> This is a perfect treat for cold winter days, providing a healthy alternative to snack foods.

Sweet Baked Pineapple and Banana

1 cup canned pineapple chunks
2 tablespoons margarine or
   butter, softened
⅓ cup brown sugar
2 tablespoons reserved
   pineapple juice

1 teaspoon Chinese rice wine
   or dry sherry
3 bananas, cut in half lengthwise
2 tablespoons untoasted
   sesame seeds

1. Preheat oven to 350°F.
2. Drain the can of pineapple chunks, reserving 2 tablespoons juice.
3. In a medium bowl, cream the butter and brown sugar. Stir in the pineapple juice and rice wine.
4. Lay out the bananas and pineapple chunks on a glass baking dish. Spread the brown sugar mixture over. Bake for about 10 minutes, until the bananas are tender but not mushy (the pineapple will retain its texture). Sprinkle with sesame seeds.

> **Serves 4**
>
> Children love this sweet treat. For an added touch, serve with a tropical fruit–flavored ice cream.

Sweetened Walnuts

½ cup chopped walnut pieces
¼ cup sugar
3 cups oil for deep-frying

1. Blanch the walnut pieces in boiling water for 5 minutes to remove their bitter flavor.
2. Spread the sugar out on a piece of waxed paper. Roll the walnuts in the sugar. Spread out on a tray and leave overnight to dry.
3. Heat oil to 275°F. When oil is hot, add the walnuts. Deep-fry until they turn golden brown. Remove and drain. Cool and store in a sealed container.

Steamed Fruit with a Surprise

4 pears   *4 Chinese honey dates*
2 tablespoons honey

1. Slice off the top of each pear and set aside. Core the pear from the top, being careful not to go through to the bottom.
2. Spoon ½ tablespoon honey into each pear. Add a Chinese honey date. Replace the lid. Steam until tender and serve hot.

🌿 Guilt-free Indulging
This healthy dessert lets you indulge and fight off illness at the same time. According to traditional Chinese medicine, pears lower cholesterol and reduce high blood pressure, while honey dates build up the blood.

Walnut Cookies

2 teaspoons baking powder
3 cups flour
¾ cup lard
½ cup finely chopped walnuts

2 teaspoons vanilla extract
1¼ cups white sugar
3 eggs
1 egg, lightly beaten

Yields 28–30 cookies

These sweet cookies
are a popular feature
in Chinese bakeries.
Food coloring is
sometimes used to
give them a yellow
color.

1. Preheat oven to 325°F.
2. In a large bowl, sift the baking powder into the flour. Cut the lard into the flour and mix with your fingers until it forms the texture of tiny balls.
3. Add the walnuts, vanilla extract, sugar, and 3 eggs. Mix into the dough to form a paste.
4. Take a piece of dough and form into a round ball the size of a large golf ball. Place the ball in the palm of one hand and press down with the palm of the other hand to form a flat circle about 2 inches in diameter. Continue with the remainder of the dough.
5. Place the dough circles on a greased baking tray. Brush lightly with the beaten egg. Bake at 325°F for about 20–25 minutes, or until a toothpick stuck in the center comes out clean. Cool and store in a sealed container.

Chinese Bakery

Need a little inspiration before you're ready to get out the rolling pin and start mixing and measuring? Try visiting a Chinese bakery. Classic treats like Mango Pudding and Sesame Seed Balls share space with sticky rice dumplings, foot-long doughnuts, and buns filled with everything from pineapple and taro to red bean paste. All reflect the Chinese belief that no one flavor should upstage any other. Indulge, and you'll leave feeling pleasantly satisfied but without a case of "sugar hangover."

Mandarin Pancakes

2 cups all-purpose flour
¾–1 cup boiling water

¼ cup sesame oil

1. Place the flour in a large bowl. Add the boiling water and quickly stir with a wooden spoon.
2. As soon as you can withstand the heat, knead the warm dough on a lightly floured surface until it is smooth. Cover with a damp cloth and let stand for 30 minutes.
3. Cut the dough in half. Roll each half into a 9-inch cylinder. Using a tape measure, lightly score and cut the dough into 1-inch pieces. You will have 18 pieces at this point.
4. Shape each piece into a ball and then flatten into a circle between the palms of your hands. Brush the top of each piece with sesame oil, and then place the pieces on top of each other, oiled sides together.
5. Using a lightly floured rolling pin, roll the pieces into a 5½–6-inch circle. (Don't worry if the edges overlap.) Continue with the rest of the dough.
6. Heat a dry pan on low-medium heat. When the pan is hot, add one of the paired pancakes and cook on each side for 2 minutes or until brown bubbles appear (the second side will cook more quickly). Remove from the pan and pull the pancakes apart while they are still hot. Place on a plate and cover with a damp cloth while cooking the remainder.

Pancakes for Dinner

Besides making a tasty snack, mandarin pancakes are served with the northern dishes mu shu pork and Peking duck. In the case of mu shu pork, the pork is wrapped in the pancakes, which are brushed with hoisin sauce. To be completely authentic, the sauce should be brushed on with Green Onion Brushes (page 73).

Sweet Red Bean Paste

½ cup dried red beans
1½ cups water

¼ cup sugar (or to taste)
1¼ tablespoons oil

1. Rinse the beans and soak overnight in water to cover, adding more water if necessary. Drain.
2. In a medium saucepan bring 1½ cups of water to a boil. Add the beans and simmer for at least 2 hours or until they are tender. Drain.
3. Place the beans and the sugar in a blender and process until smooth. Heat the oil in a preheated wok or saucepan. Add the processed bean paste and stir-fry until it is dry. Store in a sealed container in the refrigerator. The bean paste will last for approximately 1 week.

Yields 1–1½ cups

Use with Sesame Seed Balls (page 271) and Fried Pancakes with Red Bean Paste, or as a filling for steamed buns.

Fried Pancakes with Red Bean Paste

Mandarin Pancakes (page 268)
1 can red bean paste
Oil for stir-frying

When the Mandarin Pancakes have cooled, add approximately 1 tablespoon of red bean paste to each pancake and spread it out evenly. Roll up the pancake and stir-fry until golden. Serve warm.

Yields 9 pancakes

For an added treat, dust the mandarin pancakes with sugar or icing sugar after frying.

Pineapple and Ginger "Ice Cream"

1 cup sugar
½ cup water
2 cups diced fresh pineapple

1 teaspoon peeled, grated ginger
3 cups milk

1. Bring the sugar and water to a boil, stirring. Add the diced pineapple and ginger. Simmer, uncovered, for 10 minutes.
2. Strain the syrup to remove the ginger and pineapple. Add the milk to the syrup. Freeze. Chill the pineapple.
3. When the ice cream is partially frozen, stir the chilled pineapple back in. Continue freezing. Thaw slightly before serving.

Grass Jelly Dessert

1 can grass jelly
1 can lychees

1 small can mandarin orange sections

1. Remove the grass jelly from the can, slice, and cut into cubes.
2. Place the grass jelly cubes in a large bowl. Add the lychees and mandarin orange sections, and pour the syrup from the canned fruits over.

Grass Jelly Drink

A popular Southeast Asian drink consists of grass jelly cubes mixed with rock sugar. But, however you enjoy your grass jelly, it's important to neutralize its strong flavor with sugar, leaving you free to enjoy the slippery texture.

Sesame Seed Balls

¾ cup packed brown sugar
1 cup boiling water
2⅓ cups glutinous rice flour

1 cup sweet red bean paste
¼ cup white sesame seeds
6 cups oil for deep-frying

Yields 22–24 balls

Glutinous rice flour, also known as sweet rice flour, is used mainly for desserts and dim sum snacks. It is sold in bags in Asian markets.

1. Add the brown sugar to the boiling water, stirring to dissolve. Cool.
2. Place the glutinous rice flour in a large bowl, making a well in the middle. Give the sugar/water mix a quick stir and slowly pour into the well, stirring to mix with the flour. Continue stirring until well mixed. You should have a sticky, caramel-colored dough at this point.
3. Rub your hands in a bit of the rice flour so that the dough doesn't stick to them. Take a heaping tablespoon of dough and shape into a ball roughly the size of a golf ball.
4. Flatten the ball with the palm of your hand, then use your thumb to make an indentation in the middle. Take no more than 1 teaspoon of red bean paste, and use your hand to shape the paste into a circle. Place the paste in the indentation in the dough. Fold the dough over the paste and roll back into a ball. Continue with the remainder of the dough.
5. Sprinkle the sesame seeds on a sheet of waxed paper. Roll the balls in the seeds.
6. In a wok or large pot, heat 6 cups of oil to between 330–350°F. Deep-fry the sesame seed balls a few at a time, carefully pushing them against the sides of the wok when they float to the top. The sesame balls are cooked when they expand to approximately 3 times their size and turn golden brown. Drain on paper towels. Serve warm.

Bowties for Kids

1 package egg roll wrappers
1 cup brown sugar
¼ cup white sugar
2 tablespoons honey

½ cup water
Oil for deep-frying

1. Cut each wrapper vertically into 4 equal pieces. Cut a ¾-inch slit in the middle of each piece.
2. Lay one piece on top of the other and make a knot like a bow tie: Fold the top and thread the 2 pieces through the slit. Turn over, fold the bottom and thread through the other way. Spread out the folded ends slightly to make sure the entire surface is deep-fried.
3. Heat 1½ inches of oil in a heavy skillet. Deep-fry a few of the bowties at a time until they are golden brown, turning over once. Remove from the pan with a slotted spoon and drain on paper towels.
4. When all the bowties are deep-fried, bring the brown sugar, white sugar, honey, and water to boil in a medium-sized saucepan. Boil for 5 minutes, stirring constantly over low heat. Dip each of the bowties into the boiling syrup, drain, and set aside to harden. Serve cold.

Bowties for Adults

1 package egg roll wrappers   *Oil for deep-frying*
¼ cup powdered sugar

1. Cut each wrapper vertically into 4 equal pieces. Cut a ¾-inch slit in the middle of each piece.
2. Lay one piece on top of the other and make a knot like a bow tie: Fold the top and thread the 2 pieces through the slit. Turn over, fold the bottom and thread through the other way. Spread out the folded ends slightly to make sure the entire surface is deep-fried.
3. Heat 1½ inches of oil in a heavy skillet. Deep-fry a few of the bowties at a time until they are golden brown, turning over once. Remove from the pan with a slotted spoon and drain on paper towels.
4. Cool the bowties and dust lightly with powdered sugar. Serve cold. Store in an airtight container.

Yields 2 bowties for every wrapper

The trick to making these is to ensure the entire surface is lightly dusted with powdered sugar.

Marinated Cashews

½ cup honey   *1 tablespoon Grand Marnier*
¼ cup sugar   *1 cup unsalted cashews*
1 tablespoon orange juice

1. Combine the honey, sugar, orange juice, and Grand Marnier in a medium-sized bowl. Stir in the cashews. Place in a medium-sized saucepan and bring to a boil.
2. Boil for 2 or 3 minutes. Remove from the heat and pour onto a baking sheet. Separate the nuts with a slotted spoon. Leave for at least 2 hours to allow the cashews to soak up the sugar and dry. Store in a sealed container.

Yields about 1 cup

Glazed nuts are a popular Chinese snack food, similar to Italian candied chestnuts.

Spicy Roasted Peanuts

Yields 2 cups	

Spicy Roasted Peanuts are popular during the Chinese New Year season because peanuts symbolize longevity in Chinese culture.

1 ¼ teaspoons salt
¼ cup hot water

¼ teaspoon five-spice powder
2 cups unblanched peanuts

1. Preheat the oven to 300°F.
2. Add the salt to the hot water, stirring to dissolve. Repeat with the five-spice powder.
3. In a medium-sized bowl, add the flavored water to the peanuts, stirring well to mix.
4. Spread the peanuts out on a roasting pan. Pour any leftover liquid over the peanuts. Roast at 300°F for about 45 minutes or until the peanuts are a rich golden brown. Stir every 15 minutes to make sure they cook evenly. Cool and store in a sealed container.

Five-Flavor Taste Sensation
Five-spice powder contains all five flavors—sweet, sour, salty, pungent, and bitter. Its unique taste is achieved through blending popular baking spices cinnamon, fennel, and cloves with the more exotic star anise and Szechwan peppercorns.

Quick and Easy Fried Melon

2 pounds winter melon
7 tablespoons flour

½ cup flaked coconut
4 cups oil for deep-frying

1. Peel and remove the seeds from the winter melon. Cut into bite-sized pieces. Lightly dust the melon with the flour.
2. In a preheated wok or skillet, heat 4 cups of oil to 250°F. Slide the winter melon into the wok, a few pieces at a time. Deep-fry until light brown, being sure to keep the oil temperature around 250°F.
3. Remove from the wok. Dust with the coconut and serve immediately.

Winter Melon—Not Just for Soup

What can you say about a vegetable that looks like a green pumpkin, has a sweet flavor similar to watermelon, but is actually a type of squash? Winter melon is famous for making a banquet soup, but you can enjoy it anytime. Stir-fried, winter melon adds flavor to stews, curries, and even sandwiches. As this recipe shows, it can also be deep-fried.

Serves 6

Deep-frying brings out the melon's natural sweetness. Watermelon can be substituted for the Chinese winter melon.

Candied Ginger

Yields ¾ cup

The combination of ginger's sharp bite and sweet sugar is incomparable. Enjoy alone, or use to enliven salads and desserts such as Szechwan Peppered Fruit (page 277).

6 ounces fresh ginger
1½ cups water
1¾ cups sugar

1. Soak the ginger overnight and drain. Peel the ginger, removing any knobs, and cut into chunks.
2. Fill a large saucepan with water and bring to a boil. Add the ginger and simmer for about 1½ hours. Drain. Repeat again, simmering until the ginger is tender and can be easily pierced with a fork. Drain well.
3. Bring 1½ cups water combined with 1½ cups sugar to a boil, stirring. When the sugar and water have formed a thick syrup, reduce the heat and add the ginger. Simmer until the water is nearly absorbed and the hardened sugar coats the ginger. Remove and roll the ginger in the remaining ¼ cup of sugar. Cool and store in an air-tight container.

Versatile Ginger

Queen Elizabeth may have invented the gingerbread man, but Chinese cooks have been putting ginger's subtle flavor to use since ancient times. Fresh ginger is featured in soups, salads, stews, and stir-fries; it is also used to flavor oil and remove fishy odors. And nothing beats a comforting cup of ginger tea when you're feeling run-down.

Szechwan Peppered Fruit

*2 tablespoons Szechwan pepper-
corns or pink peppercorns
1 can Asian jackfruit
1 can pineapple slices (reserve
the juice)
3 tablespoons honey*

*1–2 teaspoons margarine or
butter
A few slices Candied Ginger
(page 276), optional*

Serves 4

This foolproof dessert combines sweet honey with fiery Szechwan pepper-corns. Feel free to experiment with other canned fruits like lychees.

1. Rub the Szechwan peppercorns onto the jackfruit and pineapple slices.
2. In a saucepan, add the honey and heat, stirring. Add ½ cup of the reserved pineapple juice. Turn down the heat to low.
3. Add the margarine to a skillet and heat on low. If using the candied ginger, add to the frying pan and make sure it is heated through. Remove and set aside. Add the pineapple and jackfruit to the pan. Heat, shaking and turning over the slices to make sure the Szechwan peppercorns are heated through and become aromatic. Turn the heat down to low and add the candied ginger back into the pan.
4. Bring the honey and pineapple juice to a boil and give a final stir. Pour over the fruit. Serve immediately.

Tropical Temptations
Tropical fruits live up to their exotic names. Durian is famous for its unique combination of foul odor and heavenly taste, while a single jackfruit can weigh up to 100 pounds. While fresh Asian fruit is subject to seasonal availability, canned versions can be found in Asian markets.

Glazed Bananas

Banana Fritters (page 280)
2 tablespoons oil
5 tablespoons sugar

2 tablespoons sesame seeds
Bowl of ice water

1. Prepare Banana Fritters recipe, deep-frying the bananas a second time.
2. Heat oil in a skillet. Add the sugar, stirring constantly, until it dissolves and turns a light brown. Immediately add the deep-fried banana slices to the pan, sprinkle with the sesame seeds, and toss to coat with the caramelized sugar. Remove and plunge, one piece at a time, into the bowl of ice water so that the caramelized sugar hardens.

Almond-Flavored Egg Cake

¼ cup milk
1 tablespoon sugar

¼ teaspoon almond extract
3 eggs, lightly beaten

1. In a small saucepan, scald the milk. Mix 3 tablespoons of the milk with the sugar, stirring. (You can discard the leftover milk.) Add the almond extract to the milk and sugar mixture, and add the mixture to the beaten egg.
2. Pour the egg mixture into a pie plate, and steam in a wok on medium to medium-high heat until a toothpick comes out clean.

Cooking Tips

For best results, it's important not to let too much air into the egg mixture. Lightly beat the eggs so that, if possible, no air bubbles form. Scalding the milk makes for a shorter cooking time.

New Year's Sticky Cake

6 Chinese dates
3 cups glutinous rice flour
1 cup boiling water
1¼ cups brown sugar
2 tablespoons milk or as
    required

1 egg
1 tablespoon vegetable oil
1 tablespoon sesame seeds

Serves 6–8

Sticky Cake is one of
many foods symbol-
izing good luck that
play a large role in
Chinese New Year
celebrations.

1. Soak the Chinese dates in hot water for at least 30 minutes to soften. Cut in half and remove the pits.
2. Place the glutinous rice flour in a large bowl. In a separate bowl, mix the boiling water and the sugar.
3. Make a well in the middle of the glutinous rice flour and stir in the sugar-and-water mixture. Add the milk and the egg. Stir until the batter is well mixed.
4. Prepare the wok for steaming. Grease a cake pan with the vegetable oil and pour the cake batter into the pan. Decorate with the dates and sesame seeds.
5. Set the cake pan on a bamboo steamer and place in the wok. Steam the cake for 50 minutes, or until the edges move away from the cake pan. Cool. To serve, cut the cake into wedges.

Chinese Dates
Also known as jujubes, these tiny red berries with the crinkly skin have been enjoyed in China since ancient times. Their delicate sweetness makes them a valuable addition to desserts and soups; they can also be enjoyed alone as a snack. Soak in water to soften before using.

Banana Fritters

Serves 5

Deep-frying the banana enhances its natural sweetness. For heightened flavor, deep-fry a second time at 325°F for about a minute.

½ cup flour
1 egg, beaten
2 tablespoons sesame oil
3 tablespoons water

5 bananas, cut into 1½-inch
　　pieces
Flour for dusting
4 cups oil for deep frying

1. Stir the flour into the egg. Add the sesame oil and water and stir until a smooth batter is formed, adding a bit more water if necessary.
2. Lightly dust the banana pieces with the flour. Dip the banana pieces into the batter and cover, using your fingers.
3. Heat the oil to 350°F. Carefully slide the banana pieces into the hot oil, a few pieces at a time, and briefly deep-fry until they are golden. Remove and drain on paper towels.

Sweet Orange Tea

Serves 4

This sweet soup takes the place of a sorbet at Chinese banquets. It also make a refreshing dessert soup.

4 medium oranges
4 cups water
⅓ cup brown sugar
⅓ cup white sugar
1 tablespoon cornstarch

1. Cut the oranges in half. Use a sharp knife to scoop out the pulp over a large bowl to catch the juice.
2. In a large saucepan, add the water, sugars, and cornstarch. Bring to a boil, stirring constantly.
3. Add the orange pulp and juice to the water-and-sugar mixture, stirring.
4. Serve hot or cold.

Appendices

Appendix A

Putting It All Together

Appendix B

Glossary of Asian Ingredients

Appendix A

Putting It All Together

Menu 1

Chicken Velvet Soup (page 59)
Kung Pao Shrimp (page 215)
Sweet-and-Sour Chinese Greens (page 236)
Basic Cooked Rice (page 78)

Menu 2

Spring Rolls (page 35)
Lemony Chicken Stir-fry (page 159)
Snow Pea Stir-fry (page 233)
Basic Cooked Rice (page 78)

Menu 3

Baked Oyster Sauce Chicken (page 155)
Glazed Carrots (page 234)
Basic Cooked Rice (page 78)

Menu 4

Tomato Egg Flower Soup (page 60)
Ginger Beef (page 127)
Basic Cooked Rice (page 78)

Menu 5

Hot and Sour Soup (page 55)
Traditional Mu Shu Pork (page 145)
Creamy Fruit Salad (page 66)

Menu 6

Cream Corn Soup (page 58)
Beef and Bean Sprouts in Black
Bean Sauce (page 115)
Stir-fried Bok Choy (page 235)
Basic Cooked Rice (page 78)

Menu 7

Egg Rolls (page 32)
Kung Pao Stir-fry (page 166)
Braised Baby Bok Choy (page 256)
Almond Float (page 263)

Glossary of Asian Ingredients

agar-agar: Made from seaweed, it takes the place of gelatin in Asian cooking. Agar and gelatin can be substituted for each other in recipes—just remember that agar-agar has different setting properties, requiring less time to set the same amount of liquid.

bean curd: Bean curd is made from curdled soy milk in a process that has a great deal in common with making cheese. Tofu, the name by which bean curd is commonly known, is a Japanese modification of the Chinese word for bean curd, *doufu*. Bean curd comes in a number of different textures, from firm to soft, depending on how firmly the curd is pressed. There is also fermented tofu flavored with spicy seasonings, and dried bean curd sheets and sticks.

bitter melon: A green gourd with a distinctive pockmarked skin, bitter melon has a strong chalky flavor that isn't completely removed by degorging. Bitter melon is normally paired with other strongly flavored ingredients, such as chilies.

black bean sauce and paste: Savory sauces and pastes made from dried black beans. Different varieties include hot bean sauce and yellow bean sauce.

blanch (parboil): In Chinese cooking, blanching generally refers to plunging vegetables briefly into boiling water and then draining thoroughly. Blanching helps preserve the natural color and texture of vegetables, as well as the nutrients.

bok choy: A large cabbage with dark green leaves that is available in both western and Asian supermarkets, bok choy is used in soups, stir-fries, and braised dishes. The thicker stalks require a longer cooking time than the more delicate leaves. Shanghai or baby bok choy is a smaller variety of bok choy with a sweeter flavor and more delicate texture.

chili pepper: Szechwan cuisine wouldn't be the same without these small, hot peppers. Chili peppers comes in a number of varieties, from jalapeno to hot habaneros. In general, the smaller the chili, the higher the heat content. Chili peppers are used to make Hot Chili Oil (page 23).

Chinese cabbage: Also known as napa cabbage or Peking cabbage, Chinese cabbage is the other main cabbage besides bok choy used in Chinese cooking. Its pale green leaves readily absorb the flavors of the food it is cooked with. Napa cabbage is used in soups, salads, stir-fries, and even eaten raw.

Chinese sausage: Thinner and redder than sausages normally found in supermarkets, Chinese sausages are made from a number of ingredients, including pork and liver. Look for them under their Chinese name, *lop cheong*.

cilantro: Also known as Chinese parsley, cilantro consists of the leaves of the coriander plant. While coriander is a popular Indian spice, the leaves feature more prominently in Chinese cooking. Use in sauces and as a garnish.

cornflour: Another term for cornstarch.

deep-fry: Cooking food by completely submerging it in hot oil. This is one of the three main techniques used in Chinese cooking.

dim sum: Literally meaning "touch your heart," dim sum is a meal consisting of numerous small appetizers or snacks that had its origins in Chinese teahouses. Dim sum may have been the inspiration for the Western and European custom of brunch.

dried lily buds: These are the dried unopened buds of day lilies. Their earthy flavor is featured in Traditional Mu Shu Pork (page 145) and Hot and Sour Soup (page 55).

dried mushrooms: Also called black mushrooms, although their color ranges from light to dark brown, these fungi are found on decaying logs and tree stumps. In Chinese cooking, dried mushrooms are favored over fresh, as the drying process enhances their flavor. They must be softened in water before use.

dried tangerine peel: Dried tangerine peel lends a citrusy aroma to simmered dishes, and can also be used in stir-fries. Soften in water before use.

fuzzy melon: Related to winter melon, fuzzy melon is roughly the size and shape of a cucumber, with a dark green skin covered in light fuzz. It is baked, stuffed, and added to soups and stir-fries. If the recipe does not require peeling the melon skin, be sure to remove the fuzz before cooking.

glutinous rice: Glutinous rice is made from short-grain rice kernels. In Chinese cooking, it is normally, although not always, reserved for sweets and desserts.

groundnut oil: Another term for peanut oil.

hoisin sauce: A thick sauce made from soybean paste, hoisin sauce is a mainstay of northern Chinese regional cuisine, and the base for many Chinese satay sauces. Seasonings such as garlic and chilies give hoisin sauce its unique sweet and savory flavor.

kecap manis: The Indonesian version of soy sauce, although it is much more flavorful. Kecap manis is made with an assortment of seasonings, including star anise and palm sugar. *Kecap* is the source of the word "ketchup."

oil velveting: A technique to tenderize meat or poultry by submerging it in hot oil very briefly, just until it changes color. It is then cooked by conventional methods such as stir-frying or deep-frying. Prior to velveting, the meat is frequently marinated with a mixture of egg white and cornstarch.

oyster sauce: A savory sauce made with boiled oysters and seasonings such as soy sauce and garlic. Oyster sauce is most commonly used in sauces and dips. For vegetarians, Lee Kum Kee offers an oyster sauce using mushrooms in place of oysters.

red cooking: This cooking technique consists of browning food, and then braising or stewing it in soy sauce for a lengthy period of time. Dark soy sauce is frequently used in red cooking.

rice flour: Made from glutinous rice, it is used in a few Chinese desserts, such as New Year's Sticky Cake (page 279).

rice vinegar: Rice vinegar is made from fermented rice. The three main types of rice vinegar used in Chinese cooking are red, white, and black. White rice vinegar comes closest in flavor to Western cider vinegar.

rice wine: A wine made with glutinous short-grained rice, Chinese rice wine is used frequently in marinades and sauces. The most famous rice wine comes from the Shaoxing region in northern China. If rice wine is unavailable, a good quality pale dry sherry can be used as a substitute.

rock sugar: A mixture of refined sugar, honey, and brown sugar, rock sugar is used in desserts and recipes where a stronger flavor than regular sugar is required.

sesame oil: A nutty-flavored oil made from toasted sesame seeds, sesame oil is used in sauces, marinades, and dips. It is frequently drizzled over food in the final stages of cooking. Sesame oil's strong flavor and low smoking point generally make it a poor choice as a cooking oil.

sesame paste: A richly flavored paste made from toasted sesame seeds. If unavailable, peanut butter can be used instead. Tahini, the Mediterranean version of sesame paste, is not a good substitute, as it is made from untoasted sesame seeds.

sesame seeds: The seeds that come from the Asian sesame plant, sesame seeds are used in desserts such as Glazed Bananas (page 278) and savory dishes such as Sesame Chicken (page 178). They are frequently toasted before use.

shoyu: The Japanese version of light soy sauce, shoyu can be used in Chinese cooking.

soy sauce, dark: A soybean-based sauce that is aged for a longer period of time than regular (light) soy sauce, dark soy sauce is commonly used in marinades and red-cooked dishes. Do not use in place of regular (light) soy sauce, as it has a very different flavor.

soy sauce, light: A soybean-based sauce that is one of the most important ingredients in Chinese cooking, light soy sauce has a lighter color, thinner texture, and saltier flavor than dark soy sauce. Japanese **shoyu** can be used as a substitute.

steaming: Cooking food by placing it over boiling water so that the steam reaches and cooks the food. This is the third most popular Chinese cooking technique.

stir-frying: Cooking food in oil at very high heat for a short period of time, while continuously stirring. It is the cooking technique most commonly associated with Chinese cuisine.

Szechwan peppercorn: Known for the biting sensation it leaves on the tongue, the Szechwan peppercorn gives Szechwan cuisine its distinctive flavor. It is actually not a peppercorn at all, but a berry from the prickly ash tree. Szechwan peppercorns are normally roasted and ground before use.

tapioca starch: A starch made from the tubers of the tapioca plant, tapioca starch is used as a thickener in Chinese cooking. Cornstarch and tapioca starch can be substituted for each other in sauce recipes, but cornstarch takes longer to thicken.

thick soy sauce: Used to lend flavor to fried rice and noodle dishes, thick soy sauce has been thickened with molasses.

water chestnuts: The name can cause confusion, since water chestnuts come from an aquatic plant and are not related to horse chestnuts, which grow on trees. Fresh water chestnuts have a sweet flavor reminiscent of banana. Canned water chestnuts can be substituted for texture but don't have the same flavor. Jicama is also used as a substitute.

white pepper: A seasoning made from ground white peppercorns. A little-known fact is that white and black pepper both come from the same plant; the main difference between them is that white pepper berries are allowed to ripen before processing. In Chinese cooking, white pepper makes a frequent appearance in soups and spicier stir-fries. Use sparingly as it has a sharp bite.

winter melon: A type of squash with an oblong shape and dark green rind similar to a watermelon. The inside flesh is white and pleasantly sweet. Winter Melon Soup (page 61) is a popular banquet soup.

wok: A bowl-shaped utensil designed to be used in cooking methods requiring high heat, such as deep-frying. A wok is the main piece of Chinese cooking equipment.

wood fungus: This fungus is also called cloud ear fungus because of its unusual shape. Like tofu, it has no flavor but absorbs the flavor of the foods it is cooked with. It is used in soups and stir-fries. Soak wood fungus in water to soften before use.

Index

THE EVERYTHING SERIES!

BUSINESS

Everything® **Business Planning Book**
Everything® **Coaching and Mentoring Book**
Everything® **Fundraising Book**
Everything® **Home-Based Business Book**
Everything® **Leadership Book**
Everything® **Managing People Book**
Everything® **Network Marketing Book**
Everything® **Online Business Book**
Everything® **Project Management Book**
Everything® **Selling Book**
Everything® **Start Your Own Business Book**
Everything® **Time Management Book**

COMPUTERS

Everything® **Build Your Own Home Page Book**
Everything® **Computer Book**
Everything® **Internet Book**
Everything® **Microsoft® Word 2000 Book**

COOKBOOKS

Everything® **Barbecue Cookbook**
Everything® **Bartender's Book, $9.95**
Everything® **Chinese Cookbook**
Everything® **Chocolate Cookbook**
Everything® **Cookbook**
Everything® **Dessert Cookbook**
Everything® **Diabetes Cookbook**
Everything® **Indian Cookbook**
Everything® **Low-Carb Cookbook**
Everything® **Low-Fat High-Flavor Cookbook**

Everything® **Low-Salt Cookbook**
Everything® **Mediterranean Cookbook**
Everything® **Mexican Cookbook**
Everything® **One-Pot Cookbook**
Everything® **Pasta Book**
Everything® **Quick Meals Cookbook**
Everything® **Slow Cooker Cookbook**
Everything® **Soup Cookbook**
Everything® **Thai Cookbook**
Everything® **Vegetarian Cookbook**
Everything® **Wine Book**

HEALTH

Everything® **Alzheimer's Book**
Everything® **Anti-Aging Book**
Everything® **Diabetes Book**
Everything® **Dieting Book**
Everything® **Herbal Remedies Book**
Everything® **Hypnosis Book**
Everything® **Massage Book**
Everything® **Menopause Book**
Everything® **Nutrition Book**
Everything® **Reflexology Book**
Everything® **Reiki Book**
Everything® **Stress Management Book**
Everything® **Vitamins, Minerals, and Nutritional Supplements Book**

HISTORY

Everything® **American Government Book**
Everything® **American History Book**
Everything® **Civil War Book**
Everything® **Irish History & Heritage Book**

Everything® **Mafia Book**
Everything® **Middle East Book**
Everything® **World War II Book**

HOBBIES & GAMES

Everything® **Bridge Book**
Everything® **Candlemaking Book**
Everything® **Casino Gambling Book**
Everything® **Chess Basics Book**
Everything® **Collectibles Book**
Everything® **Crossword and Puzzle Book**
Everything® **Digital Photography Book**
Everything® **Easy Crosswords Book**
Everything® **Family Tree Book**
Everything® **Games Book**
Everything® **Knitting Book**
Everything® **Magic Book**
Everything® **Motorcycle Book**
Everything® **Online Genealogy Book**
Everything® **Photography Book**
Everything® **Pool & Billiards Book**
Everything® **Quilting Book**
Everything® **Scrapbooking Book**
Everything® **Sewing Book**
Everything® **Soapmaking Book**

HOME IMPROVEMENT

Everything® **Feng Shui Book**
Everything® **Feng Shui Decluttering Book, $9.95 ($15.95 CAN)**
Everything® **Fix-It Book**
Everything® **Gardening Book**
Everything® **Homebuilding Book**

All Everything® books are priced at $12.95 or $14.95, unless otherwise stated. Prices subject to change without notice.
Canadian prices range from $11.95–$31.95, and are subject to change without notice.

Everything® **Home Decorating Book**
Everything® **Landscaping Book**
Everything® **Lawn Care Book**
Everything® **Organize Your Home Book**

EVERYTHING® KIDS' BOOKS

All titles are $6.95
Everything® **Kids' Baseball Book, 3rd Ed.** ($10.95 CAN)
Everything® **Kids' Bible Trivia Book** ($10.95 CAN)
Everything® **Kids' Bugs Book** ($10.95 CAN)
Everything® **Kids' Christmas Puzzle & Activity Book** ($10.95 CAN)
Everything® **Kids' Cookbook** ($10.95 CAN)
Everything® **Kids' Halloween Puzzle & Activity Book** ($10.95 CAN)
Everything® **Kids' Joke Book** ($10.95 CAN)
Everything® **Kids' Math Puzzles Book** ($10.95 CAN)
Everything® **Kids' Mazes Book** ($10.95 CAN)
Everything® **Kids' Money Book** ($11.95 CAN)
Everything® **Kids' Monsters Book** ($10.95 CAN)
Everything® **Kids' Nature Book** ($11.95 CAN)
Everything® **Kids' Puzzle Book** ($10.95 CAN)
Everything® **Kids' Riddles & Brain Teasers Book** ($10.95 CAN)
Everything® **Kids' Science Experiments Book** ($10.95 CAN)
Everything® **Kids' Soccer Book** ($10.95 CAN)
Everything® **Kids' Travel Activity Book** ($10.95 CAN)

KIDS' STORY BOOKS

Everything® **Bedtime Story Book**
Everything® **Bible Stories Book**
Everything® **Fairy Tales Book**
Everything® **Mother Goose Book**

LANGUAGE

Everything® **Inglés Book**
Everything® **Learning French Book**
Everything® **Learning German Book**
Everything® **Learning Italian Book**
Everything® **Learning Latin Book**
Everything® **Learning Spanish Book**
Everything® **Sign Language Book**
Everything® **Spanish Phrase Book,** $9.95 ($15.95 CAN)

MUSIC

Everything® **Drums Book (with CD),** $19.95 ($31.95 CAN)
Everything® **Guitar Book**
Everything® **Playing Piano and Keyboards Book**
Everything® **Rock & Blues Guitar Book (with CD),** $19.95 ($31.95 CAN)
Everything® **Songwriting Book**

NEW AGE

Everything® **Astrology Book**
Everything® **Divining the Future Book**
Everything® **Dreams Book**
Everything® **Ghost Book**
Everything® **Love Signs Book,** $9.95 ($15.95 CAN)
Everything® **Meditation Book**
Everything® **Numerology Book**
Everything® **Palmistry Book**
Everything® **Psychic Book**
Everything® **Spells & Charms Book**
Everything® **Tarot Book**
Everything® **Wicca and Witchcraft Book**

PARENTING

Everything® **Baby Names Book**
Everything® **Baby Shower Book**
Everything® **Baby's First Food Book**
Everything® **Baby's First Year Book**
Everything® **Breastfeeding Book**
Everything® **Father-to-Be Book**
Everything® **Get Ready for Baby Book**
Everything® **Getting Pregnant Book**
Everything® **Homeschooling Book**
Everything® **Parent's Guide to Children with Autism**
Everything® **Parent's Guide to Positive Discipline**
Everything® **Parent's Guide to Raising a Successful Child**
Everything® **Parenting a Teenager Book**
Everything® **Potty Training Book,** $9.95 ($15.95 CAN)
Everything® **Pregnancy Book, 2nd Ed.**
Everything® **Pregnancy Fitness Book**
Everything® **Pregnancy Organizer,** $15.00 ($22.95 CAN)
Everything® **Toddler Book**
Everything® **Tween Book**

PERSONAL FINANCE

Everything® **Budgeting Book**
Everything® **Get Out of Debt Book**
Everything® **Get Rich Book**
Everything® **Homebuying Book, 2nd Ed.**
Everything® **Homeselling Book**
Everything® **Investing Book**
Everything® **Money Book**
Everything® **Mutual Funds Book**
Everything® **Online Investing Book**
Everything® **Personal Finance Book**
Everything® **Personal Finance in Your 20s & 30s Book**
Everything® **Wills & Estate Planning Book**

PETS

Everything® **Cat Book**
Everything® **Dog Book**
Everything® **Dog Training and Tricks Book**
Everything® **Golden Retriever Book**
Everything® **Horse Book**
Everything® **Labrador Retriever Book**
Everything® **Puppy Book**
Everything® **Tropical Fish Book**

All Everything® books are priced at $12.95 or $14.95, unless otherwise stated. Prices subject to change without notice.
Canadian prices range from $11.95–$31.95, and are subject to change without notice.

REFERENCE

Everything® **Astronomy Book**
Everything® **Car Care Book**
Everything® **Christmas Book, $15.00**
    ($21.95 CAN)
Everything® **Classical Mythology Book**
Everything® **Einstein Book**
Everything® **Etiquette Book**
Everything® **Great Thinkers Book**
Everything® **Philosophy Book**
Everything® **Psychology Book**
Everything® **Shakespeare Book**
Everything® **Tall Tales, Legends, &**
    Other Outrageous
    Lies Book
Everything® **Toasts Book**
Everything® **Trivia Book**
Everything® **Weather Book**

RELIGION

Everything® **Angels Book**
Everything® **Bible Book**
Everything® **Buddhism Book**
Everything® **Catholicism Book**
Everything® **Christianity Book**
Everything® **Jewish History &**
    Heritage Book
Everything® **Judaism Book**
Everything® **Prayer Book**
Everything® **Saints Book**
Everything® **Understanding Islam**
    Book
Everything® **World's Religions Book**
Everything® **Zen Book**

SCHOOL & CAREERS

Everything® **After College Book**
Everything® **Alternative Careers Book**
Everything® **College Survival Book**
Everything® **Cover Letter Book**
Everything® **Get-a-Job Book**
Everything® **Hot Careers Book**

Everything® **Job Interview Book**
Everything® **New Teacher Book**
Everything® **Online Job Search Book**
Everything® **Resume Book, 2nd Ed.**
Everything® **Study Book**

SELF-HELP/
RELATIONSHIPS

Everything® **Dating Book**
Everything® **Divorce Book**
Everything® **Great Marriage Book**
Everything® **Great Sex Book**
Everything® **Kama Sutra Book**
Everything® **Romance Book**
Everything® **Self-Esteem Book**
Everything® **Success Book**

SPORTS & FITNESS

Everything® **Body Shaping Book**
Everything® **Fishing Book**
Everything® **Fly-Fishing Book**
Everything® **Golf Book**
Everything® **Golf Instruction Book**
Everything® **Knots Book**
Everything® **Pilates Book**
Everything® **Running Book**
Everything® **Sailing Book, 2nd Ed.**
Everything® **T'ai Chi and QiGong Book**
Everything® **Total Fitness Book**
Everything® **Weight Training Book**
Everything® **Yoga Book**

TRAVEL

Everything® **Family Guide to Hawaii**
Everything® **Guide to Las Vegas**
Everything® **Guide to New England**
Everything® **Guide to New York City**
Everything® **Guide to Washington D.C.**
Everything® **Travel Guide to The**
    Disneyland Resort®,
    California Adventure®,

Universal Studios®, and
the Anaheim Area
Everything® **Travel Guide to the Walt**
    Disney World Resort®,
    Universal Studios®, and
    Greater Orlando, 3rd Ed.

WEDDINGS

Everything® **Bachelorette Party Book,**
    $9.95 ($15.95 CAN)
Everything® **Bridesmaid Book, $9.95**
    ($15.95 CAN)
Everything® **Creative Wedding Ideas**
    Book
Everything® **Elopement Book, $9.95**
    ($15.95 CAN)
Everything® **Groom Book**
Everything® **Jewish Wedding Book**
Everything® **Wedding Book, 2nd Ed.**
Everything® **Wedding Checklist,**
    $7.95 ($11.95 CAN)
Everything® **Wedding Etiquette Book,**
    $7.95 ($11.95 CAN)
Everything® **Wedding Organizer,**
    $15.00 ($22.95 CAN)
Everything® **Wedding Shower Book,**
    $7.95 ($12.95 CAN)
Everything® **Wedding Vows Book,**
    $7.95 ($11.95 CAN)
Everything® **Weddings on a Budget**
    Book, $9.95 ($15.95 CAN)

WRITING

Everything® **Creative Writing Book**
Everything® **Get Published Book**
Everything® **Grammar and Style Book**
Everything® **Grant Writing Book**
Everything® **Guide to Writing**
    Children's Books
Everything® **Screenwriting Book**
Everything® **Writing Well Book**

Available wherever books are sold!
To order, call 800-872-5627, or visit us at everything.com

Everything® and everything.com® are registered trademarks of F+W Publications, Inc.